CONTRIBUTIONS IN AME

Series Editor: Robert H

THE PRESIDENCY OF RUTHERFORD B. HAYES

Kenneth E. Davison

CONTRIBUTIONS IN AMERICAN STUDIES, NUMBER 3

GREENWOOD PRESS, INC.
WESTPORT, CONNECTICUT

Library of Congress Cataloging in Publication Data

Davison, Kenneth E.
   The Presidency of Rutherford B. Hayes.

   (Contributions in American studies, no. 3)
   Bibliography: p.
   1. Hayes, Rutherford Birchard, Pres. U.S.,
1822-1893.   I. Title.
E682.D38   973.8'3'0924 [B]   79-176289
ISBN 0-8371-6275-0

973.83
H418d

Library of Congress Catalog Number: 79-176289
ISBN: 0-8371-6275-0

First published in 1972
Second printing 1974
Paperback edition 1974

Greenwood Press, a division of Williamhouse-Regency Inc.
51 Riverside Avenue, Westport, Connecticut 06880

TO MY FAMILY

Contents

Illustrations

Acknowledgments

Many organizations and individuals have generously assisted me in the writing of this book. I wish to recognize, in particular, the interest and support of The Rutherford B. Hayes and Lucy Webb Hayes Foundation. To the director of the Hayes Library, Watt P. Marchman, I am indebted far beyond any ordinary measure of an author's obligation to the keeper of the sources necessary for his work. Mr. Marchman and his entire staff, especially Ruth Ballenger and Rose N. Sberna, made my task both pleasant and rewarding. Together they make the Hayes Library an exemplary model of a scholarly research organization: well organized, easy to use, and competently staffed.

My alma mater, Heidelberg College, in several ways has encouraged my desire to write a Hayes biography. Her presidents, Dr. Terry Wickham and Dr. Leslie H. Fishel, jr., have inspired me. Twice the college board of trustees has awarded me a sabbatical leave. Dean John Allen Krout and Dean Arthur R. Porter, Jr., have secured grants-in-aid to further my work. I wish to acknowledge especially a generous grant from the recently established Allan G. Aigler Humanities Research Fund of Heidelberg College, which covered the cost of preparing the manuscript for publication. One of my greatest delights has been the privilege of using a faculty carrel in Heidelberg's beautiful new Beeghly Library. While the entire staff of the library has assisted me at various times, I would particularly like to thank Carson W. Bennett, Eva I. A. Schroeder, Richard W. Owen, Bernice Sattler, Rosemarie S. Maloney, Pamela K. Bartch, and Nancy Rubenstein for their courteous and prompt service.

Two grants from the Johnson and Penrose Funds of the American Philosophical Society were decisive in enabling me to hire a student secretary, to travel to distant libraries, and to maintain research momentum during the summer months.

Four secretaries, Mary Jo Elder, Florence Crooks, Pamela J. Bordner, and Margaret Carpenter, helped me greatly during different phases of the research. Rebecca Jane Eberly and Elaine Knutson typed the final manuscript with professional skill.

I wish also to acknowledge the interest and support of Daniel R. Porter, director, and Helen M. Thurston, editor, of The Ohio Historical Society; they have granted permission to use copyrighted material found in Chapters 2 and 14 of the present volume, which I had previously published in another form in the society's quarterly journal, *Ohio History*.

My friend and colleague, Dr. Frederick D. Lemke, chairman of the Heidelberg Department of English, read the entire manuscript and made numerous suggestions for improving coherence, emphasis, and style. I am very grateful for his help.

Several friends in Washington, D.C., made my work easier. Dr. Robert H. Walker, editor of the series, gave me much excellent and practical advice. Dr. Wilcomb E. Washburn of the Smithsonian Institution provided a valuable critique for my discussion of the American Indian in the Hayes era. Jean Stephenson and Frank Bridger introduced me to the art of genealogical research; Dr. Frank B. Evans taught me how to use archival sources. My Congressman, the Honorable Jackson E. Betts, was most generous in arranging appointments at several government agencies, in introducing me to various officials, in providing government documents and legislative reference service, and in taking me on a behind-the-scenes tour of historic rooms in the Capitol.

In the conduct of my research, I visited dozens of libraries and archival institutions, always with profit and pleasure. The following institutions and individuals were of exceptional help in my work: The National Archives (Josephine Cobb); The Library of Congress (Milton Kaplan); Smithsonian Institution, Political History Division (Herbert Collins and staff); The White House, Office of the Curator (Betty Monkman, Registrar); Office of the Architect of the Capitol (Florian Thayn); U.S. Post Office Department Library; U.S. Bureau of the Budget Library; National Society, Daughters of the American Revolution Library; National Genealogical Society Library; Harvard University Law School Library; Union League of Philadelphia (Dr. Maxwell Whiteman); Philadelphia Museum of Art; Ryerson Library, Art Institute of Chicago; William R. Perkins Library, Duke University; Louis Round Wilson Library, University of North Carolina, Chapel Hill; Earl Gregg Swem Library and Marshall-Wythe Law School Library, College of William and Mary; Bowling Green State University Library; Cincinnati Historical Society Library; Ohio Historical Society Library; The Ohio State

University Library; University of Toledo Library; and the Western Reserve Historical Society Library.

Most of all, I would remember the unending cooperation and constant encouragement of my wife Virginia, of my sons Robert and Richard, and of my mother Mildred Smith Davison, who in their several ways, made so many sacrifices to allow me time to write. It is only fitting that I should inscribe the volume to them.

Spiegel Grove KENNETH E. DAVISON
July 24, 1971

Rutherford B. Hayes,
President of the United States, 1877–1881.

Introduction

Historically, Rutherford B. Hayes is remembered primarily for his contested victory in the 1876 presidential election, while his wife Lucy Webb Hayes is usually associated with the policy of not serving liquor in the White House. Only in recent years have scholars begun to reconsider the Hayes presidency (1877–1881) and to reassess the period and its personalities; a new appraisal of Rutherford and Lucy Hayes is emerging.

Hayes was graduated as valedictorian of his class at Kenyon College, went on to Harvard Law School, and successfully practiced law in Cincinnati until he volunteered for Civil War duty. A popular officer, wounded in action three times, once severely, Hayes left the service in 1865 as a brevet major-general and began a decade of rapid rise in the Republican party. After one full term and part of another in Congress, he resigned his seat and won three close elections for the governorship of Ohio by defeating in turn the three most prominent contemporary Democrats in Ohio politics, Judge Allen G. Thurman (1867), Congressman George H. Pendleton (1869), and incumbent Governor William Allen (1875).

Many factors—especially his age (fifty-three), Ohio residence, and war record—helped Hayes attain the Republican nomination for the presidency in 1876, but more important than any of these political assets was his possession of attributes beyond mere availability, qualities vitally needed in the presidency, which set him apart from most Gilded Age politicians. In a time notorious for its spoilsmen, his strength of character and unblemished record in public and private life were important to the Republican party and the country after the shocking disclosures of corruption in Grant's second administration. "He serves his party best who serves his country best" set the theme for Hayes' administration.

His cabinet appointments made machine politicians rage and reformers rejoice. One of President Hayes' outstanding abilities was his sound judgment of men and issues.

Hayes was a man of intellectual strength. He attended private schools in Norwalk, Ohio, and Middletown, Connecticut, excelled at Kenyon College, and then, unlike so many aspiring attorneys of the time who entered the profession by reading law in the office of an established member of the bar, young Hayes went east to Harvard Law School where he studied under distinguished professors, particularly United States Supreme Court Justice Joseph Story and Simon Greenleaf. The years at Harvard (1842–1845) produced the first big changes in the outlook and thinking of Rutherford B. Hayes, and he attained greater self-control and discipline in his habits.

The atmosphere of Harvard also awakened his scholarly instincts. He attended lectures on history and literature given by George Bancroft, Jared Sparks, and Henry Wadsworth Longfellow, acquired more sophisticated taste, and polished his manners in the polite society of the East. While never a scholar by profession, Hayes enjoyed associating with men of learning, indulged a fondness for good literature, began a library, and developed the habits of a scholar. He read widely in American history and biography and purchased a large collection of Americana from Robert Clarke and Company, one of Cincinnati's leading publishing houses. He took pride in his many seventeenth-century American forebears and traveled and did research to trace his ancestry. He joined the New England Genealogical Society and the American Historical Association.

Hayes brought substantial administrative experience and skill to the White House. As Ohio's first elected three-term governor, he learned the arts of executive leadership. Events during his years as governor, including the strike of coal miners near Massillon in 1876 and the riots that followed, prepared him to cope with the great Railway Strike of 1877 while President. Once declared elected over Samuel J. Tilden, Hayes quickly took charge, appointed a strong cabinet over Senate opposition, and governed skillfully although his party never controlled both House and Senate. His success may be attributed to previous administrative experience, able advisers, men he could trust in key positions, and his rich knowledge of American history and biography.

By temperament, Hayes was generally calm and deliberate. He could never be stampeded into hasty or ill-advised action. He relied on common sense if confidential political reports seemed contradictory. Although he had many influential newspaper friends, he looked with a jaundiced eye upon the accuracy of newspaper reporting and carefully checked other sources to corroborate or refute press dispatches.

Hayes was an inveterate traveler, familiar with all sections of the United States, and well acquainted with every mode of public and private transportation of the late nineteenth century. He loved to walk, and once he trudged some forty miles each way from the Kenyon campus to his home in Delaware, Ohio, to spend Christmas with his family. He visited the New England of his ancestors several times as a young boy and as a man and continued to make pilgrimages there until his death. After deciding for reasons of health against enlisting for service in the Mexican War, he made an adventurous trip to Texas with his uncle, Sardis Birchard, to visit Guy M. Bryan, a close friend and Kenyon classmate. Soldiers' reunions, state and county fairs, official and private business, took him into virtually every state. He became the first President to make an extensive western tour while in office.

As for Lucy Hayes, she was one of the more gifted first ladies, the first to be a college graduate and the first to travel extensively with her husband. An excellent hostess, her outgoing personality complemented her husband's more reserved manner.

Today, many historians—including Arthur M. Schlesinger, Sr., and Thomas A. Bailey—rank Hayes third in achievement, after Lincoln and Theodore Roosevelt, among Republican Presidents of the United States, and his record in a single term compares favorably with the two terms of Grover Cleveland, who has generally been accorded first place among chief executives of the Gilded Age.

This book, written to mark the occasion of the 150th anniversary of Hayes' birth in Delaware, Ohio, offers a fresh study of the man and the major events of his presidency. While it is the first work to concentrate primarily on the presidency of Hayes, it places these four years within the perspective of his whole life.

Part I

THE MAKING OF
A PRESIDENT

1

The Path to the Presidency

Spiegel Grove, the beautiful Ohio home of Rutherford B. Hayes, nineteenth President of the United States, is resplendent through every season of the year. Majestic White House gates, moved here in 1928 by authorization of Congress, afford access to graceful driveways encircling an estate of natural beauty renowned for giant oaks, unusual shrubs, and lovely flowers. Prominent within the twenty-five-acre site are two large buildings. The newest, a completely rebuilt and greatly enlarged structure reopened in 1968, houses the nation's original (1916) presidential library and museum. Just behind it, a stately Victorian mansion, designated in 1963 as a national landmark for its exceptional value in commemorating and illustrating the history of the United States, commands an expanse of wooded lawn.

History abounds in the Grove. Before white settlers arrived, Indians often camped under the great trees. A portion of General William Henry Harrison's military trail of 1812 winds through the property. But most important of all, for two decades between 1873 and 1893, Rutherford Hayes and his large family lived here and entertained many famous American journalists, soldiers, and statesmen of their time.

Hayes served as America's chief executive from 1877 to 1881, between the administrations of two other famous Ohioans, Ulysses S. Grant and James A. Garfield. Relatively little is known about Hayes or his presidency because most historians have bypassed the politics of his era to concentrate upon the exciting economic expansion of the United States in the last quarter of the nineteenth century. Spiegel Grove, the homestead, and the adjoining museum and research center have preserved this part of our forgotten past.

Hayes was born in Delaware, Ohio, October 4, 1822, the youngest child of Rutherford and Sophia Birchard Hayes who migrated to central Ohio in the fall of 1817 from Dummerston, Vermont.[1]

Shortly before his birth, his father died suddenly of a fever, and the boy's mother became desperately ill and weak. Despite the gloomy circumstances, mother and child survived, and Sardis Birchard, a favorite bachelor brother of Mrs. Hayes and later a prosperous pioneer merchant and Indian trader in Lower Sandusky (now Fremont), assumed the role of father to the three young Hayes children. For half a century, Birchard was a major influence in the personal life of Rutherford Hayes, and shared many conversations and confidences. A long and steady correspondence passed between them, and they often traveled together. Sardis frequently provided funds to help young Hayes with his education, legal career, and investments. He bought the Spiegel Grove site, began building a house there in August 1859, and finally willed the valuable property to his nephew. To Sardis Birchard, Hayes owed his financial security and independence. When his uncle died in 1874, Hayes succeeded him as the town's leading citizen.[2]

Sophia Hayes, mother of the future President, was a native of Wilmington, Vermont. She, too, exerted a strong influence on the life of her son. His unfailing affection for New England, especially the state of Vermont, came from her. A strict Presbyterian, she urged him to work hard and observe the Sabbath by regular church attendance. She kept a close watch over her three children.

Young Hayes attended district school in Delaware, Ohio (1830–1835), accompanied his family on a memorable New England trip in the summer of 1834, enrolled briefly at Norwalk (Ohio) Seminary, a Methodist school (1836–1837), and completed his college preparatory studies at Isaac Webb's private school in Middletown, Connecticut (1837–1838). According to his mother's wishes, he entered Kenyon College instead of Yale in November 1838 and graduated as valedictorian in a class of nine on August 3, 1842. After Kenyon College was granted a chapter of Phi Beta Kappa in 1858, he was elected to membership.[3] That same fall he began to study law by reading Blackstone's *Commentaries* in the office of Sparrow and Matthews of Columbus, Ohio, until on August 28, 1843, in order to finish his legal preparation, he entered Dane Law School of Harvard University where he remained until February 1845.

Hayes always excelled as a student and kept up his scholarly interests throughout his life by associating with intellectuals, collecting an outstanding library of Americana, and constantly reading.[4] He liked to describe himself not as a scholar, but as a man with scholarly tastes and aptitudes. Each of his four sons went to college, and, no matter how crowded his official calendar might be as governor or President, Hayes still found time to write them affectionate letters full of fatherly advice and interest in their academic progress.

At Kenyon, Hayes received a classical education and formed important lifelong friendships, especially with two fellow students, Guy M. Bryan of Texas and Stanley Matthews of Cincinnati. The college years were happy ones for Hayes, second in his heart only to his four adventurous years in the Union Army, and he often returned to the Kenyon campus for reunion and commencement activities. In 1868, his alma mater awarded him an honorary Doctor of Laws degree, and, at the time of his death, he was president of the Kenyon Alumni Association.

At Harvard, Hayes studied with two distinguished professors of law, Simon Greenleaf and Justice Joseph Story, came in contact with John Quincy Adams and Daniel Webster, and in many other ways greatly widened his perspectives. The larger and richer environment of Boston and Cambridge quickened his cultural and literary tastes and refined his social habits. While he applied himself to his law courses and struggled to improve his ability in writing and speaking, he studied French, literature, and politics, and for the first time attended the theater. Hayes enjoyed himself at Harvard and consciously developed the manners and feelings of a true gentleman. By early February 1845, at the end of his third semester, he returned to Ohio to launch his legal career. A month later, March 10, he was admitted to the Ohio bar. His Harvard Law School diploma is dated August 27, 1845.

There followed four somewhat frustrating years in Lower Sandusky (Fremont), Ohio, as Hayes attempted to establish himself as a lawyer.[5] He probably chose this place for several reasons: Sardis Birchard and a favorite cousin, John R. Pease, were both active in business there and could help him get started; the future prospects of the town also seemed promising; and Professor Greenleaf had advised him to begin in a small town where opportunities would be greater for a beginner.[6] In retrospect these years comprise a prelude to Hayes' legal career, which does not assume importance until his move to Cincinnati late in 1849. The false start at Lower Sandusky was partly redeemed by the new experiences he had and friendships he made while living there. He formed a law partnership with Ralph P. Buckland, an established attorney and local Whig leader, later active in forwarding Hayes' political career. On a trip to Delaware, Columbus, and Cincinnati in 1847, he met for the first time, Lucy Ware Webb, whom he married in 1852. Meanwhile Hayes seriously considered volunteering for Mexican War service but finally gave up the idea upon the advice of his doctors. He joined the Sons of Temperance and the Independent Order of Odd Fellows, mingled in local society, and became a member of the Whig Central Committee for Sandusky County (1849) after strongly supporting Zachary Taylor for President the previous year.

Buckland's frequent absences gave the younger partner ample opportunity to master law office management and routine. Often restless himself, Hayes took repeated trips, visiting New England in 1847 with his cousin John R. Pease, and later Texas, in company with Uncle Sardis, to visit a college classmate. For three and one-half months nephew and uncle lived a carefree existence in Texas, traveling over much of the frontier state on horseback. The experience greatly strengthened Hayes' appreciation and sympathy for southerners, a concern he never lost.

Returning to Lower Sandusky from this exciting Texas trip, Hayes resolved to seek his fortune in Cincinnati, then the largest and most active city in the West. He arrived on Christmas Eve 1849, "a stranger seeking room among the brethren of the green bag."[7] Once more clients proved hard to find, and it took him about two years to get well established. He first formed an association with John W. Herron, sharing an office and sleeping quarters with him for several years. To fill his idle time, Hayes read more deeply in the law, attended lectures, made social calls, and, most important, joined the recently founded Cincinnati Literary Club, which afforded him excellent opportunities to improve his speaking ability and to win new clients and friends.

After his initial struggle to win recognition as a Cincinnati attorney, Hayes suddenly achieved prominence in 1852 as the defense counselor in three sensational first degree murder trials.[8] The change of fortune may be dated from January 16, 1852, when he lost his maiden effort in criminal court, a grand larceny case in behalf of one Samuel Cunningham charged with a theft of dry goods in Covington, Kentucky. Although Cunningham received a three-year sentence, Hayes conducted himself so well that Judge R. B. Warden appointed him to defend the notorious and indigent young servant girl, Nancy Farrer, suspected of poisoning four persons. The ambitious young attorney reflected on his good luck: "It is *the* criminal case of the term. Will attract more notice than any other, and if I am well prepared, will give me a better opportunity to exert and exhibit whatever pith there is in me than any case I ever appeared in."[9]

Nancy Farrer pleaded not guilty on January 15, 1852, and stood trial from February 19 to March 2, 1852, when the jury convicted her of first degree murder by arsenic poisoning. The court sentenced her to hang the following June 25. Hayes at once countered with a motion for a new trial, which was denied. He then applied to suspend sentence until the Ohio Supreme Court should meet, in order to appeal on writ of error. This was granted, and in December 1853, he successfully presented his appeal before the Supreme Court in Columbus, which fully sustained his objections to the judgment of the lower court. Throughout the legal proceedings, Hayes put forth a plea of insanity, and marshaled abundant medical and genealogical evidence to prove Nancy Farrer did not know right from wrong. In a moving speech he asserted:

> The calamity of insanity is one which may touch very nearly the happiness of the best of our citizens. We all know that in some of its thousand forms it has carried grief and agony unspeakable into many a happy home. We must all wish to see such rules in regard to it established as would satisfy an intelligent man if, instead of this friendless girl, his own sister or his own daughter were on trial.[10]

Hayes spoke with great feeling since his own family had suffered tragically from mental illness. His sister Fanny periodically lost her sanity as an aftermath of childbirth, and at times he feared a mental malady might even overtake him. Furthermore, while he was a Harvard law student, Professor Simon Greenleaf sanctioned "instruction in the medical jurisprudence of insanity and the modes of perpetrating homicide by poison or other secret means." At the same time Hayes and his classmates took great interest in the contemporary case of Commonwealth v. Rogers (1844) in which insanity was used as a successful defense against a murder charge.[11] Thus Hayes possessed both the temperament and the training ably to defend Nancy Farrer. Having won the Supreme Court appeal, he applied for a sanity inquest in probate court and convinced the jury of his hypothesis after a two-day trial in December 1854. In a strange sequel to the case, Nancy Farrer was sent to an asylum where she quickly earned the status of a privileged patient, even being put in nursing charge of ailing and sick patients. One day she escaped, however, and although it was presumed she went to Salt Lake City since she and her family were Mormons, she was never found again.[12]

Concurrently with the Farrer case, Hayes managed the defense in two other notable murder trials. In late April, 1852, he assisted in the fourth trial (three previous ones resulting in hung juries) of James Summons, a river boat captain accused of poisoning two relatives. Summons was convicted of murder in the first degree and sentenced on May 1, 1852, to hang on February 3, 1853. In the first case he presented orally before the Supreme Court of

Ohio, Hayes argued, on a writ of error, that Summons, condemned by the testimony of a deceased witness, had been unjustly denied the right to face his accuser. In addition he reminded the court that the crucial testimony was given from memory by a questionable third party. The Supreme Court, after much delay, finally decided in February 1857, by a four-to-one margin, to uphold the original verdict. Hayes, however, won the final round when Governor Salmon P. Chase commuted the sentence from death to life imprisonment.

The third murder trial involved a laborer, Henry LeCount, who while drunk on May 4, 1852, publicly attacked and unmercifully beat William Clinch over the head with a dray pin. Four days later the victim died. The trial, which lasted from June 7 to June 9, ended in a conviction of first degree murder, the third such verdict for a Hayes client in three months! This time there were no errors in the proceedings or record for the defense to gain a new trial, and LeCount was hanged on November 26, 1852. Hayes dutifully witnessed the event, however unpleasant.[13]

Firmly established as a Cincinnati lawyer through the publicity generated by his three celebrated criminal cases, Hayes steadily increased his own law business and was often retained by other attorneys to lend assistance with their practice. He formed a partnership (1853–1856) with Richard M. Corwine and William K. Rogers, a Kenyon classmate. Later, when Rogers moved to Minnesota, the firm's name changed to Corwine and Hayes (1856–1858). In November 1858, Hayes almost accepted an appointment to the Common Pleas Bench, but declined when the city council elected him in December to fill an unexpired term as city solicitor. In April 1859, the city electorate gave him a full term in his own right, a position he subsequently lost without any real regret in the election of April 1, 1861. With little prospect of adding to his luster by another term, he took pride in experience gained and the reputation for a job well done. There followed a short two-week partnership with Leopold Markbreit, which dissolved when both members volunteered for Civil War duty.

The brief service as city solicitor was significant in several respects. It was the first public office Hayes won. Second, he welcomed the fine salary of $3,500 and the agreeable duties. Third, he defeated six other candidates for the unexpired term, winning by a single vote on the thirteenth ballot after one Democrat threw his support to Hayes. It was the beginning of the famed Hayes "political luck" in winning close elections. Fourth, if he had accepted the judicial post, it seems unlikely he would ever have become a congressman, governor, or President.

Soon after the Civil War began, Hayes entered the service as an officer of the Twenty-third Ohio Volunteer Infantry. The war years brought him great satisfaction, several promotions in rank, and a modest fame as one of the "good colonels." Except for the prelude to the battle of Antietam in 1862 and some participation under Sheridan and Crook in the Shenandoah Valley campaign of 1864, Hayes spent most of his military career in the less glamorous and less dangerous West Virginia mountains and Kanawha Valley, marching and countermarching, occupying key points controlling troop movements, and fighting sporadic battles.

A popular officer, Hayes rose from major to the rank of brevet general by the war's end. He always put his war service uppermost among his experiences in life even though he recognized that his part in the conflict was "a very humble one, a place utterly unknown to history."[14] Despite this disclaimer, Hayes could nonetheless be stirred by a friendly reference to his war record. While not greatly distinguished in the army, he took pride in his successful command of small units throughout the war. In more than fifty engagements he demonstrated efficiency, self-possession, and personal daring.[15]

As the fighting commander of the Twenty-third Ohio Regiment, Colonel Hayes led numerous charges against enemy lines.[16] Several horses were shot beneath him, and he was wounded on at least three occasions, suffering bullet wounds in the right knee, left arm, and forehead. Another injury occurred when his left ankle was severely wrenched as the foot was jerked out of the stirrup at the moment his horse was killed under him at Cedar Creek, Virginia. The knee, head, and ankle injuries were relatively minor but proved bothersome the rest of his life during damp weather. At times he had to use a cane. The arm wound was quite serious. A musket ball passed through the center and above the elbow of the left arm fracturing the bone. The shattered limb might have been amputated by a less skillful Union field surgeon, but, by great good luck, the regiment's doctor, Joseph Webb, a brother of Mrs. Hayes, found the wounded colonel, took expert care of his patient, and saved the arm.[17] Mrs. Hayes won the favor of the troops by living in camp with her husband and ministering to sick and wounded soldiers.

The war experience helped Hayes in many ways. His health was never better. In the army he made friends who scattered after the war to many parts and territories of the United States where they often became active in Republican politics. While still in the army, Hayes' name was proposed for both Congress and the governorship of Ohio, but he shrewdly denied interest in either nomination as long as the war continued. An honorable service record counted heavily for political preferment in the postwar Republican party, and few candidates got far without it.

As early as 1856, Hayes had considered running for Congress but withdrew his name when the chance came. Again in 1858 he could have received the nomination had he desired it. While still in the army, friends engineered his nomination for Congress on August 6, 1864, and he was elected in October without ever taking any part in the canvass. Such behavior was typical of Hayes' attitude toward public office: "It was merely easier to let the thing take its own course than to get up a letter declining to run and then to explain it to everybody who might choose to bore me about it."[18] The office sought the man. His cause was championed by William Henry Smith of Cincinnati, who later was highly instrumental in securing the presidential nomination for Hayes. A letter written to Smith on August 24, 1864, in which Hayes wisely declined to take the stump while still on active duty, became an effective campaign document during the presidential canvass of 1876.[19] Successful in his first bid for Congress, Hayes served as a Republican member from March 4, 1865, to October 31, 1867, resigning after being nominated for the governorship of Ohio.[20]

Since the House of Representatives met for only eleven months during his entire congressional tenure, Hayes had little chance to become conspicuous or to distinguish himself. He hewed to the Republican party line, supporting the Fourteenth and Fifteenth amendments, the congressional plan of Reconstruction, including military controls over the South, and full payment of the public debt created during the war. He took no part, however, in the bitter speeches that characterized congressional debates at this time, and he deplored such tactics when used by others. He and Lucy rarely attended Washington parties or receptions. To him they were "all alike—rather a bore generally." Besides he found "being errand boy to one hundred and fifty thousand people tires me so by night I am ready for bed instead of soirees."[21] He spent a good deal of his time adjusting war claims filed by soldiers in his district. He obtained the payment of bounties and pensions for many of these former servicemen and gained the valuable reputation of being "the soldier's friend."

Perhaps his most significant congressional service involved the chairmanship of the Joint Committee on the Library of Congress. The members, all gentlemen and scholars, and the work, covering all matters of art, statuary, and painting plus general oversight of the library and Botanical Garden, brought Hayes into pleasant association with Washington cultural circles. Partly through his efforts, two new wings were added to the library. The holdings were substantially augmented by transfer of the Smithsonian Institution's collection of books and documents and by purchasing the valuable Peter Force Collection of Americana. Hayes also participated in the choice of works of art for government purchase.

In many respects, however, Hayes did not enjoy congressional life. A man of inherent modesty, he did not believe in unnecessary and intrusive eloquence, nor did he seek to make himself conspicuous through "noisy exhibition." Despite some private misgivings over Radical Republican tactics and policies, he voted as a party regular and created the kind of record that later made him acceptable to stalwarts and reformers alike.[22]

An event of considerable bearing on Hayes' future presidential career occurred during the midwinter recess of Congress in December 1866 when he visited, with his wife and several other members of Congress and their wives, New Orleans, Lynchburg, Knoxville, Chattanooga, Nashville, and Memphis. The purpose of the trip was both social and political. The Congressmen inspected for themselves conditions in the South and mingled with Southern leaders on their own ground. Hayes was particularly impressed by a meeting of "eager, earnest" black people whom he addressed briefly, and he fully enjoyed several social encounters with former Rebel officers who shared his love of war stories, if not his Negro suffrage inclinations.[23] The trip further developed Hayes' understanding of the South and helped prepare the way for the successful reception of his presidential tour of the South in 1877.

Although reelected to a second term, Hayes confided to his uncle, "I have no ambition for congressional reputation or influence—not a particle. I would like to be out of it creditably." About this time Ohio friends again began to suggest his name for the governorship, and Hayes pondered the possibility: "If this nomination is pretty likely, it would get me out of the scrape, and after that I am out of political life decently."[24] At length he consented to the wishes of his friends, and on June 19, 1867, at the Republican state convention in Columbus, he received the nomination for governor on the first ballot. Once more, as in the episode of his candidacy for Congress, it was William Henry Smith who managed to persuade him to seek the office. Hayes said repeatedly that the Second District voters must approve of his resigning to run for governor and that he would not enter a contest against other deserving Republicans. Finally, satisfied on both counts, he left Washington worries that he was glad to be rid of permanently, or so he thought, in July 1867 to launch his campaign for the governorship on August 5 at Lebanon, Ohio.[25] His Democratic opponent, Ohio's Chief Justice Allen G. Thurman, enjoyed a far greater reputation than Hayes and was expected to win. The principle of Negro suffrage, a major issue in the contest, badly divided the Republicans. Unlike incumbent Republican Governor Jacob D. Cox, Hayes favored Negro voting rights in Ohio, as well as in all the other states. His margin of victory over Thurman was less than 3,000 votes out of nearly a half million cast. Nonetheless he ran far ahead of the Republican ticket, which lost both houses of the legislature to the Democrats. At the same time, the proposed state constitutional amendment guaranteeing Negro suffrage, which Hayes supported, lost by 38,000 votes. Thurman, though defeated for governor, soon afterward became a United States Senator through election by the new state legislature. Despite the narrow victory, Hayes courageously renewed his stand for equal suffrage in his inaugural address of January 13, 1868, and squarely opposed a Democratic proposal to repeal Ohio's assent to the Fourteenth Amendment.

He enjoyed being governor. "It strikes me at a guess as the pleasantest office I have ever had. Not too much hard work, plenty of time to read, good society, etc."[26] On June 23, 1869, he was renominated by acclamation and reelected in October by 7,501 votes over ex-Congressman George H. Pendleton of Cincinnati. Negro suffrage, previously rejected when offered as an Ohio constitutional amendment, again was an issue, this time as the Fifteenth Amendment to the federal Constitution. Hayes favored ratification. Another key issue was whether the war debt should be paid in greenbacks. Hayes supported a hard money policy. In this election the Republicans managed to regain control of the legislature by a small margin.

During his two terms as governor, Hayes initiated a Geological Survey and appointed Professor John S. Newberry of Columbia University as state geologist. To his private secretary Hayes delegated the almost daily applications for railroad transportation by soldiers on furlough from the National Asylum at Dayton. Generally they went East on business connected with pensions or back pay. He also gave attention to the widespread outbreak of cattle disease in Ohio during 1868 and sought help from Governor Conrad Baker of Indiana and the British government, which had published a comprehensive report on cattle plague. Hayes also established the Soldiers and Sailors Home at Xenia and founded an Agricultural College, which, in 1878, became The Ohio State University. Meanwhile Ohio ratified the Fifteenth Amendment in 1869 with the governor's full support. In cultural affairs,

Hayes obtained portrait paintings of all the governors of Ohio, collected valuable manuscripts on the early history of Ohio, purchased the Arthur St. Clair Papers, and acquired other documents pertaining to the early Ohio governors, Return J. Meigs, Jr., Thomas Worthington, and Ethan A. Brown. He placed all of these papers in the state library and thus created its manuscript division.

While governor, Hayes took an active interest in the state's benevolent and welfare institutions, enlarging the powers of the State Board of Charities, and advocating asylum and prison reforms in his annual messages; the Reform and Industrial School for Girls created at White Sulphur Springs, Delaware County, was one result of his efforts. He studied the rehabilitation of convicts in Ireland for possible applications to Ohio's penal system and constantly sought to educate the people of Ohio on the merits of a reformatory program. An industrial arts shop was built at the Lancaster School for Boys, and a graded system introduced in the state prison provided for lighter punishment in the case of first offenders.[27]

Successful as governor, Hayes could have won a third term in 1871, although some of his admirers urged him to run for United States Senator in place of John Sherman. He declined to accept either, determined to stick to his original purpose of retiring to private life, and firmly convinced that a Republican victory was assured.[28] His forecast proved accurate; his Republican successor, Edward F. Noyes, won the governorship by 20,000 votes.

The period between 1872 and 1875 was the only time Governor Hayes was not in public service since he had first entered politics in 1858. These private years he spent improving his Spiegel Grove estate, founding the Birchard Public Library in Fremont, and developing his properties in Ohio, Minnesota, and elsewhere.

His move from Columbus to Fremont came after several curious episodes destined to affect Hayes' political future. Although unhappy with Grant's record as President, Hayes declined to join his friends in the Liberal Republican revolt of 1872, but he did attend their Cincinnati Convention in May as an observer, astutely describing it for his son Birchard:

> The Cint. Convention was large enough to show that the Republicans dissatisfied with Grant if united with *all* of the Democrats would make a force strong enough to beat us. It also showed that the Union of all these jarring elements is improbable if not impossible. There were men of talent, men wise in the management of conventions, and pure men in large numbers. But the honest men were not wise & the wise men were not honest. Three classes appeared. The free traders or Reserved reformers. These were

scholarly gentlemen of good purposes, but without experience, &
an easy prey to the scoundrels. Secondly the disappointed office
seekers—wire workers & the like & thirdly the Germans who were
dissatisfied with the Republican party quite as much on account
of Temperance & Sunday laws, as on account of Grant. The Free
Traders & the Germans represented the honesty and the power
of the Convention. Both were bitterly disappointed by Greeley's
nomination, & will not support it with unanimity, or heart. Now
come the Democrats. They divide on the question of adopting
Greeley. I hope to see the breach grow wider daily. On the whole
there is a fair chance for Grant.[29]

Hayes, however, stayed with his party, going as a delegate in
June to the Republican National Convention at Philadelphia and
supporting Grant's renomination. He always greatly admired the
general's Civil War leadership, and he also correctly concluded
that not enough Democrats would join the Liberal Republicans
to elect Horace Greeley over Grant. "My impression is they can't
do it. But of that I am in doubt—I shall make a few talks. I wish
to drift out of the political currents & shall do as little in a public
way as I possibly can."[30]

Instead, he was importuned to run for Congress in Cincinnati's
upper middle-class Second District as the only man who could
carry it for Grant against the Greeley forces. Reluctantly he
accepted, only to lose his bid for a third congressional term. Though
defeated, Hayes again ran well ahead of his party's ticket. A month
later Grant gained a second term on the strength of heavy Negro
support in the southern states. Perhaps as a reward for his party
loyalty Hayes received an appointment in March 1873 as Assistant
United States Treasurer at Cincinnati. This he respectfully
declined, and in May 1873 returned to Fremont, finished with
politics, "definitely, absolutely, positively."

In less than two years he was back in the "political rut." Republican Governor Noyes lost his bid for reelection in 1873, and Democrats won a majority of Ohio congressional seats in 1874. In the
South the restoration of white rule in all but three states spelled
the demise of carpetbag and scalawag governments. Ohio Republicans caucused in March 1875 and unanimously endorsed Hayes
for a third term as governor. Again torn between private considerations and party loyalty, Hayes confided to his diary:

A third term would be a distinction—a feather I would like to
wear. No man ever had it in Ohio. Letters tell me I am really wanted.
But the present condition of my money requires attention. The
chance of an election is not good. More important still, I do not
sympathize with a large share of the party leaders. I hate the corrup-

tionists of whom Butler is leader. I doubt the ultra measures relating to the South, and I am opposed to the course of General Grant on the third term, the civil service, and the appointment of unfit men on partisan or personal grounds. I wouldn't hesitate to fight a losing battle if the cause was wholly and clearly good and important. I am not sure that it is in all respects what it should be, and as to its importance, I am more than in doubt. Hence I have said decidedly no to all who have approached me.[31]

Yielding at length to his party's call, Hayes received the nomination for the governorship on June 2, 1875, and proceeded to organize his campaign around two issues: "Our motto is honest money for all, and free schools for all. There should be no inflation which will destroy the one, and no sectarian interference which will destroy the other."[32] To James G. Blaine he wrote, "We have been losing strength in Ohio for several years by Emigration of Rep. farmers, and especially of the young men who were in the Army. In their places have come Catholic foreigners. Last year in a tolerably full vote, they had 17,000 majority—the vote being larger than when Allen beat Noyes by a scratch. In the cities this Spring we were still more decisively beaten. Whether the reaction has spent its fire is the question. We shall down them on the school, and other state issues."[33]

The Catholic issue involved a charge that the Democratic party was part of a conspiracy to destroy the public school system and take over America for the Pope. The Ohio legislature under Democratic leadership had recently passed the Geghan Bill, which permitted Catholic inmates of state prisons and hospitals to have Catholic chaplains minister to them. The next step, according to Republican and Protestant opponents of the measure, would be a law requiring a share of public school funds for parochial schools.

The money issue emerged because Governor Allen chose to raise it as a factor in the continuing national depression of the time. He called for the issuance of more paper money and opposed resumption or putting the existing "greenbacks" on a specie basis.

Devoting his last forty speeches of the campaign to both issues, Hayes responded vigorously. He hit the Democrats hard on their subservience to Catholic demands and, as in 1869, championed hard money. Some important Democrats opposed to inflation backed Hayes, and Carl Schurz, a Liberal Republican in 1872, returned to the fold and helped the Hayes campaign among Ohio's heavy German population. The result was close: Hayes, 297,817; Allen, 292,273.

Hayes adjusted quickly to the third term: "It is like getting into old slippers to take my seat in the Governor's office once more," he wrote his eldest son Birchard; "there appears to be more business than formerly, and up to this time far more people visit the office." He pursued his old interests: "Friday I inspected the Reform Farm. Yesterday the Blind Institution."[34] Democrats had abolished the Board of State Charities; he quickly reestablished it. He made some patronage appointments and granted a few pardons, but only after personal examination of pertinent documents, and, in one case, a personal visit to a woman prisoner before finally denying her request for freedom.

In April 1876, he was suddenly confronted with a crisis when riots broke out near Massillon, Ohio, as the aftermath of a coal miners' strike. He responded swiftly. First issuing a proclamation warning the rioters to desist, he then dispatched state militia to the scene to restore law and order promptly. The governor's action contrasted favorably with the customary hesitancy of Pennsylvania authorities in dealing with their strikes.[35] Otherwise, very little occurred in the line of state policy, and the reform legislation characteristic of the first two terms was notably absent. Hayes' third term as governor is primarily important for bringing him out of political retirement, providing him with a strategic base in Republican party affairs, and advancing his availability for the 1876 Republican presidential nomination.

Notes

1. Both parents traced their lineage back to seventeenth-century New England. Although Hayes and Rutherford are Scottish names, English origins appear most often in the family ancestry. See Charles Wells Hayes, *George Hayes of Windsor and His Descendants* (Buffalo: Baker, Jones & Company, 1884), Rutherford B. Hayes Library (RBHL) copy annotated by Lucy E. Keeler; Charles Richard Williams, *The Life of Rutherford Birchard Hayes* (Boston: Houghton Mifflin Company, 1914), I, 1–14.

2. Curtis C. MacDonald, "Ansequago: A Biography of Sardis Birchard" (Ph.D. diss., Western Reserve University, 1958), passim.

3. Hayes received an honorary membership since the Kenyon Phi Beta Kappa chapter was founded sixteen years after his graduation.

4. He won first prizes in Greek, Latin, and mathematics at Kenyon. Toledo *Blade*, January 18, 1893.

5. Watt P. Marchman, "Rutherford B. Hayes and Lower Sandusky, 1845 –49," manuscript, RBHL.

6. R. B. Hayes to Fanny Arabella Hayes Platt, December 8, 1844, Hayes Papers, RBHL.

7. R. B. Hayes, Diary, December 24, 1859, Hayes Papers, RBHL.

8. For Hayes' legal career see R. B. Hayes Papers, Legal Manuscripts, RBHL, and the excellent article by Watt P. Marchman, "Rutherford B. Hayes, Attorney at Law," *Ohio History* 77 (Winter, Spring, Summer 1968): 5–32.

9. Hayes, Diary, January 17, 1852, RBHL.

10. Cited in Williams, *Life of Hayes*, I, 89.

11. See Charles Warren, *History of the Harvard Law School* (New York: Lewis Publishing Company, 1908), II, 31–34.

12. A. W. G. Carter, *The Old Court House: Reminiscences* (Cincinnati: P. G. Thompson, 1880), 445–446.

13. Hayes Scrapbook, Volume 6, p. 75, Hayes Papers, RBHL.

14. Hayes, Diary, May 13, 1886.

15. Ibid., February 1, 1876.

16. Hayes' military career is detailed in his diary and correspondence, and recently, Professor T. Harry Williams, a noted military historian, has analyzed it ably in his *Hayes of the Twenty-Third: The Civil War Volunteer Officer* (New York: Alfred A. Knopf, 1965).

17. Hayes to W. A. Platt, telegram, September 15, 1862, and Hayes to Maria Webb, September 15, 1862, both in Hayes Papers, RBHL; Rudolph Marx, *The Health of the Presidents* (New York: G. P. Putnam's Sons, 1960), 221–233.

18. Hayes to Sardis Birchard, August 31, 1856, September 15, 1858, July 30, 1864, Hayes Papers, RBHL; William Bartha, "The Early Political Career of Rutherford B. Hayes with Especial Reference to His Congressional Years" (Master's thesis, Ohio State University, 1963), 30–32.

19. "Your suggestion about getting a furlough to take the stump was certainly made without reflection. An officer fit for duty who at this crisis would abandon his post to electioneer for a seat in Congress ought to be scalped. You may feel perfectly sure I shall do no such thing." Hayes to William Henry Smith, August 24, 1864, Hayes Papers, RBHL.

20. Hayes to Governor J. D. Cox, August 7, 1867, Cox Papers, The Ohio Historical Society, Columbus, Ohio.

21. Hayes to Sophia Hayes, January 28, 1866, Hayes to Lucy Hayes, January 10, 1866, Hayes Papers, RBHL.

22. Bartha, "Early Political Career," 110. See also Felice A. Bonadio, *North of Reconstruction: Ohio Politics, 1865–1870* (New York: New York University Press, 1970), passim.

23. Hayes to Sardis Birchard, December 26, 1866, Hayes Papers, RBHL.

24. Ibid., February 2, 1867, Hayes Papers, RBHL.

25. Ibid., June 20, 1867, Hayes Papers, RBHL.

26. Ibid., January 17, 1868, Hayes Papers, RBHL. See also Daniel R. Porter, "Governor Rutherford B. Hayes," *Ohio History* 77 (Winter, Spring, Summer 1968): 58–75. His salary was now $4,000 compared to $3,500 he earned as Cincinnati's City Solicitor and $3,000 as a Congressman.

27. "The Irish Convict System was a plan of reformation based on three stages of imprisonment. The first stage was punitive and called for separate imprisonment. The second stage was one of classification by use of marks. These marks could be used by a prisoner to buy certain luxury items or to shorten his own sentence. Each prisoner could earn as many as nine marks a month—three for good conduct, three for learning in the prison school, and three for diligent work. The third stage was based on a testing program to determine the degree of the prisoner's reformation. If the convict passed these tests, he would be given a conditional pardon." Catherine S. Bartlett, "The Prison Reform Activities of Rutherford B. Hayes, 1868–1893" (Master's thesis, Ohio State University, 1958), 16–17.

28. Hayes to Josiah Thompson, June 10, 1871, Letterbook 2, p. 116, Hayes Papers, RBHL.

29. Hayes to Birchard Hayes, May 9, 1872, Hayes Papers, RBHL.

30. Hayes to W. K. Rogers, July 16, 1872, Hayes Papers, Library of Congress.

31. Hayes, Diary, March 28, 1875.

32. *Fremont Journal*, September, 1875.

33. Hayes to James G. Blaine, June 16, 1875, Blaine Papers, Library of Congress.

34. Hayes to Birchard Hayes, January 16, February 20, 1876, Hayes Papers, RBHL.

35. Hayes to Guy M. Bryan, May 7, 1876, Hayes Papers, RBHL; Hayes to General Neff, May 8, 1876, Executive Letterbook, RBHL.

2

The Contest for the Nomination

So strong was public sentiment against the corruption of Grant's administration that in 1876, for the first time since the Civil War, the Republican party faced the possibility of defeat. The Republican candidate would represent the scandal-tainted party in power; in turn his Democratic rival would hold the political advantage of attacking the policies and personnel of a weak administration. If the Republicans wished to stay in power, the choice of a safe candidate readily acceptable to a majority of their party's convention delegates, but not intimately connected with President Grant or any element within the new coalition, was of greatest importance. In the weeks preceding their convention at Cincinnati, the party press referred to this ideal nominee as "The Great Unknown."[1]

Rutherford Hayes automatically entered into the speculation for the 1876 Republican presidential nomination by winning a third term as governor of Ohio when he ousted incumbent Democrat William Allen in the 1875 election. Hayes sensed the unfolding of events. Within the privacy of his diary, he pondered his prospects: "If victorious, I am likely to be pushed for the Republican nomination for President. This would make my life a disturbed and troubled one until the nomination, six or eight months hence. If nominated, the stir would last until November a year hence."[2] Lucy shared her husband's anxiety. Awaiting the gubernatorial returns at Spiegel Grove on election night, he said, "we were prepared for either event. I told her the contest was close, the result doubtful. She spoke cheerfully of the way we would bear defeat.... We both knew well enough that victory meant the chance for the Presidency—the certainty that Ohio would present my name. Defeat meant retirement and obscurity."[3]

A few days later, his narrow victory over Allen assured, Hayes made a list of ten Ohio newspapers urging his candidacy for the presidential nomination.[4] Near the end of the month he stumped Pennsylvania with Governor John Hartranft, speaking to large crowds everywhere and garnering growing mention as a presidential possibility. In Harrisburg, the politically powerful Cameron family entertained him. Returning to Fremont, Hayes resolved "not to mix in it, or heed it; to go right along as if no such talk existed."[5] Such a course would prove impossible.

Governor J. J. Bagley of Michigan was one of the first prominent political figures to state the logic of Hayes' availability. "Your recent campaign, your location, your history all tend to give you strength. Your age is just right. You were enough of military [sic] to win our gratitude and not enough to make you known as a military candidate merely."[6] President Grant privately expressed his liking for Hayes although New York's Senator Roscoe Conkling was the nominal administration candidate. Generals William T. Sherman and Philip H. Sheridan used their influence in Hayes' behalf. John M. Harlan, a key leader of the reform-minded Benjamin H. Bristow forces, advised his candidate, "Blaine cannot be nominated—nor can Conkling—nor can Morton—I am sure that neither of them could be elected. The choice will be between yourself, Washburne, and Hayes."[7]

Ohio friends of Hayes began organizing in January 1876. Senator John Sherman, after consulting with Representative Charles Foster, put his political prestige behind the governor by writing a letter to state senator A. M. Burns promoting Hayes as the favorite son choice of the Ohio convention delegation.[8] But the canniest of all the Hayes managers was undoubtedly William Henry Smith, general agent for the Western Associated Press. Smith not only guided the Hayes movement forward but confidently predicted, nearly five months prior to the opening of the national convention, the winning ticket of Hayes and Wheeler, thus establishing Smith's reputation as a kingmaker in the annals of American political history. Hayes later acknowledged his mentor's role: ". . . your sagacity in this matter, take it all in all, is beyond that of any other friend. . . . And the way it was to come you told to a letter. Others of much sagacity have written, but nothing like yours. Not merely sagacity either—how much you did to fulfill the prediction I shall perhaps never know, but I know it was very potent."[9]

As soon as Hayes began his third term, letters and visitors on the subject of his nomination for the presidency disrupted his official duties. To his diary Hayes confided: "I say very little. I have in no instance encouraged any one to work to that end. I have discountenanced all efforts at organization or management in my interest. I have said the whole talk about me is on the score of availability. Let availability do the work then."[10]

Hayes, inwardly calm and indifferent, gave no outward sign of seeking his party's nomination. Behind the scenes, however, he kept in unbroken communication with his managers. Some of them feared he might break his public silence, declare himself an avowed candidate, and hurt his favorable position. "Write no letters," said one. "Let well enough alone," admonished another. "For God's sake avoid *all* entangling alliances with the present administration," warned another.[11] But Hayes had no need for such advice; he understood his political position perfectly, read his informant's dispatches diligently, and let the nomination manage itself. "It seems to me that good purposes and the judgment, experience and firmness I possess, would enable me to execute the duties of the office well."[12] At the very least, nearly everyone conceded, the vice presidential nomination would be his if he wished it.[13] Privately he supported Benjamin H. Bristow to head the ticket, knowing full well this would ultimately work to his own benefit if the Kentuckian's chances faded.[14]

On March 29, 1876, the 750 delegates to the Ohio Republican State Convention unanimously endorsed Governor Hayes for President, urging "earnest efforts to secure his nomination." As W. D. Bickham, editor of the *Dayton Journal*, saw it, "If the Ohio delegation stands firmly until the managers have worn out Blaine, Morton, and Conkling, the consummation will be what we pray for."[15] Hayes was less certain. "In politics I am growing indifferent. I would like it, if I could now return to my planting and books at home." Still, amid the mounting pressures, he kept his composure: "My rule and preference, however, is to do absolutely nothing to favor the movement in behalf of my nomination. I mean to keep this path to the end."[16] This air of detachment actually strengthened his candidacy. "We are all delighted," wrote Garfield, "with the sensible way in which you are bearing yourself during the chaotic period of President making."[17]

Throughout the preconvention weeks, the Hayes organization labored to line up second-choice support for their candidate among the delegations already pledged to others on the first ballot. They also carefully avoided making public attacks on any other aspirant for the nomination. But privately, and without telling Governor Hayes, for fear of his disapproval, they sought to discredit his competitors. William Henry Smith helped circulate a story about Blaine's unsavory railroad dealings, while Bristow, who came from a border state, was injured by rumors of his questionable loyalty to the Union.

In May 1876, Hayes tried to influence John Sherman to represent his interests in the convention. "I do not mean to depart from the position I have taken to remain perfectly passive on the nomination. But it is fair to assume that the time may come when I ought to be withdrawn. To be able to act on this and other possible questions it is important for me that I have friends of experience and sound judgment on the ground, by whom I can be advised of the exact condition of things and of the proper course to be taken."[18] As a rejected member of the Ohio delegation, Sherman wisely declined to interfere, and instead wielded what influence he could over the other state delegations from his position in Washington.

Meanwhile a group of Liberal Republicans—led by Carl Schurz, George William Curtis, and Charles Francis Adams—met in New York City, and indicted Grant's corrupt administration, called for reform, and backed Bristow for the nomination, although Curtis in a private letter conceded a probable compromise on Hayes because of mounting antagonisms among followers of the other candidates. Hayes himself thought Blaine's chances best because his commanding lead in delegate strength would produce a bandwagon effect among less committed members of the convention.[19]

Instead of John Sherman, Edward F. Noyes of Cincinnati, a former governor, and General Ralph P. Buckland of Fremont, a former law partner of Hayes, became his trusted spokesmen within the Ohio delegation. Noyes was subsequently elected chairman of the delegation by acclamation. On June 1 he estimated Blaine's strength at 250 on the first ballot, with 379 necessary to win. Two days later he reported Blaine's chances as fading and out of the question.[20] Governor Hayes kept up a cautious attitude, noting to William Henry Smith, "My correspondents all give me the same flattering report—sinister news doesn't reach me."[21]

On the eve of the convention, four major contenders vied for support: Congressman James G. Blaine of Maine, Senator Roscoe Conkling of New York, Senator Oliver P. Morton of Indiana, and Secretary of the Treasury Benjamin H. Bristow of Kentucky. Three other men were put forward as favorite sons by their state delegations: Postmaster General Marshall Jewell of Connecticut, Governor Rutherford B. Hayes of Ohio, and Governor John Hartranft of Pennsylvania. Since in this group the Jewell and Hartranft candidacies were designed merely as holding operations until the balloting narrowed down to two or three candidates, only Hayes was a serious contender.

Blaine, the congressional candidate, held a commanding lead in delegate strength, yet lacked nearly 100 votes to win the nomination on the first ballot. He was the only national candidate in the group having first ballot supporters in 36 of the 49 states and territories. Like Henry Clay before him, he inspired great devotion among his followers. He compensated for his lack of a military record by using his great oratorical powers to brand the South as the region of rebellion, a tactic that won both firm friends and bitter enemies. Although he had become a member of the Rules Committee and Speaker of the House, his striking weakness appeared in the notable lack of constructive legislation bearing his name and his involvement in scandal.

Senator Conkling, another brilliant orator, disliked Blaine intensely from the day Blaine mercilessly described his "turkey gobbler strut." Conkling, who controlled the New York State Republican organization, was more closely identified with President Grant than any other Republican and hence was the acknowledged administration candidate. Although he had only token support outside his own state, Conkling's large New York delegation alone represented nearly one-fifth of the votes needed to nominate a standard-bearer.

Senator Morton, Indiana's brilliant war governor and long a champion of Negro rights, controlled the party machinery in his pivotal state and held the confidence of the southern carpetbag delegations. Morton, unlike his major rivals, had a record of solid executive and legislative accomplishment, in addition to outstanding oratorical skill. His great handicap was physical; since 1865 he had suffered from paralysis of the legs. Hayes admired Morton and knew him best of the leading contenders.

Benjamin H. Bristow was the favorite of the reformers because, while Secretary of the Treasury, he had vigorously prosecuted the Whiskey Ring conspirators. His backers included most of the Liberal Republicans of 1872, eastern conservatives, Cincinnati newspaper editors, and Chicago business leaders. Although his delegate strength was thin, it was widely distributed over New England, the South, and Middle West.

A week of great excitement in Cincinnati began on Friday, June 9, as many of the delegates to the national Republican convention, unofficial supporters of the leading candidates, and mere spectators poured into the city. The Reform Club of New York, numbering about fifty or sixty men, all for Bristow, arrived early Saturday morning at the Gibson House. The New York City Republican Club, two hundred strong and accompanied by a fine band, all in Conkling's interest, put up at the Grand Hotel. Other groups from Philadelphia and Pittsburgh with two more splendid bands arrived on Monday and registered at the Arlington and Burnet

House. A host of supporters in Morton's behalf came from Indianapolis on Tuesday.[22]

The Bristow Club of Cincinnati, numbering between 2,000 and
3,000, engaged Pike's Opera House and Currier's Band for the
week of the convention. Flags were hung out all over the city,
and the hotels, draped in the American colors, were handsomely
illuminated at night. The Grand Hotel had a semicircle of colored
lights over the main entrance, and just under them a row of gas
jets arranged to spell ROSCOE CONKLING. The Burnet House had
a similar row of gas jets to spell the name of JAMES G. BLAINE.
The Bristow Club hung a strip of muslin bearing the inscription
BRISTOW and REFORM across Fourth Street in front of Pike's Opera
House. The Morton and Hayes delegations were not quite so conspicuous in their display, although they too had their respective
headquarters, flags, and banners.

Excitement and enthusiasm grew feverish long before the convention assembled on Wednesday morning. Each evening the
hotels were brilliantly illuminated, and bands played in front of
their respective headquarters. People milled about in great masses
choking traffic, and amid the din orators extolled the merits of
the Republican party or their favorite candidate. Other crowds
surged through the streets. Cheers and fireworks rent the air. Red
and green lights burned on nearly every corner. Meanwhile political workers sounded the sentiments of delegates and visitors,
attempting to win them over by argument, entreaty, or promises.

Conkling's supporters, the first on the scene, worked hard in
his cause. Theirs was an uphill struggle, however, and they generally knew before the convention even opened, that the New Yorker
stood no real chance of being nominated. The Morton men began
with more votes than Conkling, but they did not arrive so early
or work so strenuously for their candidate. By evening on Wednesday, the first day of the convention, they conceded Morton could
not be nominated either.

Great numbers of Blaine backers also arrived early. They counted
nearly two hundred delegates who were instructed or requested
to vote for Blaine, and a large number among the uninstructed
delegates who made no secret of their preference for him either
at the time they were elected or during the week of the convention.
With so many votes already secured, it was easy for his managers
to persuade other uncommitted delegates to come over to Blaine.
They assured those who were tempted by prospects of patronage
that he was destined to win, and they might as well join the
bandwagon early and thus merit his recognition and favor.
Whenever they found anyone with malice against the South, they

boasted how James G. Blaine's oratory discomfited the Rebels in the House of Representatives. They said if he were only elected President, his would be the most brilliant administration the world ever saw. They spoke of his eloquence and power as a speaker and claimed no one could make a livelier canvass or a more glorious success than he. Of course, they said nothing about his using his position and influence as Speaker of the House to forward railroad schemes in which he was interested; they said nothing about his own letters that proved him to be speculating in stocks whose value depended wholly on congressional legislation. In short, they said nothing of all the disreputable and suspicious circumstances surrounding his past life and overshadowing the future of their candidate.

Meanwhile, on Sunday, June 11, Blaine suffered a sunstroke on the steps of a church in Washington. For two days he lay unconscious, and the report went out that he was dying. No one wished to say hard things against a man who was lying at death's door, no matter how true they might be, and so, during the rest of Sunday, Monday, and Tuesday, Blaine's friends worked on the sympathies and feelings of the crowd. Even Hayes, who felt that Blaine's nomination would be fatal to the party in the November election, was nonetheless moved to send a highly emotional message, a rare response indeed for him: "I have just read with the deepest sorrow of your illness. My eyes are almost blinded with tears as I write. All good men among your countrymen will pray as I do, for your immediate and complete recovery. This affects me as did the death of Lincoln. God bless you and restore you."[23]

On Tuesday Blaine's fever passed, and he sent a message of convalescence to Eugene Hale and William P. Frye, his managers at the convention. Reassuring telegrams were sent nearly every hour of the day thereafter to some one or other of his friends to be posted in the barrooms of hotels or on bulletin boards in various newspaper offices.

Blaine's friends were jubilant and confident of victory on Tuesday night. They claimed more than three hundred votes on the first ballot and boasted they would gain enough on the second from delegations who first had to cast one complimentary vote for a favorite son to nominate their man. But their very confidence was their undoing. From the fear and depression created among other managers and delegates arose a desperate spirit to combine and defeat Blaine. At meetings of the Bristow Club on Tuesday and Wednesday nights, speakers warned of the great danger to the Republican party. The Cincinnati papers, the *Commercial* and

the *Gazette,* entered the fray, proclaiming boldly that Blaine's nomination would cause the ruin of the Republican party and that
they could not support him. *The New York Times* did the same.
Carl Schurz and other Liberals and independents warned that if
Blaine were nominated they would either support the Democratic
ticket, nominated at St. Louis, or organize a third-party movement.

Bristow's friends, however, were overly zealous and earnest in
proclaiming him to be the reform candidate. They were determined
that Blaine should not be nominated if it was possible to prevent
it, and they openly avowed their intention to "kick" against the
nomination if he won it. But their attitude automatically made
all of Blaine's backers sworn enemies of Bristow. Morton's and
Conkling's supporters were also prejudiced against Bristow since
he had been portrayed as a holier-than-thou candidate, and the
regular machine politicians were opposed to him because they
said he and all his supporters were "kickers," not true to the
party. Others resented the idea of having a candidate forced upon
them as they insisted Bristow was, and said that when people
came to them and told them they must nominate Bristow or perish,
they would rather perish. Thus Bristow's friends aroused a great
deal of opposition among the different elements in the convention,
thereby sacrificing their candidate.

The Hayes delegation, meanwhile, kept quietly in the background, voicing no preferences. They made no fuss over Hayes,
simply saying they were instructed to vote for him and should
do so while there was any chance of his success. They were friendly
with the supporters of every other candidate in the field, aroused
no opposition, and ultimately succeeded in making Hayes the
second choice of nearly every delegate. Young Webb Hayes, in
Cincinnati as his father's private observer, summarized the situation on Monday evening, June 12: "Greatest good feeling prevails
towards you on all sides. . . . The Ohio men are jubilant and willing
to sleep with any other of the delegates. All friends—no enemys
[*sic*]."[24]

At a meeting of the Ohio delegation held a day or two before
the convention, the work of visitation and conference with
delegates from other states was assigned to different members.
Among these was Clark Waggoner, alternate-at-large and Hayes'
Toledo friend. Waggoner kept a record of his activities and carefully
noted the situations of the delegations he visited.[25] Meanwhile
other Hayes' managers, William Henry Smith, James M. Comly,
Ralph P. Buckland, and A. E. Lee, the governor's secretary, worked
to promote Hayes' nomination. Another valuable ally inside the
Bristow camp was Stanley Matthews, intimate friend of Hayes

at Kenyon College and brother-in-law of Dr. Joseph T. Webb, a brother of Mrs. Hayes. Matthews could take advantage of any change in Bristow's fortunes to assist the Hayes cause, especially since Hayes himself was generally reported to favor Bristow's candidacy. By 8:00 P.M. on Monday evening Smith wired the governor: "At this hour I think I can safely predict that Ohio will win."[26]

The national convention opened on Wednesday at noon, but before it met, Murat Halstead and Richard Smith, both Bristow backers, used their Cincinnati papers, the *Commercial* and *Gazette*, to print solid columns of protest against the nomination of Blaine, and issued supplements containing Blaine's damaging Mulligan letters arranged in the order of their dates, with a running commentary on the inferences that could be drawn from them.

If the convention had balloted for President and Vice President at once, the Blaine men felt confident of victory, but the balloting was delayed by Bristow's supporters, who were endeavoring to postpone action upon the nominations as long as possible. They stalled for time so that sober second thoughts, which they expected would come to many of the delegates, would save the party from making a blunder.

The first day was consumed in effecting a permanent organization, speech making, and appointment of standing committees.[27] Repeated efforts to adjourn failed. That evening the continued speech making gave time for more earnest talk with the delegates against Blaine's nomination. Thursday morning the papers renewed their attack on him. Still, his support was so large that the Blaine forces had their way in every decision not directly connected with his actual nomination. Thus when a motion was made to exclude the territories from voting for nominees, since they had no electoral votes, the Blaine contingent succeeded in voting it down and thereby secured for their candidate twelve to fourteen additional convention votes. In debating the report of the rules committee, the proposal to recess after each ballot was defeated. Again, when a vote was taken on the report of the committee on credentials in favor of admitting the Jeremiah Haralson delegation from Alabama instead of a rival group headed by Senator George Spencer, which was favorable to Morton and Conkling, the Blaine men won by a margin of 375 to 354, gaining Alabama's sixteen votes. On this ballot, the Kentucky delegation voted against seating the Spencer group, an action which so antagonized the Indiana delegation that it probably prevented Bristow from gaining more than five votes from Indiana when Morton's name was ultimately withdrawn on the fifth ballot.

Blaine's group, however, was defeated in all its attempts to force a vote for President and Vice President. His managers could not overcome the delay, so precious to the candidate's opponents and so dangerous to him. They had tried, unsuccessfully, on Thursday morning to have a ballot taken before the committee on resolutions was ready to report the platform. That afternoon, after all the committees had reported and the platform had been adopted, they tried to force the convention to a nomination. At 2:50 P.M. the same day, the roll of states was finally called and any delegate with a candidate to present was allowed ten minutes for a speech in his favor. Ex-Governor Stephen W. Kellogg of Connecticut nominated Postmaster General Marshall Jewell. The endorsement was understood to be complimentary; perhaps it would put Jewell in a favorable position for the vice presidential nomination. Colonel Richard W. Thompson of Indiana, an orator of the old school, nominated Senator Morton in a fine speech, evoking considerable applause, and the nomination was seconded by a mulatto, ex-Governor P. B. S. Pinchback of Louisiana. General John M. Harlan rose to nominate Bristow. He made an impressive speech, more loudly applauded by the people in the galleries than by the delegates. Luke Poland of Vermont, George William Curtis, editor of *Harper's Weekly*, and Richard H. Dana of Massachusetts seconded the nomination. Curtis made a fine speech, Poland a dull one, while Dana unwisely intimated that Massachusetts would vote Democratic in November if the convention failed to nominate Bristow.

Following Dana, Robert J. Ingersoll of Illinois nominated Blaine and made the most effective speech of the day, one still considered a great masterpiece of nominating oratory. He turned to the preceding speaker, saying, "Gentlemen of the Convention: Massachusetts may be satisfied with the loyalty of Benjamin H. Bristow. So am I. But if any man nominated by the convention can not carry the State of Massachusetts, I am not satisfied with the loyalty of Massachusetts."[28] He said this with tremendous force and emphasis, inspiring an overwhelming round of applause from the Blaine delegates and heaping contempt upon Bristow's supporters. Ingersoll continued by praising his hero, James G. Blaine, who "like an armed warrior, like a plumed knight, marched down the halls of the American congress and threw his shining lance full and fair against the brazen forehead of every traitor to his country and every maligner of his fair reputation."[29]

So many in the convention hall rose and cheered until it seemed Blaine must be nominated. He undoubtedly would have been if a ballot had been taken just then, or even that afternoon before adjournment. But this was not to be. A Negro delegate from Georgia, Henry M. Turner, followed Ingersoll with such a poor speech that it provoked the laughter of the hall a half dozen times. He did not stop until the audience drowned him out with cries of "time, time, you've said enough," and the chairman told him he had better make room for others. Smiling, he yielded and said "Lord bless you—I'se got a dozen good points, I could make yet."[30] General Frye of Maine followed with a speech seconding the nomination of Blaine. When New York was called, Stewart L. Woodford arose and delivered a masterful speech nominating Senator Conkling. He gave Blaine a cruel stab by saying, "With the most loving of his friends, New York congratulates him that his strength is renewed, and his health so fully restored."[31]

Then Ohio was called, and Governor Edward F. Noyes in his rich, sonorous voice nominated Governor Hayes, stressing his candidate's war record, financial independence, political experience, and especially three successive gubernatorial victories over prominent Ohio Democrats, each considered an aspirant for the presidency. In a potent phrase designed to counter Ingersoll's reference to Blaine's "bloody shirt" oratory, Noyes characterized Hayes as "a man who, during dark and stormy days of the rebellion, when those who are invincible in peace and invisible in battle were uttering brave words to cheer their neighbors on, himself in the fore-front of battle, followed his leaders and his flag until the authority of our government was reestablished. . . ."[32] Noyes made an effective speech, which was generously applauded.

Governor Hartranft was nominated by Representative Linn Bartholomew of Pennsylvania, who made the amazing declaration that the other nominees possessed great intellectual superiority over his candidate but that Hartranft knew "enough to know that he does not know everything, and is willing to take and to follow good, sound, wholesome advice"![33]

Since there were no other candidates, the roll call of states ceased, and one of the Morton managers, Will Cumbach, made a motion to adjourn. This was yelled down by the Blaine faction. One of the Conkling men, Samuel S. Edick, then made a motion for an informal ballot (not binding upon the convention, but which would show the relative strength of the several candidates) to be followed by immediate adjournment until 10:00 A.M. Friday. Blaine supporters overpowered this motion too. William P. Frye of Maine, inquired if the hall could be lighted, and permanent chairman Edward McPherson replied: "I desire to say, for the information of the convention, that I am informed that the gas lights of this hall are in such condition that they cannot safely be lighted."[34] The motion to adjourn until Friday morning was renewed and carried by a small majority.

The opposition to Blaine had gained another night for work,

and the press got in a few more urgent protests against his nomination, while the supporters of Morton, Conkling, Bristow, and Hayes had an opportunity to adjust matters among themselves and settle on a plan of action. Late that evening Hayes received three telegrams. James M. Comly wired: "Blaine opposed adjournment gave way to evident wishes of Convention on pretext that Hall had no gas evening session Blaine prestige clouded other Candidates hopeful Ohio extremely confident Many overtures some from Blaine delegation [sic]."[35] The second dispatch from his son Webb read: "Governor Noyes instructs me to say that the Combinations are very favorable [sic]."[36] A third message came from E. Croxsey of *The New York Times*: "Chances ten to one that Blaine is beaten and that you get the nomination everybody is ready now to beat Blaine and it can't be done on Conkling, Morton or Bristow [sic]."[37]

It was conceded, then, among the anti-Blaine forces during the night of June 15 that neither Morton, Conkling, Hartranft, nor Jewell could win; that the lot must fall, if not to Bristow, to Hayes or "the Great Unknown," possibly Secretary of State Hamilton Fish or Congressman Elihu Washburne of Illinois. Jewell's name was to be withdrawn after the first complimentary ballot. Morton's supporters agreed to withdraw his name after two or three ballots if it was demonstrated that their favorite could not win, and then presumably they would cast their solid vote for Bristow. The Conkling men preferred Hayes to Bristow but would support either in preference to Blaine. It was expected that a large majority of the southern delegates would vote for Bristow as soon as Conkling and Morton were withdrawn. At the same time, it was believed that Blaine could not attain a majority until the weakness of the other leading candidates was demonstrated, and that then would be time enough to consider Hayes or someone else.

Morton's and Conkling's support dwindled steadily from the very start. Blaine gained 14 and lost 3 votes on the second ballot, for a net gain of 11, or 296 total, and remained relatively static on the third and fourth ballots gaining 6 new votes, but losing 10 for a net gain through 4 ballots of only 7 votes. His managers succeeded in offsetting a loss of 6 votes to Bristow and 3 to Hayes by picking up 11 of Morton's original votes. Conkling's net loss of 15 votes over the first 4 ballots accrued principally to Hartranft, although he lost a few each to Blaine, Bristow, and Morton. Only Hartranft, Hayes, and Bristow gained steadily through the first 4 ballots, and Bristow actually stood higher at the end of the fourth ballot than any other candidate except Blaine. On this ballot, Michigan cast 11 votes for Bristow, while Morton lost 16 votes, and it was evident his delegate strength was slipping away. On the fifth ballot, Indiana ought properly to have withdrawn Morton and cast her entire 30 votes for Bristow; Michigan might then have cast her 22 votes for him. His support then would have increased so rapidly that he undoubtedly would have combined all straggling votes and won the nomination on the sixth ballot. But the Morton men, acting under advice from Washington, still clung to their candidate. As Bristow gained nothing from any other source, Michigan decided to switch to Hayes on the fifth ballot. Her chairman announced: "There is a man in this section of the country who has beaten in succession three Democratic candidates for President in his own state, and we want to give him a chance to beat another Democratic candidate for the Presidency in the broader field of the United States. Michigan therefore casts her twenty-two votes for Rutherford B. Hayes of Ohio!"[38] This action sent the Hayes stock up at once. North Carolina gave him 11 votes more, and he gained scattered support from other states, enough to boost his strength above 100. Nine of the North Carolina votes were transferred directly from Blaine to Hayes, depressing the Blaine stock and leaving him but 286 votes, the lowest number since the first ballot.

A few days after the convention, General Harlan, leader of the Kentucky delegation, in a letter to Bristow, wrote his explanation of the turning point: "The action of the Michigan delegation in consolidating its vote for Hayes on the fifth ballot caused a stampede in our ranks.... The union of that delegation on Hayes was a surprise to us, and as soon as it was done I felt that our cause was hopeless. The failure of the Indiana delegation to change to you on the fifth ballot induced the Michigan folks to make the break to Hayes."[39] William A. Howard, chairman of the Michigan delegation, in turn, wrote to Hayes, explaining why his state voted for Hayes on the fifth ballot instead of Bristow:

On the 4th ballot 10 had voted for Bristow 5 for Hayes and 7 for Blaine. All were admirers of Blaine but believing his nomination would force upon the party a defensive campaign & perhaps defeat we felt bound to prevent his nomination. The 5th ballot commenced and 13 win [went] for Bristow 5 for Hayes & 4 for Blaine. It was certain that Conklin & Morton must soon be withdrawn & if the Bristow & Hayes strength could be united & draw to itself the greater part of the Conklin & Morton vote it would defeat Blaine. So I told the delegation if they would unite & throw the vote solid & adhere firmly we could make a nomination & perhaps save the party from defeat. The Bristow men said unite on him, the minority ought to yield to majority &c. In the absence of facts we were obliged to rely on the supposed logic of the situation. I thought the two N.Y. delegates must have exasperated the other 68 by the persistency with which they had advocated the nomination of Bristow even refusing to join in a harmless complimentary vote for Conklin. I said if we strike for Bristow we shall fail for want of New York votes. It is not in human nature while exasperated & heated that they, the 68 should take the candidate of the two. If we strike for Hayes we shall win. They reluctantly yielded—the last man after I was on my crutches to announce the vote.[40]

Spectators in the galleries and the supporters of other prominent candidates now began to count Blaine out of the race, supposing he had reached his greatest strength; therefore there was no serious effort to continue supporting an opposition candidate in the sixth ballot. Hayes gained a few more votes from Illinois, Iowa, Texas, Tennessee, Virginia, and West Virginia, some of them being transferred from Bristow, and came out two ahead of Bristow on this ballot.

Meanwhile, North Carolina, not satisfied with the slow progress Hayes was making and believing after all that Blaine was destined to win, took 12 votes from Hayes and cast them for Blaine. This produced great cheering made louder when Pennsylvania cast 14 votes for Blaine. South Carolina increased her votes for Blaine from 5 to 10. With 308 votes on this ballot, it was apparent from the way the Blaine people began to move about among the southern delegates, plus the confusion among the Pennsylvania delegation, that a big push would be made on the next ballot to nominate Blaine and that the opposition must combine now or never.

The Indiana and Kentucky delegates consulted earnestly; Massachusetts and New York retired for consultation. When the seventh ballot started, everyone knew the end was near. Blaine gained a vote from Alabama and 11 from Arkansas. California gave him 16, whereas she had given him only 6 before. And so he kept gaining from every state, until it seemed as though nothing could stop him. Every new gain was cheered wildly by his supporters. When Indiana was reached, Blaine had gained 32 votes. Amid intense excitement, Indiana was called, and chairman Will Cumbach walked slowly up to the platform. In a pathetic and dignified speech, he withdrew the name of Morton, thanked the convention for the noble support they had given him, and announced Indiana's vote as 25 for Rutherford B. Hayes and 5 for Benjamin H. Bristow. At this point the anti-Blaine forces began shouting; the people in the galleries rose to their feet, swung hats and handkerchiefs, and gave three long rounds of applause. Iowa delivered her 22 votes for Blaine as before. Kentucky was called. General Harlan rose and walked to the podium. He stood there, lips trembling with emotion, waiting for the storm of applause to be hushed, and then spoke grandly. He thanked the convention for the support they had given Colonel Bristow, and the thanks of Kentucky were especially due to those men of Massachusetts and Vermont, who when it was whispered throughout the length and breadth of the land that Benjamin H. Bristow was not to be President because he was born and reared in the South, had come forward and said they were satisfied that a Kentuckian could be loyal. He withdrew Bristow's name and cast Kentucky's entire vote for Rutherford B. Hayes. Wild and tumultuous applause broke loose.

Louisiana, which had given Blaine only 6 votes, now cast 14 for him, giving the Blaine forces another chance to cheer and so the contest wavered. When Massachusetts cast 21 for Hayes, Michigan 21, and Mississippi 16, the applause was deafening. When New York was called, there was a lull of anxious expectation. Governor Theodore M. Pomeroy advanced to the platform and said amid perfect silence, "To indicate that New York is in favor of unity and victory, she casts sixty-one votes for Rutherford B. Hayes." The remainder of his sentence, "and nine votes for James G. Blaine," was drowned out.[41] North Carolina again swung over to Hayes and cast her solid vote of 20 for him. Ohio followed as usual with 44, but now the vote seemed to count for much more, and the Exposition Hall rang with the cheers of the united opposition.

When Pennsylvania was called, there was another lull of expectation. Blaine could still win with a bloc vote here. Don Cameron, the young Secretary of War, mounted a chair in front of his delegation, withdrew the name of Hartranft, and announced 30 votes for Blaine and 28 for Hayes, which made both sides cheer long and loud. South Carolina divided evenly; Texas gave all but 1 vote to Hayes. Tennessee added 18 for Hayes, and Vermont her entire 10. Before the territories were reached, some of the reporters who were quick at figures discovered Hayes had a majority, jumped up in their seats, swung their hats and shouted: "Hayes! Hayes!" The territories were called amid great confusion and the chairmen of all but Montana and Wyoming doggedly cast their votes for James G. Blaine though they knew their man was beaten. The tally showed Blaine, 351; Bristow, 21; Hayes, 384.

Cheering lasted about fifteen or twenty minutes. The nomination of Hayes was made unanimous, and the convention proceeded to nominate a Vice President. The names of William A. Wheeler and Stewart L. Woodford of New York, Joseph M. Hawley and Marshall Jewell of Connecticut, and Frederick T. Frelinghuysen of New Jersey were presented. Early in the balloting, it became evident that Wheeler was the favorite. All the Blaine men voted for him, and Woodford withdrew his own name before New York was reached. New York cast her solid vote for Wheeler, Pennsylvania voted for Frelinghuysen, Jewell was withdrawn, and before the first ballot was completed, a motion to make Wheeler's nomination unanimous carried by an overwhelming shout. The dream ticket of William Henry Smith had been achieved. (The balloting had proceeded toward the magic number of 379 as shown in Table 1.)[42]

TABLE 1
Republican Convention Ballots (1876)

	1	2	3	4	5	6	7
Blaine	285	296	293	292	286	308	351
Bristow	113	114	121	126	114	111	21
Hayes	61	64	67	68	104	113	384
Morton	124	120	113	108	95	85	Withdrawn
Conkling	99	93	90	84	82	81	Withdrawn
Hartranft	58	63	68	71	69	50	Withdrawn
Jewell	11	Withdrawn					
Wheeler	3	3	2	2	2	2	Withdrawn
Washburne		1	1	3	3	4	
Total	754	754	755	754	755	754	756

A state-by-state reexamination of the seven ballots for the 1876 Republican presidential nomination reveals even more clearly how narrow a victory Hayes had won, and the remarkable race made by Blaine against the field not only as the front-runner on six ballots but also burdened by the doubts raised before and during the convention concerning the Mulligan letters and his illness. Despite his handicaps, Blaine might have been nominated if Hayes had not garnered barely enough votes on the seventh ballot. Composite vote figures for all seven ballots by candidate demonstrate Blaine's great appeal (Table 2).

These figures show that Blaine failed to hold forty-seven delegates who had voted for him on earlier ballots. The North Carolina delegation with twenty votes, which he controlled on five of the first six ballots, deserted him on the crucial seventh poll. A floor fight over the unit rule during the second ballot also

TABLE 2
Composite Vote Analysis

	Maximum Support over Seven Ballots	Maximum Support on a Single Ballot
Blaine	398	351
Hayes	388	384
Bristow	149	126
Morton	137	124
Conkling	105	99
Hartranft	80	71
Jewell	11	11
Wheeler	3	3
Washburne	4	4

boomeranged on Blaine's managers. When Pennsylvania was called, and her vote given as fifty-eight for Hartranft, it was challenged by one of the delegates who stated that he and another delegate wanted to vote for Blaine. They subsequently were joined by two others. McPherson, the convention chairman and loyal to Blaine, ruled that "it is the right of any and of every member equally, to vote his sentiments in this convention."[43] An appeal from this decision was put to the convention, and the chairman's decision was declared sustained. Thereupon a motion to reconsider the motion upholding the decision of the chair carried 381 to 359. On the roll call, the decision of the convention chairman was again sustained, 395 to 353. At the time, the vote was hailed as a victory for Blaine. On the seventh ballot, however, when Pennsylvania divided 30 for Blaine and 28 for Hayes, it was a major factor in defeating him. As J. C. Lee explained later to Hayes: "Had not McPherson ruled as he did on the Pa. question, or had the Convention reversed his decision, the 28 votes for you in Pa. would had been carried by the 30 Blaine votes to Blaine, and that would have given Blaine 379, just enough to nominate him & more to spare."[44] In raising the unit rule question, the Blaine faction won a minor victory that paved the way to ultimate defeat.

Hayes, on the other hand, won the nomination because his managers were shrewd enough to let Bristow's supporters make the fight against Blaine, and after it was over, they gathered in the victory. Furthermore, by concentrating on second-choice support for Hayes, he became the only candidate to gain strength on every ballot and to take votes away from each of his rivals. Hayes in the end received most of the Bristow and Conkling support, about half of the Morton and Hartranft votes, and even took votes away from Blaine. Over all seven ballots, Hayes lost only four delegates who had on some ballot voted for him, but even with this remarkable holding power he had only five votes to spare. In retrospect, Michigan's shift from Blaine and Bristow to Hayes was the decisive turning point in the balloting. A. B. Watson, a member of the Michigan delegation, later revealed how when Hayes was nominated "the Ohio delegation rushed forward, and embracing the veteran chairman of the Michigan delegation, exclaimed You have nominated the next President!' "[45] John C. Lee of Ohio conceded: "I must not forget to say that in Gov. Bagley and Wm. A. Howard of Michigan we formed original and most effective friends. They had taken in the situation much more completely than many, yes, 9/10 of our own delegates."[46]

William Henry Smith praised the leadership of Noyes:

> ... the one who above all others deserves praise. It was something to have noble men in the Ohio delegation: ... But it was of first importance to have a leader as Edward F. Noyes. Better management I never saw. It was able, judicious, untiring, unselfish, inspiring, adroit. If there was a mistake made I did not discover it. The disloyalty that attempted on the part of one or two well-known Ohioans in the interest of Blaine, was anticipated and cleverly disarmed. The General seemingly never slept. His eyes were everywhere and discipline was preserved with as much vigor as on the field of battle. He comprehended fully the situation and inspired the confidence of the men of New England, New York, Kentucky, and Indiana. His personal friendship for Gens. Bristow and Harlan did not as some mischief makers asserted would be the case, lessen his loyalty to you, but served an important purpose at a critical moment.[47]

The choice of Cincinnati's Exposition Hall as the convention site, originally expected to aid the Bristow and Morton candidacies, also ultimately worked to aid the Hayes cause. Of all the cities in America, Cincinnati alone could consider Hayes as her very own, for here he had begun his legal and political career in earnest. Here he joined the famed Literary Club, mingled in polite society, and married Lucy Webb. From here he went to war, to Congress, and the State House.

As for Bristow, if the attempt had been made to nominate him on the seventh ballot in a square fight with Blaine, it would undoubtedly have failed, since the Ohio delegation would either have held firm for Hayes or broken up to give Blaine sixteen votes. Blaine also would have picked up ten more in Pennsylvania, some in New York, and some scalawags in southern delegations. Harlan also later confessed to W. Q. Gresham that he had made a deal with the Hayes men, and Hayes carried out his part of the bargain by placing Harlan on the Supreme Court in 1877. Bristow, piqued over failure to receive the justiceship for himself, and feeling that Harlan had betrayed him, never spoke to Harlan after the latter's appointment.[48]

Two weeks after the Republican convention, the Democrats met in St. Louis and chose Governor Samuel J. Tilden of New York as their standard-bearer. Tilden, a bachelor and multimillionaire, helped expose and prosecute the notorious Tweed Ring of New York City, an activity that aided in his election to the governorship in 1874, where he further enhanced his reputation as a reformer. Aloof and shy, constantly brooding over his rather poor health, Tilden devoted many hours to his fine library. Thomas A. Hendricks of Indiana, second in the balloting to Tilden at St. Louis, received the vice presidential nomination by acclamation. With Tilden supporting the hard money views of the eastern wing of the party, and Hendricks advocating the greenback position of the western Democrats, they made a strange pair. The stage was set for the most extraordinary presidential election in American history.

Notes

1. See for example the editorial, "The Great Unknown," Boston *Journal*, May 9, 1876.
2. Hayes, Diary, October 12, 1875, Hayes Papers, RBHL.
3. Ibid., October 25, 1889.
4. Ibid., October 17, 1875. "Now come papers from all the country counties urging me for the Presidential nomination. Such as the following list: Cincinnati *Times*, Toledo *Blade*, Dayton *Journal*, Springfield *Republican*, Ashtabula *Sentinel*, Fremont *Journal*, Kenton *Republican*, Bellefontaine *Republican*, Clinton *Republican*, Pickaway *Herald and Union*."
5. Hayes to Gen. M. F. Force, November 2, 1875, Hayes Papers, RBHL.
6. J. J. Bagley to Hayes, November 11, 1875, Hayes Papers, RBHL.
7. John M. Harlan to Benjamin H. Bristow, January 24, 1876, Bristow Papers, Library of Congress.
8. John Sherman to A. M. Burns, January 21, 1876, Hayes Papers, RBHL.
9. Smith to Hayes, January 26, 1876, Hayes to Smith, June 19, 1876, Hayes Papers, RBHL.
10. Hayes, Diary, February 15, 1876.
11. M. D. Leggett to Hayes, February 21, 1876; R. C. Anderson to Hayes, March 4, 1876, Hayes Papers, RBHL.

12. Hayes, Diary, March 21, 1876.

13. Ibid., June 10, 1876; Hayes to Birchard Hayes, March 25, 1876, Hayes Papers, RBHL.

14. Hayes, Diary, March 21, 1876; Hayes to Major W. D. Bickham, April 26, 1876, Hayes Papers, RBHL.

15. Hayes, Diary, April 2, 1876; W. D. Bickham to Hayes, April 19, 1876, Hayes Papers, RBHL.

16. Hayes, Diary, April 11, 1876; Hayes to Guy M. Bryan, April 23, 1876, Hayes Papers, RBHL.

17. James A. Garfield to Hayes, May 4, 1876, Hayes Papers, RBHL.

18. Hayes to Sherman, May 19, 25, 1876, Hayes Papers, RBHL.

19. Hayes, Diary, May 19, 21, 1876.

20. Edward F. Noyes to Hayes, June 1, 3, 1876, Hayes Papers, RBHL.

21. Hayes to William Henry Smith, May 31, 1876, Hayes Papers, RBHL.

22. Most of the colorful detail used in describing the Republican Convention of 1876 is based upon an unpublished contemporary eyewitness account written by a Cincinnati lawyer, William C. Cochran, to his mother, June 18, 1876, Hayes Papers, RBHL.

23. Hayes to James G. Blaine, June 12, 1876, Hayes Papers, RBHL.

24. Webb C. Hayes to R. B. Hayes, June 12, 1876, Hayes Papers, RBHL.

25. "List of Delegates and Alternates to the Cincinnati Convention, 1876," Hayes Papers, RBHL.

26. William Henry Smith to Hayes, June 12, 1876, Hayes Papers, RBHL.

27. See *Proceedings of the Republican National Convention Held at Cincinnati, Ohio, Wednesday, Thursday, and Friday, June 14, 15, and 16, 1876* (Concord, New Hampshire, 1876) for details of the convention.

28. Ibid., 73.

29. Ibid., 74.

30. Cochran to his mother, June 18, 1876.

31. *Proceedings of the Republican National Convention*, 77.

32. Ibid., 78.

33. Ibid., 81.

34. Ibid., 82.

35. James M. Comly to Hayes, June 15, 1876, Hayes Papers, RBHL.

36. Webb C. Hayes to R. B. Hayes, June 15, 1876, Hayes Papers, RBHL.

37. E. Croxsey to Hayes, June 15, 1876, Hayes Papers, RBHL.

38. *Proceedings of the Republican National Convention*, 104.

39. John M. Harlan to Benjamin H. Bristow, June 19, 1876, Bristow Papers, Library of Congress.

40. William A. Howard to Hayes, July 4, 1876, Hayes Papers, RBHL.

41. *Proceedings of the Republican National Convention*, 108.

42. Richard C. Bain, *Convention Decisions and Voting Records* (Washington, D.C.: The Brookings Institution, 1960), Appendix D.

43. *Proceedings of the Republican National Convention*, 88, 100.

44. J. C. Lee to Hayes, June 18, 1876, Hayes Papers, RBHL.

45. Cited in Martha M. Bigelow, "The Political Services of William Alanson Howard," *Michigan History* 42 (March 1958): 17. Howard's role is also appraised by Dorothy L. Moore, "William A. Howard and the Nomination of Rutherford B. Hayes for the Presidency," *Vermont History* 38 (Autumn 1970): 316–319.

46. John C. Lee to Hayes, June 18, 1876, Hayes Papers, RBHL.

47. Smith to Hayes, June 21, 1876, Hayes Papers, RBHL.

48. Harlan to Bristow, June 19, 1876, Bristow Papers, Library of Congress; E. Bruce Thompson, "The Bristow Presidential Boom of 1876,"

The Mississippi Valley Historical Review 32 (June 1945): 28; Ross A. Webb, *Benjamin Helm Bristow: Border State Politician* (Lexington: The University Press of Kentucky, 1969), 267–274.

3

The Singular Victory

During the early morning hours of Friday, March 2, 1877, a political drama without parallel in the history of American presidential elections came to a climax. At 3:55 A.M., the House doorkeeper announced the arrival of the Senators of the United States who filed in, led by their President *pro tempore*, T. W. Ferry of Michigan, and the Senate tellers, William Boyd Allison of Iowa and John J. Ingalls of Kansas. Immediately behind the tellers, and surrounded by four men carrying revolvers, came Isaac Bassett, the venerable Assistant Sergeant-at-Arms of the Senate, who held two mahogany boxes containing the electoral returns for President from the thirty-eight states. Then some thirty Senators entered, notably John Sherman of Ohio, Simon Cameron of Pennsylvania, Hannibal Hamlin of Maine, and the paralytic Oliver P. Morton of Indiana, quite conspicuous in a chair transported by two men, and took their places among the House members. Meanwhile, ten more armed men, headed by Colonel John W. Skiles, appeared at the front of the chamber immediately to the right and rear of the Speaker's chair and directly in front of the Democratic side of the House chamber to further protect the tellers, ballot box, and Senator Ferry.

Amid the intense excitement of the moment, Congressman E. John Ellis of Louisiana yelled out: "Democrats leave your seats!" About sixty legislators got up at once and noisily made their way to the rear of the hall or hurried out to the cloakrooms. Another thirty Democrats, headed by New York City's Fernando Wood, and faithful to the leadership of House Speaker Samuel J. Randall, remained in their places.

Exhausted and visibly nervous, Senator Ferry mounted the rostrum where, as presiding officer of the joint session, he took his place beside Speaker Randall. He called upon the Secretary of the Senate and the Clerk of the House to read respective resolutions regarding the electoral count of the thirty-eighth and only state not yet reported, Wisconsin. The Republican-controlled Senate resolution called for accepting the certificate of Wisconsin and the Democratic-controlled House resolution for rejecting it. Since the two houses had failed to concur in an affirmative vote to reject, the electoral vote of Wisconsin was ordered tallied as ten votes for Rutherford B. Hayes of Ohio for President and ten votes for William A. Wheeler of New York for Vice President. At 4:05 A.M., Ferry solemnly announced: "This concludes the count of the thirty-eight States of the Union. The teller will now ascertain and deliver the result to the President of the Senate." As Ferry raised the eagle quill to sign the poll sheet, a deathlike silence stilled the House chamber. Spellbound onlookers watched from the crowded galleries while Ferry, shaking with emotion, feverishly endorsed the tally sheet and proclaimed the Republican ticket of Hayes and Wheeler elected by the slender margin of 185 to 184 over the Democratic slate of Samuel J. Tilden and Thomas A. Hendricks. Instantly someone shouted "Shoot!" but the only response was a faint hand-clapping by Hayes' longtime friend, editor W. D. Bickham of Dayton, Ohio, who stood applauding in the rear aisle. Ferry dissolved the joint session, and the Senators withdrew at 4:10 A.M. Speaker Randall, resuming the chair, called the House to order. Thereupon Representative John R. Tucker of Virginia moved the House adjourn "after such a scene as has now transpired." In three minutes, hall and galleries were cleared; in ten more, lights were out.[1]

Thus, after four months of intensive investigation, charge and countercharge, and even rumored revolution, the forces of compromise and conservatism checked the imminent danger of disunion and violence provoked by America's strangest presidential election.

The circumstances of Hayes' singular victory over Samuel J. Tilden in the contested election of 1876 are so extraordinary that they have for too long diverted scholarly attention away from any further interest in the Hayes presidency. The fact is, of course, that Hayes and not Tilden occupied the White House for four eventful years, and we need to know about that administration in its own right. It is also true that a detailed reappraisal of the 1876 disputed election, updating the 1906 monograph of Paul L. Haworth, needs to be written, certainly a formidable task for some scholar.[2] The present writer, however, has chosen to concentrate more on the less familiar circumstances of Hayes' nomination for the presidency and his performance as President of the United States, rather than to reopen the academic controversy over who actually won the 1876 election.

In retrospect, the disputed election typifies a general breakdown of political morality in the Gilded Age for which all Americans of that day must be held accountable. Both Hayes and Tilden were honorable men and outstanding as governors, but neither of them could claim a certain victory over the other in the presidential contest, or one beyond political reproach. In the end, Republican partisans prevailed only because the best laid plans of Democratic politicos went awry. The breakdown of American electoral machinery in 1876 took its toll of both major party candidates. Hayes' reputation has suffered ever since from the charge of accepting a stolen election, while Tilden, greatly embittered, largely withdrew from public life and sought some small comfort as a virtual recluse among his many books, all the while morbidly contemplating his steady physical decline until death finally overtook him in 1886.[3]

The 1876 national election, which began and proceeded in a perfectly normal way, became very complicated in the end. When the ballots for President and Vice President were counted after the polls closed on the evening of November 7, Tilden and Hendricks appeared to emerge victorious in the popular vote by about a 250,000-vote margin and seemed safe enough in the Electoral College. Early the following morning, however, the Republican party chieftains seized an opportunity to reverse the tide by claiming a Hayes triumph in certain southern states, specifically Florida, Louisiana, and South Carolina, where they controlled the electoral machinery, and with it the official count. If the electoral votes of these three states could be certified for Hayes and Wheeler, the Republican ticket would just barely win the election, 185 to 184. This explains the significance of the frantic day-after-the-election telegraph messages authorized by Zachariah Chandler, Republican National Chairman, to his southern state leaders: "Can you hold your state?"[4]

Minority counts, of course, were presented by Democratic members of the southern electoral boards, and the election ultimately depended upon which of the two conflicting sets of returns would be accepted by the President of the Senate, in the presence of both houses of Congress as provided by the Constitution. Since the Senate at the time was Republican-controlled and the House was in Democratic hands, it was highly improbable that they could reach an agreement. As a way out of the constitutional impasse, a bipartisan committee of Senators and Congressmen recom-

LIBERTY AND UNION

GOV. RUTHERFORD B. HAYES,

HON. WM. A. WHEELER

FOR PRESIDENT.

FOR VICE-PRESIDENT.

Copyright 1876, by Currier & Ives, N.Y.

GRAND NATIONAL REPUBLICAN BANNER.

NEW YORK, PUBLISHED BY CURRIER & IVES, 125 NASSAU ST

Republican Standard-bearers
Rutherford B. Hayes and William A. Wheeler, 1876.
Lithograph by Currier & Ives.

NATIONAL ARCHIVES

The secret oath of
President Hayes.

Senator Thomas W. Ferry,
president pro tempore of the Senate,
declaring the election of Hayes
as President at 4:10 A.M.,
March 2, 1877. From the New York
Daily Graphic, *March 3, 1877.*

THE RUTHERFORD B. HAYES LIBRARY

mended the creation of an electoral commission to be composed of fifteen members—five from the Senate, five from the House, and five from the Supreme Court. The plan, though vigorously opposed by many Republicans, including Governor Hayes[5] and Senator Morton, passed both houses because members of the Democratic party strongly supported it with Tilden's approval.[6]

Since the ten legislators named to the commission were evenly divided between the two political parties, and two of the Justices were Republicans and two were Democrats, the balance of power rested with the vote of the fifth jurist. Originally it was understood that this person would be David Davis of Illinois, an Independent, but a few days before the commission could meet, the Illinois legislature unwittingly elected Davis to the United States Senate. The remaining members of the Supreme Court were Republicans, and Justice Joseph P. Bradley was chosen. It was not surprising then, when by a strict party vote of "eight villains to seven patriots," the commission consistently decided all major points at issue in favor of the Republicans, and this general verdict was, in turn, accepted by the Congress.

Why the Democratic-controlled House should have yielded to such a decision has only recently been adequately explained.[7] According to the original explanation, commonly called the "Wormley House Bargain," Governor Hayes' representatives met with a group of southerners late in February 1877 and promised to remove the federal troops occupying Louisiana and South Carolina, thereby in effect abandoning Republican control of these two state legislatures and, as a consequence, the cause of Negro freedom. In return Hayes would receive southern support in his electoral contest for the presidency with Tilden. Supposedly, southerners also guaranteed to safeguard the Negro in his newly won civil rights and to forego any reprisals against their political enemies.

That this explanation is too simple is the burden of Professor C. Vann Woodward's brilliant monograph, *Reunion and Reaction.*[8] The author marshals abundant evidence to show that the Wormley Conference was only one episode in a long series of events extending over several months in which the details of a more complicated arrangement were worked out between the Hayes men and the southern Democrats. To gain support for Hayes' claim to the presidency over Tilden, the South was promised: aid for internal improvements; a subsidy for the Texas and Pacific Railway to connect the South with the West Coast; a cabinet seat; and a voice in the distribution of federal patronage in the South. In return, the South offered to abstain from a Democratic filibuster aimed at slowing the electoral count and thus defeating its purpose and

gave assurances that enough southern Democrats would absent
themselves at the opening session of the new Congress to allow
the Republicans to organize the House and elect a Hayes spokesman, James A. Garfield, as Speaker. Only as an afterthought was
it agreed that the Republicans would withdraw the remaining
federal troops from the South. This presumably would help the
southerners explain to their constituents why they had allowed
the Republican Hayes to assume the presidency when the Democrat Tilden had won the popular vote.

It is still not possible to determine with assurance who won
the contested election of 1876 or who would have won in a completely fair election. Many historians feel that Tilden was entitled
to at least Florida's four electoral votes, enough to put him across,
188 to 181.[9] But this contention rests on very slender evidence:
Democrats claimed Florida by a margin of less than a hundred
votes out of nearly fifty thousand votes cast.[10] Haworth asserts:
"Just how much the election of 1876 lacked of being 'fair and
free' in the state of Florida no historian will ever be able to determine. When all due allowances are made ... it is a not unfair
conclusion that *in equity* the electoral votes of the state of Florida
belonged to Hayes."[11] That there was skulduggery on both sides
is certain. Negroes, despite the guarantee of the Fifteenth Amendment were not permitted to vote freely in the South. The eighteen
votes of Mississippi and Alabama, for example, probably belonged
to Hayes in a fair and free election.[12]

The clouded circumstances of his election gave Hayes trouble
from the start of his term and broke out anew with the Democratic-
inspired Potter Committee Investigation of 1878, which was
designed to make the cry of "fraud" a campaign issue against
the Republicans in 1880. Nevertheless Hayes steadily maintained
he had a legal right to the presidency and the passage of time
seemed to bear him out.[13] The Electoral Commission, initially
viewed with favor by the Democrats, boomeranged on them just
as the Potter Investigation would do later when it uncovered
damaging cipher dispatches revealing more about Democratic
intrigue than Republican complicity.[14]

So far as the Compromise of 1877 is concerned, Hayes fulfilled
his party's pledges, even to the point of unwisely appointing members of the returning boards to federal offices, until the southerners
broke faith on October 15, 1877, by supporting the reelection of
Democrat Samuel Randall as Speaker, rather than Republican James
A. Garfield. After this, the President gradually backed away from
support of a subsidy for the Texas and Pacific Railway and even
openly criticized the project. By the midterm election of 1878,

Hayes' hope of reviving his party in the South and restoring the two-party system of the antebellum days was completely shattered. He had expected southerners of property to identify with the economic interests of northern Republicans, but this kind of economic rationality failed to assert itself. Southerners remained Democrats and did not support Negro rights. Although slavery had been eliminated as an institution, white supremacy reappeared in new guises, and racial policing remained of paramount interest to most white southerners.

During the weeks of anxiety and uncertainty over the contested election, Hayes did his best to maintain composure, attend to his executive duties, and rationalize his situation. "We can regard the result with comparative indifference so far as our personal futures are concerned,"[15] he assured his son. "I shall keep cool, master of all tendencies that may lead me astray, and endeavor to act as Washington would have acted under similar circumstances."[16] His one great concern was for the South and southerners, black and white alike.[17] "My feeling was and is," he said, "that a Democratic victory at this time will prove especially calamitous. . . . The South can't prosper without immigration and capital from the North and abroad. . . . The tendency of a Democratic victory is to drive off Northern people."[18] "The Amendments will be nullified, disorder will continue, prosperity to both whites and colored people will be pushed off for years."[19]

By January he resolved to be prepared for either event. If defeated, he was persuaded his family's personal comfort and happiness would be promoted by a return to private life.[20] If victorious, he must think of personnel and policy. "The Cabinet is the chief work. . . . I must urge a liberal policy towards the South especially in affording facilities for education and encouraging business and emigration by internal improvements of a national character."[21] A healer of strife, he hoped to placate the South, to promote the nation's business, and to build a Republican party south of the Potomac.

On January 31, 1877, he learned of Justice Bradley's selection for the Electoral Commission. With the odds quoted in Washington now five to one in his favor, Hayes started arranging his trip to the inauguration.[22] He wrote John Sherman inquiring if he might stay at the Senator's Washington residence until after the inauguration.[23] Many friends had advised him to avoid a hotel and to arrive in Washington secretly, lest, as the climax of the long electoral controversy, he be assassinated by some malcontent. Grant invited him to stay at the executive mansion, but to do this would have compromised Hayes' political principles and embarrassed his followers. No one could criticize, however, his acceptance of John Sherman's hospitality. The idea of a secret trip to Washington repelled Hayes. He could not begin his presidency by sneaking into town. He did not wish, however, to arrive before the official count was concluded, and thus appear to be seizing control. So he delayed his resignation as governor until February 28, 1877.[24] Before leaving Columbus for Washington, a final reception at the state house was held followed by a joint session of the legislature to honor the governor and his lady.

The next afternoon, he departed for the nation's capital with his family and several political confidants on two special cars attached to the regular Pennsylvania Railroad train. The departure from Columbus evoked memories of Lincoln and the Civil War. In a short farewell speech, Hayes, standing on the rear platform of his special car, recalled how he had marched off to war in 1861 to do what he could to restore the Union. Now he was leaving again, not to save the Union by force of arms but to seek a union of people's hearts by works of love and peace, something Lincoln died still seeking to attain.

About dawn on Friday, March 2, Hayes was awakened near Harrisburg and told the joint session of the Congress had finally declared him President-elect. Two thousand persons met his train in Washington despite a "fearful rainstorm."[25] The Sherman brothers, Senator and army commander, escorted him to a waiting carriage and drove to the former's home. A social call to pay his respects to Grant and afterward an impromptu reception at the Capitol for members of both parties demonstrated his confidence and quieted Washington jitters.

Since inaugural day, March 4, fell on a Sunday in 1877, thus postponing the formal ceremony until Monday, President Grant and Secretary of State Hamilton Fish expressed some fears about an interregnum. In the circumstances, Hayes reluctantly agreed to take the oath of office privately. The Grants gave a dinner party for the Hayes on Saturday evening, March 3. Before going into the dining room, Grant, Chief Justice Morrison R. Waite, and Hayes withdrew to the Red Room where Hayes secretly took the oath of office orally and in writing.[26]

Sunday passed quietly. Inaugural Monday dawned cold and cloudy with rain lasting until early morning. By noon, the sky brightened, and before about 30,000 people, Hayes repeated his oath, and holding his manuscript sheaves in one hand and gesturing mildly with the other, delivered a forceful address forever enshrined in American presidential oratory for its memorable line: "He serves his party best who serves his country best." The wasteland of the Grant years was over.

Notes

1. Details of this closing scene in the electoral count may be found in the *Congressional Record,* 44th Cong., 2d sess., 2029, 2068, and Thomas C. Donaldson, "Memoirs," March 3, 1877, RBHL.

2. Paul Leland Haworth, *The Hayes-Tilden Disputed Presidential Election of 1876.* (Cleveland: The Burrows Brothers Company, 1906). One important aspect of the contested election is reexamined by Norbert A. Kuntz, "The Electoral Commission of 1877" (Ph.D. diss., Michigan State University, 1969). See also the same author's article, "Edmund's Contrivance: Senator George Edmunds of Vermont and the Electoral Compromise of 1877," *Vermont History* 38 (Autumn 1970): 305–315. The role of Secretary of War J. Don Cameron in creating the electoral deadlock and the influence of House Speaker Samuel J. Randall in peacefully resolving the conflict is detailed in Frank B. Evans, *Pennsylvania Politics, 1872–1877: A Study in Political Leadership* (Harrisburg: The Pennsylvania Historical and Museum Commission, 1966), 286–309.

3. Tilden's bachelor status led to ugly rumors concerning his manhood. "The day of the election of President Hayes—Nov. 7th, 1876, sitting with Mr. Zach Chandler, Chairman of the Republican National Committee in his official room at the Fifth Avenue Hotel, New York (with others). . . . Chandler drew from a drawer in his table a bundle of papers. He read us some of them. They were a series of affidavits from physicians, nurses, and others that Samuel J. Tilden was sexless. This was believed because he was very effeminate, with a grinning beardless face, and with a sqeaky voice. Mr. Tilden was never married. These affidavits were not used of course by Mr. Chandler during the campaign." Donaldson, "Memoirs," 163.

4. William E. Chandler to Hayes, November 9, 1876, Hayes Papers, RBHL; Leon Burr Richardson, *William E. Chandler, Republican* (New York: Dodd, Mead & Company, 1940), 184–186.

5. "President Hayes continued: 'I hope no one who knew anything of the matter ever misunderstood my position as to the method of declaring who had been elected President in 1876–7. I was opposed to the Electoral Commission bill. Mr. Tilden was in favor of it, until Judge Davis went to the Senate, and then he became opposed to it. I believe that the only method is the one pointed out by Chancellor Kent, and it was the rule until the Electoral Commission expedient came up, *viz.,* by the Vice President; it is the true one, and for this we must contend. It is right." Donaldson, "Memoirs," 116.

6. The Senate passed the bill by a vote of 47 to 17, 10 members being absent. The majority was made up of 21 Republicans and 26 Democrats. Of those voting against the bill, all but one (Eaton, of Connecticut) were Republicans. The House passed the bill by a vote of 191 to 86, 14 not voting. Of the majority, 159 were Democrats and 32 Republicans; of the minority, all but 18 were Republicans. "Thus, while both parties shared equally in the drafting of the bill, and the bill could not have been passed by the Senate without the cooperation of the Republicans, the measure after all owed its existence and support much rather to the Democrats than to the Republicans. In the entire Congress only 19 Democratic votes were recorded against it and few Democratic voices were raised in opposition to its passage." Charles Richard Williams, *The Life of Rutherford Birchard Hayes* (Boston: Houghton Mifflin Company, 1914), I, 525–527.

7. A good summary is provided in *Hayes: The Diary of a President, 1875–1881*, ed. T. Harry Williams (New York: David McKay Company, Inc., 1964), xx–xxiii.

8. C. Vann Woodward, *Reunion and Reaction* (Garden City, New York: Doubleday and Company, 1956), passim.

9. See, for example, Allan Nevins, *Abram S. Hewitt, With Some Account of Peter Cooper* (New York: Harper & Bro., 1935), 373; H. J. Eckenrode, *Rutherford B. Hayes, Statesman of Reunion* (New York: Dodd, Mead and Company, 1930), 227; Alexander C. Flick, *Samuel J. Tilden, A Study in Political Sagacity* (New York: Dodd, Mead and Company, 1939), 415–416; and Richardson, *William E. Chandler, Republican*, 193.

10. Edward Stanwood, *A History of the Presidency from 1788 to 1897* (Boston: Houghton Mifflin Company, 1898), I, 383.

11. Haworth, *Disputed Election*, 57, 76.

12. Ibid., 340–341: "All things considered, it appears that both legally and ethically the decision of the Electoral Commission was the proper one."

13. The most complete statement of Hayes' position on the correctness of his legal claim to the presidency is contained in his diary entry for December 10, 1886: "Evarts, Sherman, (R. C.) McCormick, and others recently talked on the 'fraud issue' which a faction of the Democratic party still harp upon. My notions of it are clear and decided:

"1. In 1876 the Republicans were equitably entitled to the advantages of the Fifteenth Amendment under which, if it had been obeyed and enforced, they would have had *a majority of the popular vote of the country and at least 203 electoral votes to Tilden's 166*. . . .

"2. If the States which equitably belonged to the Republicans, but which were claimed by the Democrats, are excluded from the count, . . . the vote would have stood Republican, 173 (electoral votes); Democratic, 166.

"3. When the disputed election came before Congress the Democratic party decided to leave the question to the Electoral Commission. The vote on the bill was as follows: (Senate, 47 for, 17 against, 10 absent. Of the majority 21 were Republicans, 26 Democrats. Of the minority all but one were Republicans. House, 191 for, 86 against, 14 not voting. Of the majority 159 were Democrats, 32 Republicans. Of the minority all but 18 were Republicans.) Mr. Tilden advised his friends to support the measure. . . . After the result, unfavorable to the Democrats, was announced, doubts of Mr. Tilden's position were first heard of. . . .

"4. In 1880 the question was practically settled in all fairness by the action of the Democratic party and the people. The Republicans nominated General Garfield. He was identified in many ways with the result of 1876, as declared in favor of the Republicans. . . . But still more cogent was the action of the Democratic party. They declined to take issue with the Republicans in their nomination. They declined to nominate Mr. Tilden against General Garfield. . . . The Democratic party by nominating Hancock and refusing to nominate Tilden, or any one identified with the maintenance of the fraud issue, against Garfield, who was fully identified with every essential step in the series of events which gave the Republicans the victory in 1876–7, [abandoned the "fraud issue"]. Those who were closely connected with the declaration of the result in 1876–7 retain the confidence of the people." Hayes, Diary, December 10, 1886, Hayes Papers, RBHL.

14. For a recent discussion of the cipher telegrams, see David Kahn,

The Codebreakers (New York: The Macmillan Company, 1967), 221–229. The disclosures ended Tilden's presidential aspirations.

15. Hayes to Birchard Hayes, December 3, 1876, Hayes Papers, RBHL.

16. Hayes, Diary, December 7, 1876.

17. Ibid., November 11, 1876.

18. Hayes to Guy M. Bryan, November 23, 1876, Hayes Papers, RBHL.

19. Hayes, Diary, November 11, 1876.

20. Hayes to Birchard Hayes, February 1, 1877, Hayes Papers, RBHL.

21. Hayes, Diary, January 5, 1877.

22. Ibid., January 31, 1877.

23. Hayes to John Sherman, February 18, 1877, Hayes Papers, RBHL.

24. RBH to Thomas L. Young, Lieut.-Governor of Ohio, February 28, 1877, Hayes Papers, RBHL.

25. Emma Foote to Lucy Webb Hayes, March 1, 1880, Hayes Papers, RBHL.

26. Hayes to J. H. Wick, M.D., August 19, 1882, Hayes Papers, RBHL. The signed presidential oath of Hayes is unique in American history. See State Department Archives, National Archives, Record Group 59, Inventory 157, Entry 392, Tray 10 (1875–1877).

Part II

CENTENNIAL AMERICA

4

Society and Culture in
the Hayes Era

The inauguration ceremonies completed, the Grants and Hayes shared a lavish White House luncheon while others prepared for the evening's torchlight procession and a reception at the Willard Hotel. Because of the long and bitter election dispute, no inaugural parade or inaugural ball was held.[1]

The new first family quickly settled down to their duties as official leaders of Washington society and culture. Arriving as they did in Washington in the mid-1870s involved some misgivings. The first glimpses of the capital were not pleasant. Fields with stagnant pools of water and scavenging animals and muddy yards around dingy frame houses were common sights. At the railroad station, bewildering shouts and yells from passing omnibuses and hacks rang out. In the distance, the Navy Yard, the arsenal, and the penitentiary were visible and the Washington Monument remained unfinished. And the many unpaved streets prompted Lord Bryce to remark that the city was "a wilderness of mud."[2] In fact the whole metropolis seemed imcomplete, far removed from L'Enfant's envisioned symbol of national glory.[3]

Approximately 109,000 people lived in Washington in 1870, a figure which climbed to 140,000 by the end of the decade, with another 9,000 living in Georgetown across Rock Creek.[4] Roughly one-third of these inhabitants were Negroes.

Unlike other American cities, Washington, preeminently a federal city, lacked industrial development and made a slower transition from village to town, from rustic airs to an urban society. National leaders and events so wholly dominated public discussion that, for a long time, serious attention to the growing problems of local government went unheeded. During the mid-1870s, however, great changes in the physical appearance and municipal government of the District were initiated by reform-minded citizens

53

and officials. Three thousand gas lamps were installed and sixty thousand new trees planted in the numerous parks and squares of the capital. Some one hundred and eighty miles of streets were paved with wooden blocks or macadam.

In general, the city of Washington, situated on a site originally part of the states of Maryland and Virginia, exuded a southern atmosphere in the 1870s. This characteristic was especially apparent in the provincial character of the city Market District, an area developed after 1872. Here 700 stalls operated by over 250 merchants did a weekly business amounting to a quarter of a million dollars. Wives of Congressmen and Senators regularly did their marketing here.

During the four years of the Hayes administration, the capital city would achieve a cosmopolitan air unknown previously. Dramatic architectural changes were effected. Next to the White House, the new War, Navy, and State Department Building, designed by A. B. Mullett in the French Renaissance style, was completed, while across the street the new Corcoran Art Gallery beckoned to patrons. Opposite the Executive Mansion in Lafayette Square, Decatur House and Madison Place added further dignity to the neighborhood. West from Fifteenth Street and south of Florida Avenue, a fashionable district of twenty-five foreign legations and new private brick residences sprang up. Connecticut Avenue was just beginning to develop, with Stewart's "Castle" (1873) and the imposing new British legation (1875) leading the way. Meanwhile many three-story row houses with large bay windows were erected throughout the city.

Washington's social structure divided neatly into three classes in the 1870s: the first family, members of Congress, the diplomatic corps, led by Lord and Lady Thornton of England, and wealthy socialites comprised the top stratum; a large floating population of nearly 60,000 civil servants and lobbyists comprised the middle group; and finally, an underprivileged class, condemned to abject poverty, filth, and squalor, represented the lowest segment.

The upper class followed a leisurely routine, highlighted by the winter social season lasting from New Year's Day to Ash Wednesday. Afternoon entertaining followed a fixed code, which designated certain days for various officials. Monday afternoons belonged to the wives of the Supreme Court Justices, of the general of the army, and of the admiral of the navy; Tuesdays were reserved to the White House; Wednesdays to cabinet wives; and on Thursdays it was proper for families of Senators and Congressmen to entertain. Friday afternoons were left free for special occasions, especially charitable or philanthropic fund-raising activities. One hostess, the wife of General James B. Ricketts, became so well known for this type of affair that a saying was coined: "Here comes Mrs. Ricketts with a pocketful of tickets."[5]

Washington's famous hotels—the Willard, the Wormley, the National, and Ebbitt House—were often used for political and social gatherings, or if the host preferred, he might take his guests to Sam Ward's or Welcker's, fancy restaurants featuring twenty dollar dinners.

The government set formed a colony of their own, living in boarding houses, private residences, or one of the city's thirty-six hotels where excitement always abounded, despite the rather high cost of board and room priced at between four to five dollars a day. Many of the government employees were young female clerks, and males were naturally attracted by so many unattached young women and also by the new opportunities open to professional lobbyists. With an abbreviated workday lasting from only nine to three, the government workers had ample time to court mischief. A hundred gambling houses operated in the heart of the city. In the one run by John Chamberlain in the old British legation, thousands of dollars were lost each night and famous midnight suppers were served to those less inclined to test the laws of chance.

Within the black community, a few persons managed to become prominent in Washington society. John M. Langston was dean of the law department of Howard University (1869–1876) and later consul general to Haiti (1877–1885). The House had several distinguished black members, including Mississippi's John R. Lynch (1873–1877; 1882–1883), while the Senate was noted for the presence of Blanche K. Bruce, also of Mississippi. Frederick Douglass served as Marshal and Recorder of Deeds in the District. Other blacks acquired middle-class status as barbers, cobblers, merchants, contractors, or government workers.

Toward the end of the decade, the city finally achieved a measure of maturity in its governmental affairs with the passage of the Organic Act of June 1878, creating a municipal corporation ruled by a board of three commissioners appointed by the President of the United States. Coincident with progress in government, improvements in public transportation, growth in population and residential areas, and intellectual and cultural advances, gave Washington a more modern character.

No less than 150 newspapers maintained press representatives in the capital, and a growing corps of female correspondents regularly reported social doings in their columns. There were Miss Grundy and her mother (Austine and Fayette Snead) of the New

York *Daily Graphic* and the Louisville *Courier-Journal;* Raymonde (Mrs. R. B. Mohun) of the Cincinnati *Commercial;* and the dean of Washington's lady observers, Mary Clemmer of the New York *Independent.* The Washington *Post* began publication in 1877.

Men of science began to congregate in Washington as their work with the Department of Agriculture, the Naval Observatory, the Weather Bureau, or the Smithsonian and the National Academy of Science required their presence in the District. Literary men, Henry Adams and George Bancroft, for example, took up permanent residence in the city. President Hayes knew them both and frequently visited in Bancroft's home. Meanwhile dozens of famous personages climbed the stairs to Matthew Brady's photographic studio just off Pennsylvania Avenue to have their portraits preserved for a grateful posterity. Painters organized the Washington Art League, and the sculptors found an additional outlet for their talents with the opening of Statuary Hall in the Capitol and the granting of commissions for works to adorn Washington's many traffic circles and public parks. Such was the nature of the city of which Rutherford and Lucy Hayes became the first citizens in March 1877.

What of the larger American social and cultural scene during the Hayes era? The year 1876 is a memorable one in American history. The United States entered her second century with unmistakable signs of growing maturity. The great Philadelphia Centennial Exposition of 1876 not only helped to unify Americans, but it also marked a new departure in their taste and daily living habits. In the 1870s for the first time, Americans lived in flats, raided iceboxes, mailed postal cards, walked on concrete sidewalks and linoleum floors, rode the elevated, harmonized the new science with Genesis, patronized five-and-ten-cent stores,[6] popularized mail order catalogs, and purchased goods on the installment plan.

The Hayes years in the White House also witnessed a strong economic recovery after five years of depression going back to the panic of 1873. While the President and his Secretary of the Treasury, John Sherman, believed their hard money policy and the return to specie payment in January 1879 effected the business upturn, they were, in fact, the beneficiaries of economic forces beyond their control and understanding.[7] Nonetheless, the prestige of both men increased in the public eye, and Sherman became a serious contender for the 1880 Republican presidential nomination.

Perhaps the greatest economic development of the 1870s was the rise of businesses national in scope. Corporations destined to become industrial giants of their era were founded—John D.

Rockefeller's Standard Oil Company and Andrew Carnegie's steel works were among them. At the same time Philip Armour and Gustavus Swift rose to prominence in the meat-packing business.

Farming followed the lead of industry. The centering of milling operations in Minneapolis heralded not only the development of Minnesota and Dakota wheat farms but also the demise of thousands of small gristmills scattered throughout America. Meanwhile, the Central Plains developed into another major agricultural area as homesteaders worked thousands of new farms. In the world market, the balance of trade finally shifted in favor of the United States. Americans were selling more than they were buying.

Before the bonanzas in grain, other fortunes were made and lost in mining and cattle raising. Gold on Indian lands in the Black Hills of Dakota and silver near Leadville, Colorado, produced new rushes to ruin or fortune. The 1870s marked the golden age of the Texas cowboy who drove his cattle northward to railheads like Dodge City and Abilene, Kansas.

Several railroads reached the Pacific Coast in the 1870s, spurred on by the completion of the Union Pacific and Central Pacific connection in 1869. What had started with a few miles of Baltimore and Ohio track about 1830 now spanned a continent. Further improvements in safety and comfort pioneered by George Westinghouse and George Pullman made travel and shipment across America easy and practical for the first time in American history. But the railroad also brought about clashes between capital and labor, capital and the farmer. Indeed, the Great Railway Strike of 1877 was America's first nationwide labor dispute and caused President Hayes to use federal troops to quell the violence.

When one considers that the average wage earner made only about two dollars a day for ten hours work, it is easy to understand why the first real labor union movement, the Knights of Labor (1878), originated in this decade. Another important feature of the American economy to appear at this time was standardization in older industries. Ready-made clothes, boots, and shoes led the way.

By 1881 a mature industrial capitalism dominated American life, and most men of ambition aspired to a business rather than a political or professional career. For this reason, the political history of the era received little attention until in the 1960s a group of younger scholars began to take a fresh look at the Gilded Age. The result is a more accurate, balanced, and sympathetic picture of a much maligned era. Many of the forgotten figures of the time, like Hayes and Garfield, are becoming better known.[8]

Political life in the 1870s was marked by many issues crying

for solution, but too few public servants were devoted to the general
interest instead of to their own personal profit. Standards of political morality have seldom sunk lower in a democratic government.
Offices were bought and sold by brazen bribery, politicians openly
mingled with notorious speculators, and public confidence was
badly shaken by scandals involving the highest officials in the
government. A brilliant maneuver, no matter how dishonest, could
put James G. Blaine within a whisker of the White House, while
the honest and less dramatic officeholder seldom found public
favor.

Although the Republican party ruled the executive and legislative branches most of the time from 1865 to 1913, during Hayes'
presidency his party never achieved a majority in the House of
Representatives, and controlled the Senate only during his first
two years of office.[9] The elimination of military occupation of
the South, begun by Grant and completed by Hayes, enabled the
Democrats to resume control of the House of Representatives in
1874, and to challenge seriously the Republicans in every election
thereafter. Each party suffered from internal divisions. The Grant
men, or Stalwarts, who clung to their idol despite his obvious
weakness as a chief executive, were led by New York's crafty
Senator, Roscoe Conkling. James G. Blaine of Maine, minority
leader of the House, headed the Republican Half-Breed faction,
while a minority of reform-minded crusaders represented by Carl
Schurz were dubbed the Mugwumps. Democrats of the South,
many of Whig origins, spoke of themselves as Conservatives or
Redeemers, but were often called Bourbons by their opponents.
These leaders, mostly industrialists plus a few planters, assumed
power after Reconstruction, disfranchised the Negro in part, and
cooperated with the North to secure capital to finance mills, fac-
tories, and furnaces of the New South. Rank-and-file Democrats,
farmers, laborers, and small businessmen comprised yet another
wing of the Democratic party, which rarely held the leadership
reins until the 1890s.

Campaign tactics avoided real issues and concentrated instead
upon emotional appeals evoking memories of the Civil War.
Republicans "waved the bloody shirt" by labeling the Democrats
a southern party noted for rebellion and treason.[10] In response,
the southern Democrats warned of the danger of Negro rule and
called for white supremacy. One can scarcely overestimate the
power of these suggestions, nor the appeal of candidates with
a military record.[11]

In every election, New York and Indiana received major attention
as "doubtful states." The prominence of Ohio in providing leader-

ship in the Hayes years should not be overlooked. Chief Justice Morrison R. Waite and his colleague, Noah H. Swayne, were both Ohioans and the only two members of the Supreme Court from the same state. President Hayes and his chief cabinet officer, Secretary of the Treasury John Sherman, were natives of Ohio. Sherman's brother, General William T. Sherman, dominated the army as commanding general (1869–1883). James A. Garfield functioned as House minority floor leader, and Allen G. Thurman piloted Democrats in the Senate. Furthermore, census records show that the nation's population fulcrum centered in Ohio from 1860 to 1880.

The 1870s witnessed the first sustained assault on the evils of patronage since the advent of the spoils system under Andrew Jackson. By his presidential proclamations and especially by his dramatic attack on the single most glaring example of the patronage system, the New York Custom House Ring, President Hayes established important precedents for the Pendleton Act of 1883. In asserting executive power on behalf of civil service reform, Hayes, as in the fight to name his own cabinet officers, won still another presidential victory over the United States Senate, then at perhaps its highest ascendancy in American history.[12]

The most interesting aspects of the Hayes period, however, involve social, cultural, intellectual, and literary trends. In combination they make the era important as a cultural epoch in American civilization, not just an age dominated by big business and handicapped by ineffective politicos.

One of the most significant occurrences was the Philadelphia Centennial Exposition of 1876. As much as any single event, this exposition symbolized America's coming of age. Ostensibly held to commemorate a century of independence, the Philadelphia Exposition, sixth of the world's fairs and the first to be held in the United States, served to focus international attention upon the new machines and processes of industrial America. Secondarily it also awakened aesthetic and social consciousness in the United States. Nearly 10 million visitors, including Hayes and his family, thronged to the Fairmont Park exhibition grounds in five months. Railroads offered safe and comfortable transportation at bargain round-trip rates to lure the populace to Philadelphia where they marveled at the many rows of exhibits featuring art objects, goods, and recent inventions like the typewriter. The exposition succeeded educationally, if not financially, and helped to foster national spirit and unity.

Americans coming to the Centennial filled with thoughts of the Liberty Bell and august patriots discovered instead a new era of inventive ferment and fascinating machines. Cavernous Industrial Hall—a third of a mile long—and the almost equally vast Machinery Hall thrilled the crowds who thronged the exposition grounds. They saw machines to lift, machines to crush, machines to spin and weave and make decoration, and the mighty Corliss steam engine made to power all the other machines. To prove to chronic worriers that the machine was no threat, even to the most refined sensibilities, the exposition announced a wholly new branch of human achievement known as "industrial art." A proud array of machine-made iron beds, iron lamps, iron rocking chairs, and hatracks was exhibited to show that the newfangled machine could produce as many frilly gewgaws as the most artful medieval craftsman. When the exposition was finally closed in the autumn, Americans knew that the age of progress and machinery had arrived. Simultaneously the Smithsonian had acquired twenty-one freight-car loads of foreign exhibit displays from thirty countries! When the institution discovered it had no place to put the treasure, Congress responded more quickly to this situation than it had to the original bequest of James Smithson. It formally established the national museum in 1879 and also provided a red brick structure (now known as the Arts and Industries Building) to house its exhibits.

The exposition also fostered other areas of science and invention. It displayed Edison's duplex telegraph, the Westinghouse air brake, and a refrigerator car, besides many products to lighten household chores for women. Of the latter, sewing machines made the greatest impression. The newly patented Bell telephone was a late and obscure entry, but in dramatic, last-minute consideration by the judges, it won a gold medal award and accompanying public acclaim. Many practical inventions such as Edison's electric light and phonograph were patented shortly after the Centennial.[13]

The business of inventing was humming along. At the time of the Hayes presidency, Edison was in his early thirties and at the height of his creative power. Great Wall Street money men (as he called them) battled for possession of his patents, testifying to their importance in the industrial system. Alexander Graham Bell also would experience a long struggle over his patent rights. Elsewhere in the realm of science, the creation of a National Weather Service in 1870, Clarence King's work on the United States Geological Survey, and John Wesley Powell's leadership of the Bureau of American Ethnology, both dating from 1879, should not be omitted. Edison's chief rival, Charles A. Brush of Cleveland, patented his arc light in 1878, and two years later, illuminated New York's famous Broadway with these lamps. Nor should the

significance of George Selden's automobile patent of 1879 be overlooked. Science and technology took giant strides, indeed, during
the Hayes era.

Another notable area of new departure in the Gilded Age was
the founding of major museums.[14] President Hayes participated
in the dedication ceremonies for new buildings housing the Metropolitan Museum of Art and the American Museum of Natural
History in New York. The 1876 exposition had spurred both
academies in Philadelphia to construct new buildings. In addition,
Memorial Hall, which had been built specifically for the art exhibits
of the exposition, survived the Centennial as the home of the
new Pennsylvania Museum of Art.[15] Although the institution
ultimately was renamed the Philadelphia Museum of Art and
moved to other quarters, it maintained Memorial Hall as the home
of its extensive industrial arts collection, making it until recently
the oldest public art museum building standing in America.

The year of the Centennial also saw the construction of the first
wing of Boston's Museum of Fine Arts. The United States National
Museum, a branch of the Smithsonian Institution, took shape
shortly after the Exposition. Although today it is separated into
a Natural History Museum and a new Museum of History and
Technology, the latter a virtual history book written in artifacts,
it still displays many of the finest objects exhibited at Philadelphia
in 1876. Along with new buildings came changes in museum
organization. Earlier institutions had been initiated by individuals, societies, and academies. The new plan that evolved provided
for a corporation governed by a board of trustees and aided, in
New York, by municipal tax funds; in Boston, by public subscrip-
tion. In return for such financial help, New York City expected
the American and Metropolitan museums to be "as important and
beneficial an agent in the instruction of the people as any of the
schools or colleges."[16]

Meanwhile, the new awareness of the museum movement's
importance led to active support across America. Congress
increased its appropriation to the National Museum. Four state
museums, functioning with state funds, were established. Smaller
communities established their own local museums in growing
numbers. By 1870 about two dozen state and more than thirty
local historical societies existed. The first historic house museum
had been established in 1850 at Newburgh, New York, the site
of George Washington's headquarters during the last two years
of the Revolution. By 1876 six more buildings in various states
were permanently preserved in the fashion of their periods, and
more than a dozen cities possessed natural history societies with

museums. On its hundredth birthday, the nation boasted more than two hundred museums, most of which would survive well into the next century. The movement spread westward—to Cincinnati, Detroit, Grand Rapids, Milwaukee, Chicago, Davenport, and as far as San Diego. And from Washington to Sacramento, from Baltimore to Boston, rich men amassed art collections that would, in a few generations, be made available to the public. Typical of these benefactors was William Wilson Corcoran of Washington, D.C., whose justly famed Corcoran Gallery was offically opened in 1871 by the arrival of President and Mrs. Grant at a Gala Ball for the benefit of the Washington Monument Fund. The Walker Art Center of Minneapolis has a similar history. T. B. Walker, a wealthy lumber merchant who had been privately collecting paintings and art objects, opened his residence to the public in 1879. In addition to the two new buildings in Philadelphia already mentioned, the 1876 exposition was responsible for the development of at least one other institution. Three women from Providence, in comparing the Rhode Island display with those of other states, found their own state wanting, and decided upon their return home that local improvement was in order. They agitated for and received an appropriation to start the Rhode Island School of Design and its now famous museum.

The Philadelphia Exposition made other significant cultural contributions. The founding of the American Library Association in 1876 and its great influence in fostering interest in the American past and the founding of numerous patriotic organizations should be especially noted.

Several enterprising librarians assembled in May 1876 and proposed a larger meeting of their colleagues in connection with the centennial exhibition in Philadelphia. Originally planned for August, the convention was postponed until October in the hope that the more comfortable fall weather would attract greater participation. The Centennial Conference of Librarians held in the quarters of The Historical Society of Pennsylvania, October 4–6, marks the birth of modern librarianship in America and establishes 1876 as the most eventful year in the history of the American library profession. In addition to forming a major professional association, the same pioneers launched the *American Library Journal*, still the most widely read of the profession's magazines. Meanwhile, the United States Bureau of Education published its massive survey on *Public Libraries in the United States*, and Melvil Dewey of Amherst College compiled his decimal classification and subject index. Dewey also became the first executive secretary of the American Library Association and was given the honor of being listed as the first member of the new organization.

Other professional associations and agencies came into existence about this same time and constituted a fundamental transformation of American scholarship and scientific activity. The opening of Johns Hopkins University in the centennial year of 1876 was highly significant for its doctoral program and the use of the German seminar method as a vehicle of graduate instruction. Professional education in law and medicine was also upgraded. University extension courses and presses came into being. University libraries began to develop into genuine research institutions and to take the place of the older private libraries collected by dedicated scholars. New learned societies, each with its own scholarly journal, were formed. The American Chemical Society, founded in 1876, the Modern Language Association of America (1883), the American Historical Association (1884), which Hayes joined, and the American Economic Association (1885) are outstanding examples.[17]

The fine arts made new departures and gained significantly in popular attention and achievement during the Hayes period. In the 1870s, art history was introduced into the curriculum at Harvard. By the 1880s, Princeton, Smith, and Wellesley had constructed their own art centers, and educational interest increased steadily thereafter. Hayes had his portrait painted by both Thomas Eakins and William Merritt Chase.[18] The Eakins portrait, now lost, was the artist's first real commission and earned him a $400 fee from Philadelphia's prestigious Union League whose members then rejected the finished work owing to its realism. Tradition says that the heat of an August day in Washington caused Hayes to appear florid while he was sitting for the portrait.[19]

America's other old masters, Winslow Homer and Albert Pinkham Ryder, the latter like Eakins in disfavor with the contemporary public, painted genre and seascapes. Meanwhile, Mary Cassatt, John Singer Sargent, and James McNeill Whistler forsook American residence for the friendlier artistic climate of the Continent. In architecture, the brilliant Beaux-Arts designs of Richard Morris Hunt and the Romanesque Revival plans of Henry Hobson Richardson foreshadowed the early work of Adler and Sullivan and the birth of the skyscraper in the 1880s. Already sculptors Augustus St. Gaudens and Daniel Chester French had begun to challenge their field with highly realistic monuments like *Admiral Farragut* and *The Minute Man* respectively. In the graphic arts, documentary photographic work by William Henry Jackson and Timothy O'Sullivan, skilled cameramen accompanying government expeditions exploring the Far West and Caribbean regions, is most outstanding. Jackson's views of the Yellowstone country persuaded a reluctant Congress to preserve the area as a public park or "pleasuring

ground." Meanwhile, musicians made American music respectable in this country and abroad. Schools of music, founded at
Harvard, Columbia, and Yale, were led by John Knowles Paine,
Edward McDowell, and Horatio Parker respectively. George Chad-
wick served as head of the New England Conservatory.

Social life underwent profound transformation in the 1870s as
the city increasingly dominated American society. The pace of
life accelerated; personal and group relationships changed; and
the use of leisure time altered with the commercialization of recrea-
tion and the professionalization of sport. The city, compressing
humanity, created disease-infested slums, higher crime rates, and
notoriously corrupt boss-ridden political machines. Only gradually
did sanitation, street lighting, paving, and transportation improve.
Adequate fire and police protection lagged sadly behind.[20]

Immigration patterns fluctuated sharply during the Hayes years.
In place of the largely Protestant people from northwestern Europe
and the British Isles who had comprised the older wave of immigrants during the colonial period and the first century of the new
nation, the immigrants of the Hayes era began to come increasingly
from central, eastern, and southern Europe. For the most part
they were poverty-stricken, and of Catholic, Jewish, or Greek
Orthodox faith. While they provided a source of cheap labor supply
and enriched the cultural fabric of American life, they also gave
the United States a case of acute indigestion as the older stocks
found it more difficult to assimilate so many diverse peoples, customs, and habits. Not only the Negro question, but also the plight
of the city, two very basic mid-twentieth century problems,
emerged in this era.

America's population jumped from slightly less than 40 million
in 1870 to over 50 million in 1880, with immigrants accounting
for about 3 million of the increase. While Hayes was President,
immigrant arrivals showed a substantial upsurge:[21]

1877	141,857
1878	138,469
1879	177,826
1880	457,257
1881	669,431

Nearly nine hundred a day arrived in 1880 at New York, the single
greatest port of entry, marking the largest influx in any year since
the peak of the Irish immigration in the early 1850s. Most of the
new migrants came from the Continent, especially from Germany,
the Scandinavian countries, Hungary, Italy, Bohemia, Russia, Turkey, and Greece.

A separate immigrant problem of the era involved the growing unpopularity of Chinese laborers in California where their foreign ways and low standard of living produced several riots against them in the summer of 1877. A "Workingmen's party" demanded the exclusion of Chinese immigrants, but President Hayes stood squarely on the terms of the Burlingame Treaty of 1868, which allowed unrestricted admission of Americans to China and the same privilege for Chinese migrants coming to America. Any violation of the treaty might have imperiled American missionaries and traders inside China. Hayes subsequently sent a special commission to China to revise the treaty.[22]

Increasing urbanization and immigration automatically affected religious and educational life. Catholicism gained in strength. Some urban churches began to lead movements for social amelioration by teaching that the principles of Christianity should form the base for the reconstruction of the social order. Their new fellowship halls and gymnasiums provided a wholesome social environment for youth and adults during the week. Simultaneously, education became more vocational in outlook as it sought to fit city dwellers for the new urban occupations. Women took jobs as secretaries, office clerks, and sales ladies in department stores. Many men found employment as factory workers requiring a variety of skills.

Recreational habits changed too. Sports became standardized and professionalized as spectators willingly paid a fee to watch others take their exercise for them. Meanwhile the seaside resort developed as a new pleasure for the more affluent classes. Even eating habits underwent a change with the advent of refrigeration, commercial bakeries, and canned meats. Reading tastes centered on newspapers and a myriad of periodicals. Among the outstanding papers of the day were the *Times, Tribune, Post, Sun, World,* and *Daily Graphic* of New York City; the Springfield *Republican;* the Washington *National Republican;* Chicago *Tribune* and *Inter-Ocean;* and the Louisville *Courier-Journal. Frank Leslie's Illustrated Newspaper* published a huge 324-page volume in observance of the centennial celebration. The New York *Daily Graphic* regularly printed a remarkable series of black and white sketches of newsmakers and events of the era during its short life. Quality magazines of the age included the *North American Review, Scribner's Monthly, Atlantic,* and *Harper's Monthly. Puck,* a satirical weekly, carried the superb political cartoons of Joseph Keppler, rivaled by those of Thomas Nast in *Harper's Weekly,* which in turn competed with *Frank Leslie's Illustrated Weekly* in the excellence of its artistry. Another cartoonist, J. A. Wales of Clyde, Ohio, deserves to be ranked with Keppler and Nast but is all but forgotten. *The Nation,* a journal of opinion, concentrated on social and political issues while the *Scientific American* appealed to yet another type of intellectual audience. Frank L. Mott, the historian of the American periodicals, estimated that the average life of American magazines after the Civil War was less than four years. In the twenty-year period after the Civil War, 9,000 different magazines were published, but never more than 3,300 in a single year.[23]

The one subject that seemed to dominate this effervescent era was the "woman question." With greater education and leisure time came increased purchasing power, and with the gradual perfection of the typewriter and the telephone came new job opportunities. Advertisers, in emphasizing fashion, femininity, and fragrance, showed their complete awareness of the new circumstances. Shrewd publishers of newspapers and general interest magazines began to build their circulation by adding features on home-management, social etiquette, and clothes design, and by including sentimental romances in serial form.

Thus, the period from Hayes' nomination and election through his presidency and retirement coincides with the birth of a new age: the modern economic and social world. In the year of the centennial and the two or three years following this historic event, there were invented the telephone, the electric light, the phonograph, and the automobile, all of which profoundly influenced the family and the individual. Not only does 1876 mark a dividing line between a new and an old life in social and industrial America, but a similar line of demarcation may also be drawn in the history of the American presidency. Why this is true forms the subject of the remainder of this book.

Notes

1. Joseph N. Kane, *Facts About the Presidents* (New York: The H. W. Wilson Company, 1959), 138, 317–318.

2. Cited in H. Wayne Morgan, *From Hayes to McKinley* (Syracuse: Syracuse University Press, 1969), 8.

3. The description of Washington, D.C., that follows is based upon an honor's thesis in history written by one of my former students, Jacqueline Wires, "Society and Culture in Washington, D.C., during the Gilded Age" (Heidelberg College, 1967).

4. Constance McLaughlin Green, *Washington, Capital City, 1879–1950* (Princeton: Princeton University Press, 1963), 3.

5. Marian Gouverneur, *As I Remember* (New York: D. Appleton and Company, 1911), 362.

6. Frank W. Woolworth opened a five-and-ten-cent store in Utica, New York, on February 22, 1879, thereby initiating the limited-price variety store. The original stock was limited to no more than five-cent items.

See James T. Adams, ed., *Dictionary of American History* (New York: Charles Scribner's Sons, 1940), II, 279. For a graphic picture of the United States at the time of the centennial, consult Dee Brown, *The Year of the Century: 1876* (New York: Charles Scribner's Sons, 1966) and William Pierce Randel, *Centennial: American Life in 1876* (Philadelphia: Chilton Book Company, 1969).

7. Irwin F. Unger, *The Greenback Era: A Social and Political History of American Finance, 1865–1879* (Princeton: Princeton University Press, 1964), passim.

8. Examples of the revisionist literature include: Morgan, *Hayes to McKinley*; John A. Garraty, *The New Commonwealth, 1877–1890* (New York: Harper and Row, 1968); John Thomas Houdek, "James A. Garfield and Rutherford B. Hayes: A Study in State and National Politics" (Ph.D. diss., Michigan State University, 1970); Kenneth E. Davison, ed., "Rutherford B. Hayes Special Edition," *Ohio History* 77 (Winter, Spring, Summer 1968); and the essays found in H. Wayne Morgan, ed., *The Gilded Age*, rev. ed. (Syracuse: Syracuse University Press, 1970).

9. The following discussion of party politics is based upon the analysis by Vincent P. De Santis, "The Republican Party Revisited, 1877–1897," in H. Wayne Morgan, ed., *The Gilded Age: A Reappraisal* (Syracuse: Syracuse University Press, 1963), 91–110.

10. The phrase "waving the bloody shirt" referred to the action of Representative Benjamin F. Butler, who showed his colleagues the blood-stained shirt of an Ohioan who had been flogged in Mississippi in 1866 to support the argument that southerners were unwilling to accept the results of the war and should be treated harshly. R. S. Holzman, *Stormy Ben Butler* (New York: Macmillan, 1954), 180.

11. An interesting study is Mary R. Dearing, *Veterans in Politics: The Story of the G. A. R.* (Baton Rouge: Louisiana State University Press, 1952).

12. A recent monograph is Ari Hoogenboom's *Outlawing the Spoils: A History of the Civil Service Reform Movement, 1865–1883* (Urbana: University of Illinois Press, 1961).

13. Walter Karp, *The Smithsonian Institution* (Washington: Smithsonian Institution, 1965), 15; Melville Bell Grosvenor, "Alexander Graham Bell" in the *Encyclopedia Americana* (New York: Americana Corporation, 1968), III, 504. The first telephone was placed in the White House in 1878 while Hayes was President. See Wayne Andrews, ed., *Concise Dictionary of American History* (New York: Charles Scribner's Sons, 1962), 930.

14. See Herbert Katz and Marjorie Katz, *Museums, U.S.A.: A History and a Guide* (Garden City, New York: Doubleday and Company, Inc., 1965), 17–20; Karp, *The Smithsonian Institution*, 76–77; Leonard Carmichael and J. C. Long, *James Smithson and The Smithsonian Story* (New York: G. P. Putnam's Sons, 1965), 19–24; 205–222.

15. It also became one of the earliest American buildings to be a prototype for European structures such as the Reichstag.

16. Cited in Katz and Katz, *Museums, U.S.A.*, 18.

17. "The Centennial Exposition provided the setting for the formation of the American Library Association and the resultant beginning of the free public library movement. It also gave an educational impetus to the museums of the country." *Collier's Encyclopedia* (New York: Crowell Collier and Macmillan, Inc., 1967), I, 130; Wallace Evan Davies, *Patriotism on Parade* (Cambridge: Harvard University Press, 1955), 46–50. See also

Edward G. Holley, *Raking the Historic Coals: The A.L.A. Scrapbook of 1876* (Chicago: Lakeside Press, 1967), 3–19, and Arthur E. Bestor, Jr., "The Transformation of American Scholarship, 1875–1917," *The Library Quarterly* 23 (July 1953): 164–179.

18. Hayes, Diary, October 7, 8, 1881; Hayes to Webb C. Hayes, October 6, 1881; Hayes to Fanny Hayes, October 11, 1881, all in Hayes Papers, RBHL. The full-length portrait of Hayes by Chase is owned by Harvard University and is on display in the law school building.

19. Lloyd Goodrich, *Thomas Eakins, His Life and Work* (New York: Studio Publications, 1933). The portrait, could it now be found, would command a small fortune.

20. Arthur M. Schlesinger, *The Rise of the City, 1878–1898* (New York: The Macmillan Company, 1933), especially pp. 78–120.

21. Richard B. Morris, ed., *Encyclopedia of American History*, Revised ed. (New York: Harper & Row, Publishers, 1961), 471.

22. See Gary Pennanen, "Public Opinion and the Chinese Question, 1876–1879," *Ohio History* 77 (Winter, Spring, Summer, 1968): 139–148.

23. Robert H. Walker, *Everyday Life in the Age of Enterprise, 1865–1900* (New York: G. P. Putnam's Sons, 1967), 196.

5

The First Family

Friends and foes of Rutherford Hayes often commented on his remarkable luck in winning six close elections[1] but the President was even more fortunate in his personal life.[2] Probably no statesman of his time enjoyed a happier marriage or closer family ties. Shortly before he died Hayes referred to his marriage to Lucy Ware Webb as "the most interesting fact" in his entire life.[3] Eight children, seven boys and a girl, blessed their union between 1853 and 1873. Of these, five lived to maturity; the remaining three, all boys, died during infancy. Lucy and Rutherford Hayes frequently spoke of their surviving children as comprising two distinct families: three older boys, Birchard, Webb, and Rud, born between 1853 and 1858 before the Civil War; and two younger children, Fanny (1867) and Scott (1871), both born during the Reconstruction era. Fanny and Scott, together with Webb, who acted as his father's confidential secretary, lived in Washington throughout the Hayes presidency. Birchard and Rud visited off and on while the former practiced law and the latter attended college.

Fifty-four years of age and in excellent health, Hayes was in the prime of life at the time of his inauguration. Of medium height, five feet eight and one-half inches, he appeared taller in photographs showing him wearing a Prince Albert coat. Although he possessed broad shoulders and a powerful torso, his contemporaries overlooked these features and noticed instead his high forehead, dark blue eyes, and full beard, which accentuated his profile. His slightly graying fair hair and sandy beard grew more so in the presidential years, and finally turned silver white during his retirement. Sedentary habits and a heavy diet gradually increased Hayes' weight from 180 to 192 pounds while he was President. The return to Fremont and private life with more open air and accustomed exercise helped him lose eight pounds within a few months.[4] Hayes rarely used glasses, which he may have needed since his right eye was weaker than the left one, and occasionally he complained of sore eyes. Generally he possessed good health throughout his life, and, by a self-imposed regimen of calisthenics before breakfast, long walks by day, and a brisk rubdown before retiring, he kept himself physically fit.[5] His rapid recovery after the serious arm wound at South Mountain and his ability to withstand the rigors of steady traveling in crude conveyances attest to his rugged constitution. During the Civil War, when Hayes was in his early forties, he boasted of being the healthiest man in the regiment.[6] Thomas Donaldson once remarked, "Hayes was always young to me." His "laughing face... seemed to light up with a warm glow as his years passed."[7] Another contemporary, Judge William Johnston, graphically portrayed the Hayes visage: "No painful, care-worn wrinkles, indicative of infirmities or misfortunes, to provoke a grudge against nature, or engender sourness toward mankind. Nor does he wear a smirking face, as if he were a candidate for admiration; but a fine sunny countenance."[8]

The President dressed simply and used little jewelry except a watch and ring and the lapel emblems of the Grand Army of the Republic or the Loyal Legion. For public occasions "he wore a silk hat, frock coat, plaited linen shirt, black shoes and varied his costume only in hot weather and then only to the extent of replacing his black tie for a white one and having his clothing made of thinner material."[9] In private, his appearance at times, like Thomas Jefferson's, was careless. His hair and beard might be unkempt, his comfortable slouch hat old and worn. Personal display did not concern him, and he often delighted in appearing incognito.[10]

Mrs. Hayes described her husband as "always calm."[11] No orator, his voice was agreeable and mild, yet still easily heard in a crowd, a skill he developed by constant practice starting with his days as a college debater.[12] A conciliatory manner won him many friends, and he was often asked to preside at meetings and to introduce speakers. He responded to criticism dispassionately and preferred to let his public record speak for itself. He studiously avoided personal attacks. Sometimes he would draft a short memorandum of the facts in a dispute and then request a friend quietly to circulate his rejoinder.

Hayes made friends readily and felt at ease in any society. "Well, what do you know?" was a favorite greeting.[13] His remarkable memory for names and faces often surprised men and women he had met only casually perhaps years earlier. His intellectual curiosity seemed unbounded, and his diary is replete with persons met or places visited, although his phonetic spelling of them was likely to be wrong. A favorite habit he retained even while governor and President was to purchase ordinary day coach railway tickets in order to talk informally with other passengers around him. Even conductors were fooled by this practice.[14] While frank and outspoken to his friends, Hayes kept his own counsel on private affairs and once cautioned a son not to write personal information on a post card.[15]

Despite his attractive personal qualities and admirable family life, Hayes suffered from a general abuse in the press, which affected the public's view of him and prevented general popular success. Chauncey M. Depew noted that "President Hayes, although one of the most amiable, genial, and companionable of our Presidents, with every quality to attach men to him and to make warm friendships was, nevertheless, one of the most isolated."[16] He inherited the presidency with a contested title, plus all the business troubles, economic disorganization, and currency disturbances that grew out of the panic of 1873, but, with rare courage and good nature, he introduced essential reforms and created conditions that made possible the success of his party in 1880. His strong sense of duty sustained him, and he left the presidency convinced history would justify his policies.

For relaxation, the President enjoyed family gatherings, visits with old friends, musicales, sports, travel, genealogy, and books. The executive mansion seldom lacked for visitors or house guests during his tenure. His son Rud, a student at Michigan and Cornell, and often a White House visitor, declared: "Never, during the time my father was President, did I have a bedroom or even a bed to myself."[17] When all the other guests were provided for, Rud curled up on whatever was left—a hallway cot, a couch in a reception room, the billiard table, or even a bathtub—as his bed for the night. But everything was very jolly in spite of the crowding.

Hayes was a good shot with a rifle and he knew how to hunt. He also liked to fish, skate, and swim. While President, he took walks and carriage rides daily. Fond of travel, he made several extended trips as national spokesman into the South, Central Plains, and Minnesota, climaxed by the first journey of a President to the West Coast. Many shorter trips took him to Philadelphia, New York, Boston, county fairs, and military reunions. Lucy Hayes teasingly accused him of being "scenery mad," and the Chicago *Tribune* dubbed him "Rutherford the Rover."[18] Whenever possible, he combined his interest in genealogy with these trips and took great pleasure in tracing a family connection or adding a volume of family history to his extensive library collection. Hayes enjoyed books immensely, especially if they pertained to American history and biography. At one time he purchased six thousand volumes, a valuable collection of Americana, from Robert Clarke, the prominent Cincinnati bookseller.[19] The President did not play cards or gamble.

Compared with past Presidents, Hayes enjoyed a high degree of financial independence. He achieved his wealth through success in law and politics, inheritance from his uncle Sardis Birchard, and his own wise investments. With an estate of $1 million at death, he probably was the wealthiest President of the nineteenth century.[20] Like George Washington, however, he sometimes owed others because much of his capital was tied up in land that he could not or would not sell at a loss when he needed cash. Entertaining on a grand scale, he lived graciously as President. In a single month, the bills totaled $6,000! Of the $200,000 he earned as President for four years, he left Washington with only about $1,000.[21] Nonetheless, his ban on alcohol in the official and private life of the executive mansion led to the charge that he was too frugal. Innumerable "begging letters" from friends, former employees and servants, soldiers or their kin, and even total strangers, plagued him throughout his public life. It is unusual how many times he responded favorably and generously, lending money never repaid, endorsing debts of others, and granting gifts of cash, food, or clothing.

Hayes never joined a church because doctrinal emphasis and denominational disputes displeased him.[22] Nonetheless he attended worship service each Sunday and gave liberally to the support of church work. Reared as a Presbyterian, he turned after marriage toward Methodism, his wife's faith. In Washington, the Hayes family deliberately attended the modest Foundry Methodist Church—just a five-minute walk from the executive mansion, rather than the more fashionable Metropolitan Methodist Church to which the Grants had belonged.[23]

Rutherford Hayes first met Lucy Ware Webb in Delaware, Ohio, in July 1847, shortly before her sixteenth birthday. Her childhood and youth resembled his in several respects. Born in Chillicothe, the first state capital of Ohio, on August 28, 1831, Lucy, like her future husband, was the youngest child in the family. Both of her brothers, Joseph and James, became doctors, and she looked up to them in the same devoted way Hayes admired his older sister, Fanny. In 1833, Lucy's father, Dr. James Webb, a veteran of the War of 1812, died of cholera in Kentucky where he had gone on a visit to free some slaves he had inherited. Left a widow with three small children to rear, Maria Webb, like Sophia Hayes, capably discharged her added responsibilities aided by her bachelor brother, Matthew Scott Cook.[24]

Originally Presbyterians, Lucy's father and mother left the denomination in 1831 when a majority of the Chillicothe congregation took issue with the proslavery sentiments of the pastor. The Webbs then became Methodists, and, in 1844, the widow moved her family to Delaware, Ohio, so the two boys might attend Ohio Wesleyan, a new college recently started there. Lucy took courses in both the preparatory and college departments, and in the fall of 1847 she enrolled in another new Methodist institution, Wesleyan Female College, located in Cincinnati. Here, like Hayes at Kenyon, she had several southern roommates, and she acquired life-long friendships, especially with Eliza Given, later Mrs. John Davis. Hayes, who had just moved from Fremont to Cincinnati to improve his prospects as a lawyer, discovered she was in the city and renewed the acquaintance at a college reception. After this, he was a frequent caller and attended her commencement in June 1850. Her education, unusual for its day, made her the first college graduate among presidential wives. Another year of courtship preceded their bethrothal in June 1851, followed by their marriage in her mother's home on December 30, 1852. The fact that it took the young Hayes two years to establish his legal practice probably accounts for the rather long engagement.

Since home and family always afforded Lucy Hayes her greatest pleasure, the first eight years of her marriage, before her husband became a public man, were very happy ones. A trip to Niagara Falls, visits with Chillicothe and Columbus relatives, a long delayed honeymoon in 1860 up the St. Lawrence to Quebec and Montreal returning through Vermont, New York City, and Philadelphia, plus numerous concerts, lectures, and church activities, highlighted her early years of marital bliss in Cincinnati. The birth of Birchard in 1853 prompted Hayes to purchase a home on Sixth Street for his growing family. Three boys were born in the first five years of the marriage. Only a family death marred these years for the happy couple. Fanny Hayes Platt, Rutherford's elder sister died tragically after a difficult birth of twin daughters, who also died. Fanny's death affected Hayes grievously, but the strength of his marriage and his growing family responsibilities soon compensated for the loss.

The Civil War years held further personal sorrow for the Hayes family. A fourth son, Joseph Thompson Hayes, born in December

1861, died at Camp White, West Virginia, while Lucy and the boys were visiting their father. Hayes consoled himself that since the death occurred in camp Lucy would at least not associate their Cincinnati house with the baby's death.[25] Mrs. Hayes often left home to be near her husband during the war and earned the respect of his troops by her kindness and sympathy in sewing garments and nursing wounded men. After Hayes' serious arm wound at South Mountain, she searched Washington hospitals for a week before locating him in a Middletown home. Another war baby, George Crook Hayes, born in 1864, died of scarlet fever in his second summer. Death struck the family circle twice more in 1866 with the passing of both grandmothers, Maria Webb on September 14 and Sophia Hayes on October 30.

Meanwhile Hayes started his congressional career, and Lucy made a six-week visit to Washington. Each afternoon during the debates over Reconstruction, she observed the House of Representatives in session. In the winter of 1866–1867 she accompanied her husband on a congressional junket to New Orleans. Later, as first lady of Ohio (1868–1872), she shared the governor's deep interest in the state's welfare institutions, and she is particularly credited with enlisting key support for the Soldiers' Orphans Home at Xenia and advocating the cause of deaf and dumb pupils at the Reform Farm. Prison policies, correctional institutions, and hospitals for the mentally ill also stirred her humanitarian concern.

Two more children, Fanny and Scott were born in Cincinnati and Columbus respectively. At the conclusion of his second term, Governor Hayes returned briefly to Cincinnati with his family and then, in May 1873, accepted his uncle's offer to make Spiegel Grove their permanent home. Lucy had resisted an earlier move to Fremont because she wished to be mistress of her own household and because most of her friends lived in southern Ohio. Uncle Sardis, however, removed the first obstacle by moving into the household of his ward, Sarah Jane Grant, on Birchard Avenue, a short distance from the Grove. Two months later, Dr. James Webb, Lucy's younger brother died of a mental malady. The sadness partly abated with the birth of Manning Force Hayes on August 1, 1873, only to return with the baby's fatal illness the following summer, the third Hayes boy to die in infancy.

Hayes reentered the political arena in 1875, won his third term as governor, and once more moved the family to Columbus where he rented a small house across the street from the State Capitol grounds. From this modest home he left for Washington and the White House on March 1, 1877.

Lucy Hayes, nearly nine years younger than the President, was only forty-five when she became first lady. A little above average size in height (five feet four and one-half inches) and weight (161) for women of her generation, she arranged her blue-black hair madonna style, parted in the middle and braided at the back. Preferring a comb or flower in her hair, she seldom wore a hat. Always fond of flowers, she sent countless gifts of them to friends and institutions. Her gowns, although fancier in the second half of her husband's term than in the first, were always less extravagant than Mrs. Grant's and never décolleté.[26]

Mrs. Hayes possessed a vibrant and magnetic personality, which perfectly complemented her husband's more serious and dignified demeanor. When he proposed to her, she confessed she thought herself "too light and trifling" for him.[27] Nonetheless her dark eyes and lovely musical voice captivated him, and for her twentieth birthday he sent five pieces of sheet music.[28] In his diary he confided: "Intellect, she has, too, a quick sprightly one, rather than a reflective, profound one. She sees at a glance what others study upon, but will not, perhaps, study out what she is unable to see at a flash. She is a genuine woman, right from instinct and impulse rather than judgment and reflection."[29]

Lucy Hayes enjoyed having people around her. She made friends readily and quickly put visitors at ease. Children, servants, and animals loved her. With her natural gaiety and wit, unusual education, social background, and long experience in official circles as the wife of a successful attorney, army officer, and governor, she raised the prestige of the executive in the public eye. Though not a crusader in the usual sense, she put "a new spirit of purity and conscience in the White House."[30] While having little direct influence on politics she had great sway among her family and friends and did much to overcome hostility and promote harmony throughout her husband's administration. She most enjoyed and much preferred informal receptions to state dinners. Letter writing always seemed tedious and difficult for her. Instead Mrs. Hayes relied upon conversation, frequent entertaining, and innumerable small courtesies and gifts to preserve her social position. She was especially cordial toward "ladies of the press" and freely granted them invitations and interviews.

The first lady loved to fish and to ride horseback. On a visit to Vice President Wheeler's home in New York State she caught a fifteen pound trout, which the President proudly served to male guests back in Washington.[31] She read a good deal, often out loud, and her favorite book was Harriet Beecher Stowe's *Old Town Folks*.[32] She sang beautifully and even her call to breakfast—"Familee-ee-ee"—was sweet and full voiced.[33] Lucy's optimism and zest for living attracted all who knew her.

When they moved to Washington, Rutherford and Lucy Hayes

had three grown sons, Birchard (twenty-three), Webb (twenty-one), and Rud (eighteen), besides two smaller children, Fanny (nine) and Scott (six). The President took great pride in his three older boys, who later strongly reflected aspects of their father's career and interests. Hayes taught his sons to abide by rather strict rules: no cards, billiards, liquor, or tobacco. He advised them to be attentive to ladies—"the wee small courtesies of life"—if they wished to succeed and be popular socially.[34] He particularly instructed them to exercise, to be outdoorsmen, and to practice at every opportunity to improve their ability in speaking and writing. He urged them to read and have favorite authors.[35]

Birchard (1853–1926), the eldest son, won a prize for scholarship and good conduct when he was eleven years old, and later graduated from Cornell (1874) and Harvard Law School (1877). Shy and introspective by temperament, he did not marry until he was past thirty-three. A poor speaker, not quite as fond of books in youth as later when he developed an antiquarian bent, Birchard enjoyed baseball, the theater, and, like his father, genealogy, and statistics. His ability to analyze statistical data led him to specialize in taxation and real-estate law.[36]

Webb (1856–1934), the second and perhaps the favorite son, while not scholarly, was honest, sensible, and sociable. He liked to ride and visit, and especially enjoyed boyhood trips to see his father as a soldier in West Virginia camps and as a legislator in Washington. At Cornell (1872–1875), Webb played football and attended the Saratoga regatta, but withdrew without graduating to serve as his father's confidential secretary (1875–1880) at the state house and the White House. He attended the Cincinnati convention as family observer, and then for a time acted as a bodyguard after a mysterious shot was fired into the Hayes Columbus home during a family dinner. Webb regularly attended cabinet meetings and also supervised the Spiegel Grove property while his father was President. An extrovert and a sportsman, who shared his father's love of outdoor life, Webb played polo and hunted elk, deer, and antelope in the Wyoming territory with Hayes' old army commander, General George Crook. When two disastrous fires in 1886 and 1889 temporarily paralyzed his business ventures, he turned toward a military career and served as a cavalry officer in Cuba, Puerto Rico, the Philippines, and China at the turn of the century, and along the Mexican border and on the Italian front in World War I. He was wounded in the Spanish-American War and awarded the Congressional Medal of Honor for gallantry during the Philippine Insurrection.[37]

Rutherford Platt Hayes (1858–1927), the third son, came closest of the boys to the President's own personality. Fond of wit and

Lucy Webb Hayes,
First Lady, 1877–1881.

Scott and Fanny Hayes, 1877, youngest children of President and Mrs. Hayes.

THE RUTHERFORD B. HAYES LIBRARY

President Hayes with his two oldest sons, Webb C. and Birchard Austin, 1877.

PRINTS AND PHOTOGRAPHS DIVISION, LIBRARY OF CONGRESS

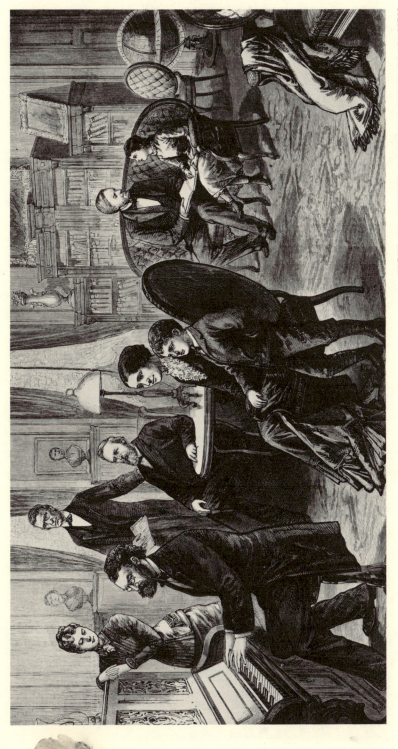

Secretary of Interior Carl Schurz playing the piano for President Hayes and his family at the White House, 1880. From Frank Leslie's Illustrated Newspaper, April 3, 1880.

President and Mrs. Hayes at worship in the Foundry Methodist Church, Washington, D.C. From Harper's Bazar, *April 19, 1879.*

The Hayes cabinet in session. Left to right:
Carl Schurz, Secretary of the Interior; David M. Key, Postmaster General;
George W. McCrary, Secretary of War; William M. Evarts, Secretary of State;
President Hayes; John Sherman, Secretary of the Treasury;
Richard W. Thompson, Secretary of the Navy; Charles Devens, Attorney General.

company, he delighted in the social life of Columbus and Washington and mingled easily among the many visitors and guests. After some graduate work in civil engineering at Boston Polytechnic Institute, he became in 1882 a Fremont banker and trustee of the Birchard Library. He developed a children's reading room program, sponsored traveling libraries, helped organize the Ohio Library Association in 1895, and for many years was secretary of the American Library Association. In later life he developed real-estate projects, especially around the resort area of Asheville, North Carolina. Thus his life reflected his father's inordinate love of books and Sardis Birchard's flair for financial enterprises. After his graduation from Cornell in 1880, he functioned as personal secretary to his father and managed the ex-President's financial affairs until the elder Hayes died in 1893. Troubled with poor health and eyesight, Rud took extended trips to New Mexico (1880) and Tennessee (1891) in search of improvement, and finally moved to Clearwater, Florida, in 1920. He and Birchard also accompanied their parents on the memorable 1880 trip to the Pacific Coast.[38]

Fanny Hayes (1867–1950), the sole daughter, was born in Cincinnati during her father's first canvass for governor. In fact, he had to ride thirty-eight miles by handcar to get home for her birth. She was nine years of age at the time her father became President. As the only girl, Fanny received much attention and pampering from her family and grew up to be a grand lady.[39]

In February 1878, when President and Mrs. Hayes attended the Methodist Fair in Baltimore, Maryland, a local carpenter and builder, George C. Brown, presented Mrs. Hayes with a three-story Victorian doll house for Fanny. Miss Grundy (Austine Snead), a lady correspondent in Washington during the Hayes administration, mentioned the gift in her column after a White House tour: "Most agreeable reminders of the presence of children are the two large 'baby houses' [the second one built in Washington] standing in the hall, in which the President's only daughter, little Fannie, between 10 and 11 years of age, and the youngest child, Scott, some three or four years younger, take great delight. . . ."[40] Fanny Hayes attended dancing school in 1875, and after the White House years continued her education at Miss Mittlebarger's School in Cleveland (with her friend Mollie, President Garfield's daughter) and Miss Porter's School in Farmington, Connecticut. Fanny was more liberal than her parents in her attitude toward amusements, and was fond of cycling and lawn tennis. After her mother's death in June 1889, she became her father's closet confidante and traveling companion and, as mistress of Spiegel Grove, strove to make his last days happy.

Scott Russell Hayes (1871–1923) was the youngest child to survive infancy. His large head and weight of eleven pounds made his birth difficult, and Lucy suffered more than usual. Always large for his age, he weighed 180 pounds by his fifteenth birthday. As a child, he enjoyed riding his velocipede and pony. He received private instruction in Washington, attended Fremont schools, transferred to boarding school at Green Springs (Ohio) Academy in 1883, and later studied manual training in Toledo before following his brothers' footsteps to Cornell. Scott entered business and became an officer of several companies manufacturing railroad equipment. Scott Hayes died somewhat prematurely at age fifty-seven, his death probably hastened by a physical breakdown in 1919 following a strange and horrible experience at sea. He had started with his wife on what was to be an extensive business trip through Central and South America but, in a terrible storm, was shipwrecked and forced to abandon ship off the coast of Peru. Just before the ship sank, the passengers were placed on two tankers. All their possessions were lost. In the continuing storm, the metal tankers were picked up by a vessel carrying wild animals, and in the storm the tigers, boa constrictors, and other terrified beasts broke loose, adding to the horrors of the rescue operation. In answer to repeated wireless calls, however, the passengers were again rescued and safely landed in Peru.[41]

The family kept several pets in the White House, giving "a Robinson Crusoe touch to our mode of life," as the President put it.[42] Scott's goat hauled him all over the premises and two dogs added to the fun. Lucy kept a mockingbird and Siamese cat simultaneously without incident. The cat, Siam, was sent to Mrs. Hayes from Bangkok in November 1878 by U.S. Consul David B. Sickels, who informed her it was the first attempt ever made to send a Siamese cat to America.[43] Siam became a great White House favorite and always entered the room when Mrs. Hayes had visitors. During the autumn of 1879, while the President and Mrs. Hayes were in Ohio, the cat sickened, and despite all the White House physician, Dr. J. H. Baxter, and William T. Crump, the family steward, could do, died in October. Crump sadly wrote Mrs. Hayes that he had taken Siam to Commissioner of Agriculture William G. LeDuc and given orders to have her stuffed.[44]

President Hayes brought with him from Ohio one pair of black horses not remarkable for beauty. As he owned only one carriage not worth bringing to Washington, he bought a fine landau from Brewster and Company on March 22, 1877, for which he paid $1,150. This he used as a family and official vehicle throughout his residence in Washington and even loaned it to President Garfield until the latter acquired a proper presidential carriage of his own. When returned to Fremont, the Hayes carriage was used continuously by the family until the death of the former President on January 17, 1893. President Hayes also spent $900 for a pair of carriage horses, but his secretary, William K. Rogers, to whom he entrusted the purchase, was such a poor judge of horseflesh that considerable newspaper criticism of the Hayes horses in contrast to Grant's finely matched teams compelled the President to purchase another pair in May 1877 for $800. This assignment Webb Hayes, the chief executive's second son, discharged effectively.[45]

Among the staff of official servants, the chief place was held by the steward, a virtual autocrat of the official table fare at the executive mansion who did all of the marketing and shopping and was entrusted with the care of plate, furniture, and the general housekeeping.[46] Edgar R. Beckley, Grant's steward, purchased a large store of foodstuffs, except for perishable meats and vegetables, just before the Hayes moved in, and Grant thoughtfully left behind a stock of fine wines in the cellar.[47] John A. Simms, like his predecessor a black man, took over from Beckley about March 20, 1877, and functioned until June 1879, when William T. Crump, Hayes' orderly in the Civil War, replaced Simms whose extravagance and acceptance of commissions on White House purchases displeased Hayes.[48] Whereas Grant bought food at cost from the army commissary, Hayes issued instructions that he wished to buy his provisions "like other men."[49] Simms and Crump patronized many Washington merchants in purchasing groceries, vegetables, meat, fish, oysters, ice, poultry, confections, butter and eggs, and baked goods at separate stores. The fact that yearly expenses of the steward totaled between eight and nine thousand dollars helps to explain why the Hayes family earned a reputation for setting an excellent table. The Hayes' state dinners were catered affairs costing six to eight dollars a plate, not including extra waiters and incidentals.[50] Meanwhile the family cook prepared up to two thousand meals a month for the presidential family, domestic servants, and house guests.[51] Crump remained in Washington as Garfield's steward but strained his back so badly while nursing the mortally wounded President that he was finally forced to tender his resignation to President Arthur in 1882. He then took an ocean voyage to England and tried hydropathic baths in a vain search for a cure. Compelled to wear a brace and to have help in putting on his own shoes and socks, Crump never adequately recovered from his injury. For a brief period he operated "The Garfield Dining Rooms" in Washington, but repeated financial reverses reduced him to borrowing money from Hayes and selling his few mementos of the White House years.[52]

Other presidential servants under Hayes included a doorkeeper, four assistant doorkeepers, a messenger, four assistant messengers (two mounted), a watchman, and a fireman.[53] Three members of this group were veteran executive mansion employees. The fireman, T. S. Herbert, had been appointed by President Fillmore; the chief doorkeeper, T. F. Pendel, by Lincoln; and the chief usher or messenger, Charles Leoffler, by Grant.[54] Pendel began his duties as one of the four original Lincoln bodyguards in November 1864, but his appointment soon afterward as doorkeeper created the vacancy filled by Crook. In 1902 Pendel published his official memoirs, *Thirty-Six Years in the White House*.[55] Loeffler, a German, started as a messenger presenting visitor's cards to the office secretaries, but soon advanced to the position of chief usher and keeper of the President's door, a station he retained until retired as a quartermaster-major of the United States Army in 1901.[56]

Another group of about twenty employees, mostly Negro domestic servants, came under the jurisdiction of Colonel Thomas L. Casey, Commissioner of Public Buildings and Grounds.[57] Only three of them remained from the Grant era: Henry Harris and Beverly Lemos, waiters, and Jerry Smith, house servant. Harris lost his job in 1881 but secured a place in the War Department.[58] Lemos probably was a relative of Charles H. Lemos, the White House barber. "Old Jerry" stayed until the McKinley period.[59]

Several experienced domestic servants accompanied the Hayes family to Washington and still others were employed as required. Winnie Monroe, an excellent Negro cook and nurse, had lived in the Hayes home in Cincinnati as far back as 1857 and was the daughter of "Aunt Clara," another servant in the early days of the Hayes household. Winnie, widow of a "shiftless husband," was a large woman of about thirty-three years of age in 1877. A native of Kentucky, she enjoyed Washington society and as housekeeper for the President spoke of herself as "the fu'st culled lady in de lan'! " Her fifteen-year-old daughter, Mary T. Monroe, assisted her as a housemaid in the executive mansion. Census data indicate Winnie could read but not write. Her temper sometimes created trouble with other servants and Mrs. Hayes, but she remained in the family employ until a short time after they retired to Fremont, and then, unable to be content in Ohio after four years of Washington excitement and attention, Winnie returned to find new employment in the capital city and buy a house there. At her death in 1886, Hayes paid her funeral expenses of seventy dollars.[60]

Isaiah E. Lancaster, the President's Negro valet, a young man of twenty-three in 1877, first met the Hayes when he worked at the Carlisle House in Cincinnati where they stayed briefly in 1873 before moving to Spiegel Grove. He became a Hayes servant in September 1876 and remained at least until 1881. Other domestic servants at one time or other during the Hayes presidency included Jane Humphreys, Mrs. Stanard, Maria Meredith, and Margery Daw, all cooks; Ann Maria Rustin and Mary Waters, laundresses; Edgar Beckley, messenger; Oscar L. Berger, clock winder; and Telemachus Ford, watchman. Several of them posed for a very rare and historic group picture of White House servants in May 1877.[61]

An unusual and prominent feature of the President's official residence in the Hayes era was the large rambling conservatories which leaned against the west side of the mansion.[62] Removed in the major renovation of 1902 to make way for the present executive office wing, these greenhouses played a prominent part in the Hayes administration. The first lady loved flowers, and more than one dollar out of every four appropriated for the upkeep and improvement of the executive mansion in these years went toward the expense of the greenhouses. Colonel Casey employed a staff of ten people solely for conservatory maintenance. Henry Pfister, an Ohioan, served as head gardener assisted by four other men, a fireman, two laborers, a bouquet maker, and a lady with horse and cart who presumably delivered the many floral gifts Mrs. Hayes loved to bestow upon her friends and favorite charitable institutions.[63]

Hayes paid some servants out of his own pocket. When he became President, he sat down with Colonel Casey and struck from the list of items paid by congressional appropriation those which seemed to him more personal than public in nature. Maintenance of the White House stable fell into this category as the President's cash book reveals. (George) Albert Hawkins, Grant's coachman, continued through the Hayes period and drove also for President Garfield. Hayes paid him sixty dollars per month and gradually increased the wages of his hostler, James Simms, from fifteen to thirty dollars a month. In his first year as President, the executive stable account alone cost Hayes nearly six thousand dollars. In addition he assumed or supplemented the government salary of other personal servants. Although cooks normally received thirty dollars a month, he paid Winnie Monroe and Isaiah Lancaster an extra twenty dollars in addition to their government pay of thirty and fifty dollars respectively. He paid the laundresses an extra five dollars beyond the government rate of twenty to thirty dollars a month.[64]

Contemporaries attest to a general revival of society and presidential hospitality during the Hayes administration reminiscent of the proud tradition of Abigail Adams, Dolley Madison, and

Harriet Lane.[65] The tone of official society had unfortunately dropped considerably in the maelstrom of the Civil War years when the ill-fated Mary Todd Lincoln presided over a White House that resembled more a New York hotel in atmosphere than the nation's stately executive mansion. The Grants, in turn, reflected the poorest taste of the Gilded Age with its thin veneer of cheaply gotten-up four-in-hand teams, flashy liveries, and snobbish feasts. The Hayes restored a natural, simple dignity and sincerity to White House social functions. Garfield's tragically brief term missed the social season entirely. His successor, President Arthur, instituted a much more exclusive entertainment policy and kept very late hours, some of his private parties lasting until two o'clock in the morning.[66]

Rutherford and Lucy Hayes entertained openly and liberally, straining their presidential purse. Dinners for not only the members of both houses of Congress, the Supreme Court, the cabinet, and the diplomatic corps, but also in honor of other federal and state officials visiting the city, and the yearly increasing throng of notable private visitors from the several states and from all quarters of the world, constituted a steady drain on the President's annual salary. A single state dinner for thirty-six people, like the famous one (including wine) given by Hayes in honor of the visiting Grand Dukes of Russia, cost him $507.[67] After the ban on alcohol, the annual dinner to the diplomatic corps was given up in favor of an evening reception to which hundreds of other persons of note, civil and military, were invited. Hayes gave instructions to make up for the absence of wine by having the very choicest decoration and entertainment that could be obtained. These diplomatic receptions were, by general agreement, the finest entertainment given in Washington up to that period.[68]

One of these receptions in February 1879 cost the President $1,571, not to mention damage to the premises from souvenir hunters. "After every public reception a man had to go rounds with a basket of crystal pendants to replace those taken from the chandeliers. They cut pieces off the bottoms of curtains, and carried off everything in sight."[69] During part of the term, Congress was so hostile to Hayes that it refused to make appropriations for the upkeep of the White House, and it became an added financial burden to keep it presentable. Mrs. Hayes resorted to reversing the ends of curtains, covering worn spots in the carpets with furniture, and other sorts of subterfuges. She ransacked the attic and cellar to find furniture that could be restored to use, and, when this sometimes failed, she spent her own money to purchase furniture and accessories for the executive mansion.[70]

Some house guests, usually young ladies in their teens or early twenties, stayed at the White House for weeks or months at a time to assist Lucy with her social duties and virtually became part of the family. Some were favorite nieces or daughters of old friends, others daughters of close associates in the administration. Thus, a bevy of attractive young girls who, by common consent, helped Mrs. Hayes stage some of the handsomest and most lavish receptions in Washington, compensated for state dinners without wine.[71]

During the many public receptions, Mrs. Hayes usually stood with the President, and everyone, regardless of social station, received a hearty grasp of the hand from the President and the first lady. A thousand or more would pass in line, and Mrs. Hayes' white gloves would quickly lose their shape and color. Ushers had a difficult time keeping the crowd moving along. For one hour, an hour-and-a-half, and sometimes two hours, the President and Mrs. Hayes would stand and shake hands. No one was ever turned away, and the function closed only when the last caller had been greeted. The President's dignified greeting and Mrs. Hayes' winning smile were never lacking from beginning to end.[72]

Lucy instituted regular Saturday afternoon receptions for the public in the Blue Parlor. At these affairs, guests passed along to the Green Parlor where as many as sixteen young hostesses greeted them. The President's sons often escorted visitors through the White House and squired young ladies to the theater or on tours of the city. Rud confessed, "In case I wished to get rid of them quickly, I would take them to the museum and show them the Egyptian mummies, prehistoric skeletons and reptiles. By the time they had seen these they had had enough."[73]

At one of the crowded diplomatic receptions, Lady Thornton, wife of England's Sir Edward Thornton, then the dean of the Washington diplomatic corps, apologized to Mrs. Hayes for being obliged to leave early and inquired if she might depart quietly by a side doorway. There was not a single side or back door available.[74] The ground floor was simply a basement where coal, old furniture, and other odds and ends were stored. Rud, in whose charge the first lady placed the distinguished visitor, remembered a door near the coal bin and led Lady Thornton through the dark, musty basement and out of this door. "She was very jolly and laughted heartily over the escapade."[75]

Mrs. Hayes was always at home in the Red Parlor of the White House to her friends living in Washington or visiting the city for a few days. These nightly assemblies became quite noted, and happy was the person who had unwritten permission to be present. Sometimes the President honored the occasion for a few minutes, but his official duties more often called him upstairs to the Cabinet Room. The family and guests usually went from the dinner table directly to the Red Parlor. Some evenings thirty to fifty people called, not the usual sycophants of Washington life but the leaders and brilliant men and women of that day. The cabinet officers with their wives and daughters came regularly. The army and navy officers always made an effort to call, if only for a moment, either going to or returning from dinners or receptions. Noted writers and artists of the day used this time to call when in Washington and created perhaps the most brilliant White House social life since the early days of the Republic. General Sherman, Admiral Porter, George Bancroft, Albert Bierstadt, William Wetmore Story, Bishop Matthew Simpson, Lord Dufferin of Canada, and young Major and Mrs. William E. McKinley all inscribed their names in Lucy's guest book. These assemblages usually broke up at ten o'clock when the President and Mrs. Hayes went to their room and the young people all adjourned to the library, used as a family room during the Hayes administration; and very frequently Crump, the steward, would lay out a light lunch for them on the table in the upstairs hall. These were moments when fun and wit prevailed. General Russell Hastings courted the President's niece, Emily Platt, in such circumstances, and the young couple were subsequently married in a White House ceremony on June 19, 1878.[76]

In the winter months, Mrs. Hayes held many afternoon receptions. These were grand affairs, and all the parlors of the house were thrown open to the guests. She received in the Blue Parlor and with her were always some wives of government officials, usually cabinet ladies, while ranged behind her were the young ladies of the house and their invited friends. As the visitors came in from the Red Parlor, they were introduced by Colonel Thomas L. Casey, Commissioner of Public Buildings and Grounds. Those intimate with the family went behind the line and were greeted by the young belles, while the rest went on to the Green Parlor and from there to the East Room. A few moments before the hour for the function to close, the coterie in the rear of Mrs. Hayes in the Blue Parlor broke up and circulated among the guests scattered about the many parlors. Gentlemen were seldom very numerous at Mrs. Hayes' afternoon receptions.[77]

Another kind of assemblage at the White House in the Hayes era involved Vice President William A. Wheeler. Usually a President and Vice President go their own way in line of duty and see little of each other. Hayes and Wheeler, however, were very friendly, and the Vice President was frequently a social visitor at the White House. A widower of about sixty years of age, Wheeler was passionately fond of psalm singing, his one major diversion. Each Sunday evening the first family and a few close friends met in the White House library, the Vice President supplying copies of *The Presbyterian Hymn and Tune Book* for "a revelry of sweet sounds and mingling of souls." Carl Schurz, who was Hayes' Secretary of the Interior, accompanied them on the piano.[78]

Hundreds of private citizens signed Mrs. Hayes' social register, including such different personalities as Emma C. Thursby, Thomas A. Edison, and J. Franklin Jameson. Miss Thursby, a church soloist who became a famous coloratura soprano of the era, was one of the first American singers to achieve renown in Europe where she studied voice and presented numerous recitals. While on a month's tour of eastern American cities in 1877, she made two highly successful concert appearances in Washington's Lincoln Hall. President and Mrs. Hayes expressed their pleasure in her singing by honoring her with a reception and musicale in the East Room of the White House on the evening of November 28, 1877. Miss Thursby made several return visits to Washington and again called on her good friend, Mrs. Hayes.[79]

In April 1878, at the age of thirty-one, Edison came to Washington to demonstrate his recently invented phonograph to the American Academy of Science and the members of Congress. His last stop during this triumphal tour was an unusual audience at the executive mansion. As Edison relates:

> About 11 o'clock word was received from the President that he would be very pleased if I would come.... I was taken there and found Mr. Hayes and several others waiting, among them I remember Carl Schurz who was playing the piano.... The exhibition continued till about 12:30 A. M., when Mrs. Hayes and several other ladies who had been induced to get up and dress, appeared. I left at 3:30 A.M.[80]

A young graduate student at Johns Hopkins University, J. Franklin Jameson, who was destined to win fame as one of the nation's greatest archivists and historians, paid an informal Sunday evening call at the White House on the chance that he might meet the President. The next day he described the memorable experience in a letter to his mother:

> The introduction and cards were sent up, and after waiting some time in a room, we were conducted to the foot of the big stairs by one attendant; at the top of them another met us, and conducted us into a sort of study where the President was. We were fortunate

enough to find him alone. He isn't quite as goodlooking as his
picture, his face being somewhat pitted. But he was very pleasant
indeed, and I liked him ever so much. To tell the truth, I hadn't
much liked the idea of calling there, for I thought it must be an
awful bore to the President. Very likely it was, but as he didn't
in the least show it, but appeared very kind and cordial, I didn't
feel uncomfortable at all. He talked about the things to be seen
in Washington, and about the odd characters who drifted to the
city, and a little about Johns Hopkins. . . . I thought Mrs. Hayes
very pleasant, as I suppose every one does.[81]

Somewhile after Hayes retired from the presidency, Jameson
summed up the opinion of very many other White House callers
of the era when he prophesied, "I think we shall some time look
back with pride to Hayes as one of the best presidents."[82]

Notes

1. See the comment of William Disney in the Cincinnati *Commercial
Gazette*, January 31, 1893. Disney was one of the candidates who lost
the city solicitorship of Cincinnati to Hayes in December 1858.

2. Carl Schurz to Hayes, June 26, 1889, O. L. Pruden, an executive
clerk under several administrations, spoke of the Hayes family "as the
best he had known." See reference in Hayes, Diary, February 2, 1890,
Hayes Papers, RBHL.

3. Hayes to Albert English, July 14, 1892, Hayes Papers, RBHL.

4. Hayes, Diary, May 26, 1876, March 11, 1881, December 7, 1881.

5. Ibid., April 9, 1876. "He was a great walker. A kind of Caliph of
Bagdad, *in cog.* traveling the capital at night." Thomas C. Donaldson,
"Memoirs," January 30, 1880, p. 126, RBHL.

6. Hayes, Diary, October 3, 1861.

7. Donaldson, "Memoirs," May 6, 1879, p. 89.

8. Judge William Johnston, Speech at Avondale, Ohio, July 21, 1876,
Hayes Papers, RBHL.

9. "I heard him once say that the Grand Army button he wore on
his coat was the grandest decoration he had ever had." Gov. Wm. E.
McKinley, "Life and Character of R. B. Hayes," May 16, 1893, in the
*Proceedings of the Twenty-Seventh Annual Encampment of the Department
of Ohio, Grand Army of the Republic* (Sandusky: I. F. Mack & Bro., 1893),
240; David S. Barry, *Forty Years in Washington* (Boston: Little, Brown and
Company, 1924), 25–26.

10. "The President had an old slouch hat, and a black alpaca coat on. . . .
The President has a fashion I don't like and I don't think it becomes
him of wearing his hair long and turning it ends under; it is awfully
country like. His clothes are never extravagant. I dislike an old alpaca
coat he wears dreadfully." Donaldson, "Memoirs," April 28, 1877, pp.
13–14. "The President said to Mrs. Hayes, 'Mr. Schurz the other day,
in speaking of a shocking bad hat which some gentleman present with
him was wearing, said, "Go get another one. That hat is almost as bad
as the President's or Mr. Evarts." ' . . . The truth is, the President does
manage to wear some horrid hats." Ibid., December 12, 1879, p. 113.

11. Lucy Webb Hayes to Birchard Hayes, February 6, 1879, Lucy Hayes
Papers, RBHL.

12. See Allen Boyd Bogarad, "A Historical and Rhetorical Analysis of Rutherford Birchard Hayes" (Master's thesis, Ohio State University, 1957), 76–103; Upton S. Palmer, "An Historical and Critical Study of the Speeches of Rutherford B. Hayes" (Ph.D. diss., University of Michigan, 1950), 267–273.

13. Cited in Charles Richard Williams, *The Life of Rutherford Birchard Hayes* (Boston: Houghton Mifflin Company, 1914), II, 416.

14. Hayes, Diary, November 28, 1879.

15. Hayes to Rutherford Platt Hayes, August 11, 1873, Hayes Papers, RBHL.

16. Chauncey M. Depew, *My Memories of Eighty Years* (New York: Charles Scribner's Sons, 1922), 100.

17. Rutherford Platt Hayes, "The Age of Innocence in the White House," *Literary Digest* 92 (February 5, 1927): 41–42.

18. Calvin Dill Wilson, "Our Presidents Out of Doors," *Century Magazine* 55 (March 1909): 709; Hayes to Mary Sherman Hayes, September 29, 1889, Hayes Papers, RBHL; Chicago *Tribune*, September 6, 1878.

19. Hayes to Austin Birchard, May 14, 1874, Hayes Papers, RBHL: "You know I am given to antiquarian and genealogical pursuits. An old family letter is a delight to my eyes. I can prowl in the old trunks of letters by the day with undiminished zest." See also Williams, *Life of Hayes*, II, 432–433.

20. "Gen. Hayes left an estate of near a million dollars. Much of it is in real estate. He has large tracts of land in Minnesota and property in Nebraska. He owned several good business properties here, and a number of houses in Toledo. . . . he owned a large block of stock in the savings bank here, and he and his son Webb, have, perhaps $100,000 invested in the Thomson-Houston carbon works. Gen. Hayes inherited $500,000 in money and property from his uncle Sardis Birchard, and by judicious investments, has nearly if not quite doubled the sum. But in all his public life as congressman, governor or President, he never used his position to further his private interests." Toledo *Blade*, January 19, 1893. Records of the Executors of the Estate of Rutherford B. Hayes, Hayes Papers, RBHL.

21. "I never received in any office more than I expended. . . . My habits were not expensive, and my family never lacked carefulness, but we had enough to warrant it and we lived freely—travelled always a good deal, and did not pinch ourselves in any respect. . . . We spent in hospitality, charities, and generous living the whole amount of my salary. My belief is that no other ever spent as much in the White House as we did. . . . Special entertainments were frequent. And the regular routine of affairs was made exceptionally brilliant and expensive. Many new dinners and entertainments were added to the "of course" affairs. Mrs. H. was busy with her whole hearted energy in looking up poor and needy. When we left Washington a story was started that I had saved about $20,000 during my term. This was shown by the reduction of my indebtedness to that amount. This had an appearance of truth and was perhaps derived from one of the family. But on looking up affairs at home it turned out that a large part of this reduction of my debts was from collections on real estate sales made before I left home. I left Washington with less than $1,000." Hayes to Donaldson, March 10, 1891, Hayes Papers, RBHL.

22. "I do not belong to any church; I never have. I can not subscribe to any of the creeds. Religion is as natural to men as anything else.

One wants some one to look up to, to lean upon, a Supreme Being. As to the Bible, I do not care to discuss it, or its origins. Christ's religion is to me the best." Donaldson, "Memoirs," April 17, 1887, p. 187.

23. "Your act last Sabbath [attendance at the Foundry M. E. Church in preference to the more pretentious Metropolitan Church], has given to our church a lesson in humility and practical piety which we feel we need to keep ever in view." D. C. Knowles, Pastor M. E. Church, Malden, Mass., to Lucy Hayes, March 14, 1877, Lucy Hayes Papers. RBHL.

24. The best biography of Lucy Hayes is Emily Apt Geer, "Lucy Webb Hayes: An Unexceptionable Woman" (Ph.D. diss., Western Reserve University, 1962).

25. Hayes to Lucy Hayes, July 26, 1863, Hayes Papers, RBHL.

26. Receipted bills indicate the cost of her dresses ranged from $104.80 to $400.00 each. Receipts for Mrs. Hayes' White House gowns, RBHL.

27. Hayes, Diary, June 14, 1851.

28. Ibid., August 26, 1851.

29. Ibid., May 23, 1851.

30. Carl Schurz to Hayes, March 6, 1881, Hayes Papers, RBHL.

31. Hayes, Diary, June 3, 1878; Webb C. Hayes, Journal, June 2, 1878, Webb Cook Hayes Papers, both in RBHL.

32. Hayes to Mrs. Clara Hanson Mohun, August 26, 1889, Hayes Papers, RBHL.

33. Hayes, Diary, August 16, 1889, Hayes to Fanny Hayes, February 4, 1886, Hayes Papers, RBHL.

34. "Your mother fears you may be led astray—get wild and reckless at that great College [Cornell]. I must therefore suggest that you never play cards or billiards either at the college or in Ithaca. Liquor and tobacco in all its forms you will I am sure eschew wherever you are. But I need not lay down rules. I feel confident you will do what is sensible." Hayes to Birchard Hayes, October 31, 1870, Hayes Papers, RBHL. "You may join the Society you prefer. But do not allow yourself to drink or smoke or gamble. No swearing. Be always a gentleman. If others behave badly to you try to have character enough to be kind and manly always." Hayes to Rutherford Platt Hayes, October 17, 1876, Hayes Papers, RBHL.

35. Hayes to Birchard Hayes, April 24, 1868, April 23, 1871; Hayes to Webb C. Hayes, December 1, 1872, all in Hayes Papers, RBHL.

36. "I am in no hurry about having my boys learn to write. I would much prefer they would lay up a stock of health by knocking around in the country than to hear that they were the best scholars of their age in Ohio." Hayes to Sophia Birchard Hayes, September 28, 1863, February 6, April 21, 1865; Hayes, Diary, August 13, 1874, April 12, 1886, May 9, 1887, all in Hayes Papers, RBHL. Fremont *News Messenger*, January 24, 1926.

37. Hayes to Rutherford Platt Hayes, October 15, 1878, Hayes Papers, RBHL; Hayes, Diary, March 21, 1879, February 27, 1886, October 30, 1889. See also "Colonel Webb C. Hayes" (n.p., 1913?), RBHL; Eugene M. Fusco, "The Last Hunt of General George Crook," *Montana* 12 (Autumn 1962): 36–46; "Webb Cook Hayes," *The National Cyclopedia of American Biography* (New York: James T. White & Company, 1937), XXV, 136–137.

38. Hayes, Diary, February 22, 1875; Hayes to R. P. Hayes, telegram, April 17, 1880, Hayes Papers, RBHL. Fremont *Daily News*, May 8, 1891. "Rutherford Platt Hayes," *The National Cyclopedia of American Biography* (New York: James T. White & Company, 1931), XXI, 198.

39. See the article in the centennial edition of the Fremont *News Messenger*, Summer 1949, for a short biographical sketch of Fanny Hayes, who was still alive at the time.

40. Miss Grundy (Austine Snead), "How Presidents Live ... A Glance at Mr. Hayes's Domestic Arrangements," March 28, 1878, in Hayes Scrapbook, Vol. 112, p. 100, RBHL; Flora Gill Jacobs, *A History of Dolls' Houses* (New York: Charles Scribner's, 1965), 114–116.

41. Newspaper obituary by Lucy E. Keeler pasted in Charles Wells Hayes, *George Hayes of Windsor* (Buffalo: Baker, Jones & Co., 1884), copy in RBHL.

42. Hayes to Birchard Hayes, April 13, 1879, Hayes Papers, RBHL.

43. David B. Sickels to Mrs. R. B. Hayes, November 1, 1878, Lucy Webb Hayes Papers, RBHL.

44. Wm. T. Crump to Mrs. R. B. Hayes, October 5, 1879, Lucy Webb Hayes Papers, RBHL.

45. The Cincinnati *Commercial*, Sunday, April 1, 1877; R. B. Hayes, Ledger Kept While in the White House, Executive Stable Account, 60, Hayes Papers, RBHL. The Washington *National Republican*, March 22, 1877, and March 31, 1877. The Hayes carriage, now handsomely restored, is on exhibit in the Hayes Museum at Spiegel Grove.

46. Gilson Willets, *Inside History of the White House* (New York: The Christian Herald, 1908), 181; "White House Secretaries, Messengers, etc., March 4, 1877," manuscript, Hayes Papers, RBHL.

47. Margarita Spalding Gerry, ed., *Through Five Administrations: Reminiscences of Colonel William H. Crook* (New York: Harper and Brothers, 1910), 218.

48. Donaldson, "Memoirs," June 14, 1881, pp. 159–160. Beckley became one of the messengers after his service as steward.

49. Gerry, *Five Administrations*, 225.

50. See Rutherford B. Hayes, "Ledger Kept While in the White House," 1–2, 30, Hayes Papers, RBHL.

51. "Total Number of Meals served at the White House during January, 1881," manuscript, Hayes Papers, RBHL.

52. Hayes, Diary, October 28, 1888; Gerry, *Five Administrations*, 272; W. T. Crump to Hayes, April 29, August 4, 1882, March 1883, April 1884, Hayes Papers, RBHL.

53. "Regular Force of the Executive Mansion paid by Executive Mansion Appropriation," manuscript, Hayes Papers, RBHL.

54. Willets, *Inside History*, 175.

55. Ibid., 177–178; Thomas F. Pendel, *Thirty-Six Years in the White House* (Washington: The Neale Publishing Company, 1902).

56. Willets, *Inside History*, 176–177.

57. "Executive Mansion Force Employed by Commissioner of Public Buildings and Grounds Col. T. L. Casey, December 1, 1880," manuscript, Hayes Papers, RBHL.

58. W. T. Crump to Webb C. Hayes, March 31, 1881, Hayes Papers, RBHL.

59. For a picture of "Old Jerry," see Amy La Follette Jensen, *The White House and Its Thirty-Two Families* (New York: McGraw-Hill Book Company, Inc., 1958), 164.

60. A. S. Stevens to Governor Hayes, December 17, 1868; Hayes, Diary, December 26, 1870, both in Hayes Papers, RBHL; U.S., Department of Interior, Bureau of the Census, *Ninth Census of the United States: 1870*.

Population, Ohio, Vol. XIX, Franklin County, Third Ward, Columbus, 46, original in the National Archives; U.S., Department of Interior, Bureau of the Census, *Tenth Census of the United States: 1880. Population, Ohio,* Vol. LVI, Sandusky County, First Ward, Fremont, 12, Microcopy T–9, Roll 1063, National Archives; Charles Richard Williams, *The Life of Rutherford B. Hayes* (Boston: Houghton Mifflin Company, 1914), II, 301n.; Mary F. Monroe to Hayes, June 14, 1886; W. H. Crook to Hayes, June 17, 22, 1886, Hayes Papers, RBHL.

61. Jensen, *The White House,* 113, reproduces this first photograph ever taken of a White House staff.

62. Ibid., 112, 165.

63. Thos. Lincoln Casey to Hayes, June 21, 1881, enclosing "Statement of Expenditure of Appropriation For care of and repairs, refurnishing, and fuel for the Executive Mansion, and care of and necessary repairs of the Green Houses, and fuel for the same"; "Force in Executive Mansion Greenhouses"; both manuscripts, Hayes Papers, RBHL.

64. Manning Force, "Reminiscences of Rutherford B. Hayes," manuscript, 1893; Rutherford B. Hayes, "Cash Book, 1878–81," passim; Rutherford B. Hayes, "Ledger Kept While in White House, Executive Stable Account," all items in Hayes Papers, RBHL.

65. Donaldson, "Memoirs," January 5, 1882, p. 161.

66. See newspaper clipping entitled "A Change of Social Base," enclosed in a letter from John D. Martin to Hayes, March 6, 1877; Thomas C. Donaldson to Hayes, January 9, 1882, both in Hayes Papers, RBHL.

67. Hayes' son Rud said the expenses of the White House and family were between $32,000 and $35,000 a year. Donaldson, "Memoirs," May 17, 1880, p. 134. Manning Force, "Reminiscences of Rutherford B. Hayes," manuscript, RBHL; R. B. Hayes, "Ledger Kept While in White House," 2, RBHL.

68. Force, "Reminiscences of Hayes," 6–8.

69. Hayes, "Ledger," 30; Hayes, "Age of Innocence," 42.

70. Geer, "Lucy Webb Hayes," 213.

71. Hayes, Diary, January 2, 1881; Hayes to Guy M. Bryan, March 26, 1880, Hayes Papers, RBHL.

72. "Genealogy and Autobiography of Russell Hastings," manuscript, Chap. 16, pp. 8–10, RBHL.

73. Hayes, "Age of Innocence," 42.

74. "Webb said, 'What a queer house this is, only one door, and that in front, so that you must come in and out the one way. About 3 days after Father came in here, in March, 1877, he wanted to go out for a walk. We discovered there was but one door to the house, so we went out the front door where we were met by an immense crowd, and forced our way through it. As the President was squeezing through the people, he said laughingly, "It's almost as much trouble to get out of this house as it is to get into it," referring, of course, to his fight for the position.' " Donaldson, "Memoirs," January 30, 1880, p. 126.

75. Hayes, "Age of Innocence," 41–42.

76. Hastings, "Autobiography," chap. 16, pp. 6–8, 13–14.

77. Ibid., 9.

78. Ibid., 11–12.

79. Richard McCandless Gipson, *The Life of Emma Thursby* (New York: The New York Historical Society, 1940), 181–182, 241, 249, 394. Numerous other musicians appeared at the executive mansion during the Hayes

administration. Madame Gerster, the Hungarian prima donna, performed in 1879, singing several airs from "Sonnambula" and the jewel song from *Faust*. Hayes, Scrapbook, Vol. 113, p. 68, RBHL. "In the Red Room we found Mrs. Hayes, Prof. Widdows, and Prof. Aptomas, the Welsh harpist.... Aptomas was a wonderful musician." Donaldson, "Memoirs," July 18, 1879, p. 108.

80. Matthew Josephson, *Edison* (New York: McGraw Hill Company, Inc., 1959), 169. See also William H. Bishop, "A Night With Edison," *Scribner's Monthly* 18 (November 1878): 88–99.

81. J. Franklin Jameson to Mrs. John Jameson, quoted in Elizabeth Donnan and Leo F. Stock, eds., *An Historian's World: Selections from the Correspondence of John Franklin Jameson* (Philadelphia: The American Philosophical Society, 1956), 18.

82. Ibid., quoted from Jameson's diary, May 4, 1882.

6

The New Administration

At the end of Grant's presidency in March 1877, the official executive office staff consisted of a private secretary, an assistant secretary, two executive clerks, a steward, and one messenger, each one a salaried employee from a congressional appropriation established in custom and law.[1] Upon his induction into office, President Hayes left the Grant system largely intact and added a few more positions only as the need arose. When Grant had felt he required extra administrative assistance, he borrowed staff personnel from other government departments. Hayes continued this practice so that during his tenure some White House employees were paid through Interior, Post Office, Treasury, or War Department funds; others through the executive mansion appropriation; still others through that of the Commissioner of Public Buildings and Grounds; and some few out of the President's private purse.[2]

The post of private secretary, first acknowledged and underwritten by Congress in the Buchanan era, involved opening, referral, and distribution of mail.[3] U. S. Grant, Jr., held this job in the final year of his father's administration. Hayes hoped to appoint one of two old and trusted Ohio friends, either William Henry Smith or Manning Force, but when both men felt the low-salaried position beneath their dignity, he appointed William K. Rogers, a former Kenyon classmate and law partner. Rogers was educated for the Episcopal ministry, and since politics and society did not suit him, he should have followed his chosen profession.[4] Although Hayes knew his secretary was not popular with officialdom and lacked genuine executive ability, he liked Rogers and retained him despite criticism.

The assistant secretary's duties required him to submit important papers to the President for his action and to bear his messages and executive orders to Congress. C. C. Sniffen, assistant private

secretary to Grant, served briefly under Hayes, and then was promoted to major and paymaster in the army. O. L. Pruden of New
Jersey, one of the two executive clerks, became the new assistant
secretary partly through his friendship with Sniffen.[5] Destined
to hold his new job for twenty-five years until death overtook
him in 1902, Pruden earned the sobriquet of "the Sphinx of the
White House" because of his extraordinary reticence concerning
all matters pertaining to official business. In 1873 Grant had transferred him from the War Department to the executive office to
record all presidential appointments, commissions, and pardons.[6]
An excellent penman, Pruden later, at the behest of Webb C. Hayes,
prepared by hand a beautiful multicolored social register of White
House state dinners, luncheons, and receptions, which today is
one of the treasures in the Hayes Library manuscript collection.[7]

The two executive clerks, each paid $2,000, briefed and recorded
incoming mail, kept records of nominations, confirmations, and
commissions of federal officers—civil, military, and diplomatic—besides recording bills and resolutions which passed Congress.[8] Pruden's promotion to assistant secretary created a vacancy
filled by the appointment of his brother-in-law, Charles M. Hendley of Cincinnati. Hendley kept the job twelve years before taking
a better paying position as private secretary to William Windom,
Secretary of the Treasury in the Benjamin Harrison administration.[9]

The other executive clerk, William H. Crook, began his career
as a metropolitan police officer. Originally assigned in January
1865 as one of President Lincoln's bodyguards, he later assumed
charge of the new reception room instituted during Grant's term
and took the honorary title of "Colonel." Crook ultimately served
under ten presidents from Lincoln through Theodore Roosevelt
and became one of the best-known employees in executive office
annals. Crook also functioned as paymaster and keeper of the
White House scrapbooks. Staff employees could conveniently
claim their salary anytime during the month from him.[10]

President Hayes added a few new clerks, principally Henry C.
Morton and J. S. Bolway, transferred from the Treasury Department
in March 1877 and April 1880, respectively, and W. R. Duke who
began his service in November 1879. Morton, an Ohioan, worked
as executive clerk in the administration of Governor Edward F.
Noyes (1872–1874) and secured the same post again during Hayes'
third gubernatorial term. Later he joined the White House staff
for eight years until discharged by the Democrat Grover Cleveland.
Morton blamed Pruden and Hendley for his dismissal. Under
Hayes he read newspapers to sample friendly and hostile public

opinion about the administration, and pasted pertinent clippings in scrapbooks for the President's perusal.[11] Two other very important members of the Hayes staff were George A. Gustin, his stenographer, who always sat in the President's office,[12] and the bantam telegraph operator, Sergeant Benjamin F. Montgomery. Detailed from the army signal service, Montgomery, who wore lifts to compensate for his short stature and size, climaxed a long executive office career when he was named chief intelligence officer in charge of the War Room during the McKinley administration.[13] Rutherford Hayes liked to think of his office clerks and secretaries as "my second family." Each year at Thanksgiving and Christmas, he and Lucy entertained the staff families at a private dinner party and distributed gifts to both children and adults.

In conducting official business Hayes followed a simple routine. He rose at seven; wrote until breakfast at eight-thirty; observed family devotion about nine; attended office business until ten; received congressional and cabinet visitors in the Cabinet Room to noon; met other visitors seeking office or favors from twelve to two; lunched at two; read selected correspondence for a half-hour; enjoyed a carriage ride from three-thirty to five; answered more correspondence; took a nap and dressed for supper; dined at eight; greeted more callers until ten or eleven at night; and finally took a short walk, unaccompanied by secret service agents, before retiring. He ordinarily did not grant interviews on Saturday, and he met his cabinet from twelve to two on Tuesdays and Fridays instead of receiving visitors. So habitual was this pattern that the cabinet once arrived only to find the President away on a trip!

The President rarely dictated letters. He either wrote a short note in his own hand or indicated the nature of the desired response and left the exact phrasing to a secretary. Typewriters were not then in use, and all work was done laboriously by hand. The telephone and phonograph were just being introduced. One of the very first telephones was installed in the White House, but it was a crude wall instrument, and, as there were virtually no other telephones in use, it was of little practical value. Both inventions, however, were immediately recognized to have almost unlimited potential.

The White House basement and attic space was not nearly so effectively utilized as it is today, and the present office wing was still a full quarter century in the future. The few clerks somehow found working accommodations. Emily Platt, the President's niece (who later was married in the White House) once described for Rud Hayes, away at college, the improvised, seemingly haphazard regime: "Birchard [eldest son] is in the act of ousting Mr. Rogers [private secretary] from his sanctum in the corner of the house. The barbershop has been moved into the hall and a partition has been built around it. The telephone and telegraph office has likewise been moved into the hall with a corresponding partition built around them. This having been accomplished the room is undergoing a thorough renovating and then Birchard will occupy it as a bedroom, study, office, sanctum and all combined."[14]

Presidential privacy proved hard to find with numerous employees, visitors, and house guests roaming through the official residence. Hayes often conducted some of his most confidential business during frequent carriage rides around Washington with close associates and legislators. At other times he retired to a bathroom to prepare some important state paper.[15]

Hayes assembled one of the stronger cabinets in American history if one measures by the personal achievements and public performance of the members. In selecting his cabinet officers the President followed three basic guidelines: "1. A new Cabinet—no holdovers from the Grant administration; 2. no presidential candidates; 3. no appointment to 'take care' of anybody."[16] His civil service philosophy of personal merit and fitness for office determined the choice of key departmental advisers. The record of the Hayes cabinet proved he was an excellent judge of these qualities and that he could keep the loyalty of his appointees. Whereas Grant made eighteen changes after his original seven-member cabinet was named, Hayes replaced just three men (McCrary, Key, and Thompson) and only one of these for cause. The Senate oligarchy, which had expected to impose its will in constructing the new cabinet, met an unexpected rebuff as Hayes coolly designated his own advisers, and public opinion supported his nominees. Only Secretary of the Navy Richard W. Thompson was appointed primarily for partisan reasons, and Hayes ultimately dismissed him in the public interest. Compelled to govern without benefit of majority control in the legislature, Hayes necessarily put together a strong administrative team, studiously avoiding the Grant men, Zachariah Chandler, J. Don Cameron, and Roscoe Conkling, as well as their bitter opponent, James G. Blaine.

Hayes started screening likely names during the first week of January 1877. Many letters of advice reached him, none more influential than those of Carl Schurz. The gradual evolution of the Hayes cabinet appears in an inquiry to Schurz:

Whatever occurs to you on the following names will be confidentially treated:

Forbes and Rice of Boston
Frelinghuysen, New Jersey
Settle, North Carolina
Harlan, Kentucky
Sherman, Ohio
Booth, California
Alcorn, Mississippi
McCrary—Iowa
Who from Pennsylvania besides Grow?
And how stands Grow in that State?
Morrill of Vermont.[17]

He also consulted with Vice President William A. Wheeler, Senator
John Sherman and former Governor Jacob D. Cox of Ohio, William
Henry Smith, Manning Force, Ralph P. Buckland, and William
D. Howells.

Hayes soon decided upon William M. Evarts, an outstanding
New York lawyer, for Secretary of State. For the Treasury post
he considered Governor Alexander Hamilton Rice of Massachusetts, John Murray Forbes of Boston, or John Sherman of Ohio
acceptable.[18] The lot fell to Sherman. John Marshall Harlan, Bristow's manager at the Cincinnati convention, seemed destined for
Attorney General but was eliminated when Senator Oliver P. Morton, whom Hayes greatly admired, voiced his personal objection.
George W. McCrary of Iowa, one of the authors of the Electoral
Commission plan, who figured prominently in Hayes' early speculation over the cabinet, became Secretary of War. Schurz, offered
his choice of the Post Office or Interior portfolio, accepted the
latter. The President-elect briefly considered Confederate General
Joseph E. Johnston for a place, but when his confidants advised
him otherwise, he picked David M. Key, a Chattanooga Democrat,
as the southern member of the cabinet, and installed him as Postmaster General. Charles Devens, a Massachusetts Supreme Court
judge and former Union officer, became Attorney General after
he declined to be Secretary of War. The Navy Department, as
already indicated, went to Richard W. Thompson, an odd choice
since Thompson came from Indiana rather than a coastal state.
Hayes undoubtedly hoped to court favor with his old friend Oliver
P. Morton whose oratory would be a valuable asset for the Hayes
program in the Senate. If so, this prospect vanished with Morton's
untimely death on November 1, 1877. Sherman, Schurz, and Evarts
comprised the "big three" of the cabinet, with Devens and McCrary
close behind. Key and Thompson, who both resigned in 1880,
proved to be the weaker members. Among others Hayes rejected
were John A. Logan of Illinois, Thomas A. Platt, backed for Postmaster General by Roscoe Conkling, and William Pierce Frye of

Maine, urged by both Blaine and Hannibal Hamlin after Eugene Hale, their first choice, refused to be Secretary of the Navy. Blaine and Conkling, who hated each other, were thus united in a common hostility to Hayes when the President ignored their favorites.[19]

When the President was in Washington, the cabinet officers met every Tuesday and Friday for two hours to discuss the larger issues of state and the many details of patronage appointments. They assembled in the President's private office on the second floor of the executive mansion, a high ceilinged room about thirty-five to forty feet in depth and thirty feet wide. Long lambrequin curtains of a dark bluish gray color hung at the two windows, and a large map of the United States was on the wall. A long table stood in the center of a red carpet. The general effect of the room was that of a library without books.[20] Cabinet sessions were rather informal and very harmonious. Hayes sat at the head of the table with Schurz at the foot. Sherman, Thompson, and Devens sat to the President's left, and Evarts, McCrary, and Key to his right. Some ten or fifteen minutes of casual conversation and banter normally preceded the agenda of the day.

Presidential cabinets figure perhaps less than they deserve in the political history of the United States. Only a few books have appeared in this century on the cabinet as a presidential institution, and just one outstanding study of a particular cabinet comes to mind, Burton J. Hendrick's fine volume, *Lincoln's War Cabinet.* Many cabinet officers are even more obscure than the lesser known Vice Presidents of the United States. The Hayes cabinet, though comprised of a distinguished group of men, is no exception. At least three of the original seven members, Devens, Key, and Mc-Crary, are lost men of American history.[21] Thompson is remembered most as an Indiana orator and party politician while John Sherman, a central figure in the Hayes administration and one of the most prominent American statesmen for fifty years, still merits more attention. Evarts, one of the truly great constitutional lawyers of the nineteenth century, is seldom mentioned in the ordinary textbook. Only Carl Schurz, the "red-eyed Dutchman," is a well-known personality and this for reasons other than his four-year tenure as Secretary of the Interior under Hayes.

Charles Devens became the New England member of the cabinet after Hayes passed over Governor Rice of Massachusetts and the national committeeman and Boston merchant, John Murray Forbes. Forbes had supported Grant in 1868 and 1872, but joined the Bristow movement in 1876 and attended the Cincinnati convention as a Massachusetts delegate-at-large along with Richard H. Dana and Judge E. R. Hoar. Devens formed a law partnership with future United States Senator George F. Hoar, brother of Judge Hoar, in 1856. Thus the Devens appointment represented an acknowledgment by Hayes of important convention support from the New England reform element originally behind Bristow. Although Hayes had perhaps not actually met Devens, he must have known of him, because he succeeded Ambrose Burnside as national commander of the Grand Army of the Republic in 1874. Devens and Hayes formed a lasting friendship, and the bachelor Attorney General became a great social favorite during the Hayes administration, calling more frequently at the White House than any other cabinet officer. Lucy Hayes especially admired the handsome and urbane Devens, and the entire presidential family soon grew very fond of the "Beau of the Cabinet."[22] Devens often accompanied President Hayes on official trips around the country.

The chief executive and his Attorney General had much in common.[23] Both graduated from the Harvard Law School; both won an excellent legal reputation as a city solicitor; both served as Union officers throughout the Civil War; and both preferred to be remembered as a soldier more than as an officeholder. Devens attended the Boston Latin School and graduated at age eighteen from Harvard in 1838 with James Russell Lowell, who later received two high diplomatic posts from Hayes. Devens received his Harvard law degree in 1840. He practiced law nine years in Northfield and Greenfield, Massachusetts, served one term as a state senator, and then four years as a United States marshal, before moving to Worcester where he quickly earned a reputation as an advocate and public speaker. Meanwhile he advanced steadily in the state militia, rising to the rank of brigadier-general. Devens entered the Civil War as a major in the Third Battalion of Massachusetts Rifles, became colonel of the Fifteenth Massachusetts Regiment, and left the service at war's end as a brevet major general. He was saved from death by a metal button in the battle of Ball's Bluff, but suffered wounds at Fair Oaks and Chancellorsville. At Fredericksburg he commanded the advance and rear guard as it crossed and recrossed the river. His last major action was the Battle of Cold Harbor. Devens led the advance into Richmond, became its military governor, and later commanded the federal troops in South Carolina until 1866. In this period, exercising all the powers of government, he decided without appeal all important questions of military law and civil rights, experience valuable to him later as Attorney General.

After a brief renewal of his legal partnership with George F.

Hoar, Devens served as Justice of the Superior Court (1867–1873) until promoted to Associate Justice of the Massachusetts Supreme Court (1873–1877). He resigned this position in March 1877 to accept the Hayes cabinet appointment. He hesitated before accepting Hayes' offer since, at fifty-six, he already occupied a good judgeship with little expectation of getting it back once he resigned. Moreover his private means were not sufficient to support him without professional income, and he preferred living in Massachusetts among his friends. He took the cabinet post as a matter of duty and held it faithfully to the end of the Hayes administration, although he was offered the First United States Circuit Court judgeship by the President in 1878. In 1881 he was again appointed Associate Justice of the Massachusetts Supreme Court and held this position until his death in Boston on January 10, 1891. He was buried with military honors from famed Trinity Church in a service read by the Reverend Phillips Brooks.

Devens won great distinction as an orator. Notably handsome, possessed of a strong and flexible voice, he drew upon the events and men of the Revolution and the Civil War as his main themes. He often spoke at reunions of veteran's organizations, especially the Loyal Legion and the Grand Army of the Republic. Today Fort Devens commemorates his army career and leadership.

Among the original Hayes cabinet officers, Devens appeared most distinguished and best looking. A courtly and polished gentleman with white hair, mustache, and side-whiskers, always the best dressed member in sober black, he looked strong and dignified.[24] He possessed vigorous health, commanding height, a mild temperament, and excelled in conversation enlivened by a sense of humor, which won him many friends. Senator Hoar, his old associate, felt he should have chosen a political career after the war rather than the bench, but Devens disliked the strife and bitter antagonisms of political life. Hayes eulogized Devens as a model gentleman, a distinguished soldier, and a man much honored for character, ability, and life.[25]

David McKendree Key of Tennessee became the southern member of the cabinet after Hayes decided not to name Confederate General Joseph E. Johnston as Secretary of War or Interior. Hayes, who thought highly of Johnston as able, patriotic, and wise, felt that his relationship with men in Richmond unable "to forget the past, or rather to act on the new situation" would embarrass both Johnston and him.[26]

A. J. Kellar, editor of the Memphis *Avalanche*, first suggested Key for Postmaster General in a letter of February 16, 1877, to

William Henry Smith, close friend and political adviser of Hayes. Key had recently served in the Senate, filling part of Andrew Johnson's unexpired term. Like Johnson, Key opposed Tennessee's secession, but when it came, unlike Johnson, he chose to fight for the South. Hayes, by appointing a former Confederate officer to his cabinet, hoped to build up the Republican party in the South and also demonstrate his administration's sincerity toward all southern people. For his part, Key promised to support the Hayes southern policy and incorporate his fortunes and self with it. Key wired to Kellar his acceptance of the President's invitation to come to Washington and, when he arrived, had a lengthy interview on the evening of March 6, 1877, at the end of which he accepted the Postmaster Generalship. Key, however, agreed to share post office patronage control with the retiring incumbent, James N. Tyner, regarded as the best informed person in the country on post offices and post roads. The latter was requested to remain in the department as First Assistant Postmaster General. Key handled southern patronage, and Tyner supervised northern appointments, in addition to running the department during Key's rather frequent absences.[27] Actually, as far as the number of removals is concerned, the record of the Hayes administration was excellent. Only sixty-seven Presidential postmasters were removed in four years (most of these for just cause), and more than half were reappointed when their commissions expired. Even among the fourth-class offices, the number of removals was small. Only 2,500 out of 40,000 were removed.[28] However, Key's administration of the Post Office Department was not overly successful because he allowed too much latitude to his subordinates. Under Key (1877–1880) and his successor, Horace Maynard (1880–1881), great frauds in "Star Route" contracts were perpetrated. Neither Key nor Maynard had any knowledge of the frauds, but they were made possible by their easy rule.[29]

Key, of Scotch and English lineage, was born January 27, 1824, near Greenville, Tennessee.[30] He received his early education while working on the family farm. Later he attended the common schools of Monroe County and, working his way through Hiwassee College, became one of its first graduates in 1850. While attending college, he read law in the office of H. H. Stevens and was admitted to practice in 1850. After a short legal career in Kingston, he moved to Chattanooga in February 1853, where he formed a law partnership and met his future wife, Elizabeth Avery Lenoir, whom he married on July 1, 1857.

During the Civil War, Key was appointed adjutant general of the first Tennessee troops and soon became lieutenant-colonel of the Forty-third Regiment. He was wounded, captured, and paroled at Vicksburg in July 1863 and later served with Longstreet in Tennessee and Virginia and with Kirby-Smith and Bragg in Kentucky. At the end of the war, Key temporarily grew corn and potatoes in North Carolina to raise some money. He resumed law practice, ran unsuccessfully for Congress in 1872, and served as chancellor of the Third Chancery Division (1870–1875) until August 18, 1875, when he took the United States Senate seat made vacant by the death of Andrew Johnson. He was unsuccessful as a candidate to fill the vacancy in 1876. The next year, Hayes named him Postmaster General. His financial situation prompted his cabinet resignation on August 26, 1880, to accept the President's appointment as United States District Judge for the Eastern and Middle District of Tennessee, and he kept this post until he retired on January 26, 1894. He died in Chattanooga on February 3, 1900.[31]

Of his twenty-four years in public life, twenty were spent on the bench, and fifteen of these on the federal bench where he tried many cases under Internal Revenue laws involving the mountaineers of East Tennessee whom he generally let off with mild penalties, judging more by equity than precedent. Although he was not especially active or energetic, he disposed of cases rapidly and his docket was never crowded.

David M. Key was a large, erect, but corpulent man, above six feet tall and weighing 240 pounds. Big-hearted and public-spirited, his dark eyes and luxuriant silver-gray hair, which he wore "roached," gave him a dignified and judicial demeanor. Neither Key nor his wife belonged to any church but both were reared by Methodist parents. Of the cabinet wives, Mrs. Key had "the most commanding figure and genial dignity of manner." Emma Key, eldest of the Postmaster General's eight children, "a tall, well-developed blonde, with blue eyes," reigned as a belle of Washington society in the Hayes era. She married Colonel William B. Thompson, general superintendent of the Railway Mail Service in 1883.[32]

An important personality in the early years of the Hayes presidency was George W. McCrary of Keokuk, Iowa.[33] Only forty-one when he became Secretary of War, McCrary was by far the youngest and liveliest man in a cabinet whose members averaged fifty-four years of age. His forebears had emigrated from Scotland in the early eighteenth century and settled near Gettysburg, Pennsylvania. Other ancestors migrated to North Carolina, then to Tennessee, and finally to Indiana where George was born on August 29, 1835. The next year his parents moved to the Iowa Territory, then a frontier of civilization where Indians still roamed and white settlements were scarce. Young McCrary helped on the farm while attending common schools and an academy near his home. By the age of eighteen, he was teaching in a country school, studying law, and professing free-soil Whig politics.

Considered a prodigy, he entered the office of John W. Rankin and Samuel F. Miller, later Associate Justice of the United States Supreme Court. In 1856 he was admitted to the bar after passing a rigid examination without an error. On March 11, 1857, he married Helen Gelatt of Van Buren County and began a notable public career. By winning election to the Iowa House of Representatives, he became at twenty-two the youngest member of the legislature. By the age of forty-five, he had spent six years in the Iowa House and Senate, eight years in Congress, nearly three years as Secretary of War, and had become a United States Circuit Judge, altogether a remarkable and rapid rise in public life. McCrary led his ticket in every election and was never defeated as a candidate for nomination or election or as an applicant for appointment or confirmation.

McCrary joined the Republican party at its inception and voted for Frémont in 1856. Unlike most other politicians of the Hayes era, he did not have a military record. Throughout the Civil War, McCrary occupied a seat in the Iowa Senate where he chaired in turn the Indian Affairs and Judiciary committees. During Grant's presidency, he held a congressional seat and served on the committees of Naval Affairs, Revision of Laws and Elections, Railroads and Canals, and Judiciary. McCrary became an authority on contested elections and election law, publishing a standard work, *A Treatise on the American Law of Elections* (1875). His report on the constitutional power of Congress to regulate interstate commerce became the basis for later legislation. He also developed in part the Electoral Commission device and appeared as Republican counsel before it during the contested election of 1876. The decision in favor of Hayes helped put McCrary in the new President's cabinet. Iowa Republicans supported him strongly. Senator William Boyd Allison, boss of the Iowa Republican organization, removed a strong rival for the 1878 senatorial nomination by getting the popular McCrary out of the state.

Originally slated to be Attorney General, McCrary at the last moment expressed an opinion favorable to the McGarrahan claim, which Hayes opposed. Not wishing an Attorney General on record about it, and learning that Charles Devens did not wish to be Secretary of War, Hayes made a switch, and Devens became Attorney General, and McCrary Secretary of War.[34]

As head of the War Department, McCrary participated in several key events of the time. He acted promptly on the executive order of President Hayes in dispatching troops during the Railroad Strike of 1877. He used other troops along the Mexican border. Meanwhile he reassigned, at Hayes' direction, the last of the occupying forces in the South, thus officially ending Reconstruction. Without legal sanction he authorized the issuing of tents, blankets, and rations to persons rendered destitute by the yellow fever epidemic of 1878 in the southern states. He also began the first systematic work toward the publication of the official records of the Union and Confederate forces and improved the Signal Service Bureau by connecting it with similar agencies abroad. McCrary became the first original member to depart from the Hayes cabinet, resigning on December 12, 1879, to accept the President's appointment as a United States Judge of the Eighth Circuit (1880–1884).

As a United States Circuit Judge, McCrary was again brought into close touch with his former law teacher, Justice Samuel Miller of the Supreme Court. The five volumes of McCrary's *Circuit Court Reports* show him to be a man of excellent judicial temperament. McCrary again resigned, this time to accept a well-paid position as general counsel for the Atchison, Topeka, and Santa Fe Railroad so that he could better provide for his family of five children and spend less time traveling. Nevertheless, he died poor while visiting his daughter in St. Joseph, Missouri, June 23, 1890.[35]

McCrary never entirely gave up his legal practice except for the four years on the bench. Even while a member of Congress and a cabinet officer, he argued important cases in court. Iowa College at Grinnell honored him with an LL.D. in 1877. Like his friend, Justice Miller, McCrary belonged to the Unitarian church in which he served as an active leader for thirty years. In an "age of beards" McCrary was "smoothfaced" and bald. Stout, somewhat puffy, decidedly homely, he generally wore a brown frock coat with velvet collar and carried a walking stick.[36] An intellectual, he liked to read and contributed articles to the *North American Review.* Although his manner was mild, amiable, and even-tempered, he was a fine debater, excellent storyteller, and speaker. He enjoyed camping and trout fishing in the upper waters of the Rio Grande in Colorado. He did not smoke, drink, or play cards. The President characterized his Secretary of War as a sound, painstaking, upright lawyer of unselfish patriotism. Mrs. McCrary's delicate health prevented her from joining fully in Washington social life, although she did support the temperance advocates in the White House.[37]

By tradition, a President may reserve a seat in his cabinet for someone from his own state. The most obvious candidate in 1877 was John Sherman, to whom Hayes offered the Treasury portfolio. Since exceptional fitness for financial leadership blended effectively with political considerations, he was an admirable choice.[38]

Sherman and Hayes had mutual feelings of respect and friendship ever since 1872 when Hayes, while governor, steadily refused to participate in moves to deny Sherman renomination and to promote Hayes as the party's choice for the Senate seat. Thereafter their political fortunes and honor were closely connected. Moreover the preferences of each man were better served. Hayes did not enjoy his brief congressional career but felt very comfortable in the governor's chair. Sherman missed the governorship he did not seek and found his natural niche in the United States Senate. From this vantage point, the Senator played a key role in helping Hayes secure the Ohio Republican endorsement for president in 1876. Later, after the onset of the contested election struggle, Sherman assumed a very uncomfortable role as one of the party's five "visiting statesmen" assigned to the Louisiana investigation. Back in Washington he sought to mediate the electoral impasse.

In addition to his close association with Hayes, John Sherman possessed excellent qualifications for Secretary of the Treasury. During his six years in the House of Representatives, he rose to chairmanship of the Ways and Means Committee and then followed this experience with sixteen years service in the United States Senate where he specialized in the intricacies of financial policy. Thus by party loyalty, knowledge, and temperament, he was well suited to head the Treasury Department and readily accepted Hayes' offer.

As it turned out, Sherman not only emerged as the strongest and most important man in the Hayes cabinet, but also as one of the more outstanding Secretaries of the Treasury—certainly the best one in the generation from Grant to McKinley.[39] Hayes often left the White House in his company and the two took long rides around Washington in the President's Brewster landau where they could discuss affairs of state in assured privacy.[40] To his future political disadvantage, however, he was intimately connected with the five great problems of the Hayes administration: an opposition-controlled legislature; the continuing electoral controversy; the southern policy; patronage reform; and the money question.

Sherman's achievement in handling the monetary crisis of the Hayes era amounted to the most brilliant success of his long public career, but his close identification with the President and the other problems of the administration robbed him of a middle stance so important to statesmen with presidential aspirations. His very success as Secretary of the Treasury denied him the Republican nomination in 1880. Other factors, too, hurt his chances, as Jeannette P. Nichols so aptly summarizes: "In 1880, as in 1888 and to a less degree in 1884, Sherman failed of the nomination because he lacked unscrupulousness in the use of patronage, color in personality and appeal, cordial unity in the Ohio delegation, and skill in manipulating politicians, and because he had an abundance of inflationist opposition."[41]

Hayes favored Sherman as his successor in 1880 and paid deserving tribute to his "faithful servitor": "On the whole, I am exceedingly gratified by the results and the closing scenes of my Administration. To no one am I more indebted—to no one am I so much indebted—for the career in public life which is now closed, as I am to you. I want you to know that I know and appreciate this fact."[42]

He also preferred Sherman to head the party ticket in 1888 although Benjamin Harrison emerged victorious: "We like Harrison of course and think the ticket 'good politics' in the sense of availability. But you were so clearly entitled to it by service and fitness, and our personal feelings were so enlisted that we cannot think of it without great disappointment. I try to find comfort in the reflection that it has become usage in our country that the man of great and valuable service in civil life must be content to leave the presidency to the less conspicuous and deserving."[43] Again in 1892 Hayes alluded to Sherman "as our best equipped statesman."[44]

After Garfield's election as President in 1880, Sherman took the Senate seat originally intended for Garfield and served another sixteen years in the Senate before resigning to become McKinley's Secretary of State, a post beyond his vigor and understanding, from which he retired to private life in 1898, in the wake of his failing health and disapproval of the decision for war with Spain. He died in Washington on October 22, 1900.

Sherman was fifty-three years of age when he entered the cabinet, some seven months younger than the President. Born in Lancaster, Ohio, May 10, 1823, the eighth child in a family of eleven children, he was the son of Charles Robert Sherman, who became an Ohio Supreme Court Justice and died when John was only six years old. The straitened circumstances limited Sherman's education to the common schools of Lancaster, plus two years at a local academy and some private law instruction. He was admitted to the Ohio bar in 1844 and started practice in Mansfield, his new home. The young lawyer entered politics as a Whig and served as a delegate to and secretary of the 1848 Whig National Convention in Philadelphia, which nominated Zachary Taylor. With the demise of the Whigs in the early 1850s, Sherman joined the new Republican party and was president of the first Ohio Republican state convention in 1855, the year he commenced his long legislative career in Washington as a Congressman (1855–1861) and Senator (1861–1877; 1881–1897).

During the Civil War, Lincoln caused a Senate vacancy by appointing Senator Salmon P. Chase of Ohio as his Secretary of the Treasury. Sherman won the seat after a hard-fought caucus struggle. The President then prevailed upon him to forsake a possible military career because of the administration's great need for experienced financial leadership in the Senate. Thus Sherman never attained the military glory so useful for political advancement.

A word portrait of the Hayes cabinet, penned by Thomas Donaldson, mentions "Sherman, thin as a rail, over six feet high, with close cropped beard," and possessed of bad teeth and a divine laugh, "when he laughs."[45] Other contemporaries agree that Sherman's customary demeanor was usually one of cautious reserve and great self-control. This aloof and cold temperament only occasionally gave way to genuine affection and warmth. Sherman married the former Margaret Stewart, the only child of a Mansfield judge, on August 31, 1848. The marriage was childless except for an adopted daughter, Mary. Mrs. Sherman won the distinction of being the most attractive of the cabinet wives in Washington society.[46]

While the Secretary of the Treasury held the job of greatest significance in the Hayes cabinet, the Secretary of State occupied the place of highest prestige despite the relative quiescence of a presidency termed the "dead center" in the history of American foreign relations between 1865 and 1898.[47]

William Maxwell Evarts, a distinguished lawyer considered by many of his contemporaries as the outstanding leader of the American bar when Hayes selected him as his Secretary of State, fitted the needs of the time and his office well. Senator Sherman acted as Hayes' trusted intermediary in proffering the State Department to Evarts. Hayes did not know Evarts prior to inviting him to join the cabinet, but they soon became good friends and often took long walks together about Washington. Neither overly serious like his predecessor, Hamilton Fish, nor openly reckless like his successor, James G. Blaine, Evarts followed the relaxed routine of a cultivated, urbane gentleman, who simultaneously maintained a summer retreat in Windsor, Vermont, and other homes in Washington and New York City. He summed up his philosophy of diplomacy at a dinner at Delmonico's two years after he left the State Department:

> Saying common things and doing common things make up human life, and being able to say them and do them with propriety, with ease, with elegance, with justice, makes the difference in private life between good manners and bad; and makes the difference between governments, and their subjects or citizens, of oppression or of confidence and allegiance; makes in diplomacy the difference between a bad foreign secretary, a bad foreign minister, a bad foreign consul, and a good one.... And it is better by far that the friction of common life and of public life should be lubricated by this oil and cheered with this wine, than that it should be embittered and soured even when the substance and sense are all meant to be right.[48]

Petty details and dull routine bored the Secretary. Complaints reached the President's ear about Evarts' dilatory habits in conducting State Department business. One secretary of a legation reported that the foreign representatives generally criticized Evarts' slowness, delay, and incapacity. Sir Edward Thornton, the British minister, said he had called and called scores of times over a six-month period for answers to some urgent matters and had been turned away.[49] Vice President Wheeler did not like his lack of frankness in handling office seekers: "He does not say no, but by an equivocal, noncommittal way of talking allows them to hope." Donaldson added, "When there is no hope, tell the man so. He will be disappointed at the time, but it [is] the best way." Hayes agreed with the criticism: "Prompt and square talk is in the long run safest and is just to the parties concerned."[50] At the same time, the President recognized redeeming qualities in Evarts and resisted pressure to dismiss him. During his tenure, Evarts raised the standard of the consular service and originated the idea of regular consular reports on a great variety of topics. From long experience and natural inclination, Evarts moved easily in diplomatic circles and social gatherings. John Hay once remarked, "He had the rare faculty of saying at the dinner table the best things that were said there." Furthermore his ready wit sparkled without wounding any hearers, and the stiffness of many a White House reception was enlivened by his gift of graceful repartee.[51] While neither popular with party politicians because of his strongly independent inclinations and contempt for party control over his actions nor effective as a stump orator, Evarts won distinction in political life by his strong intellect, powerful pen, and gracious manners.

The Secretary's physical appearance gave political cartoonists a field day. He was "thin as a lath," erect and dignified, with a prominent forehead and nose, and although only fifty-nine in 1877, "had a dried leaf or brown parchment look to his skin that all gourmets get when about 70. To see him look sideways out of his carriage is to regret that Hogarth is dead." He dressed simply, wore a frock coat even at receptions to which others came attired in dress suits, and, in his peculiar way, a high hat tilted back on the crown, "so that a plumb line dropped from its center would fall about twelve inches behind his heels."[52]

William Evarts came from a distinguished New England back-ground.[53] On his father's side, he traced his descent from Welsh ancestors who had migrated to Connecticut around 1635, while his mother was the daughter of Roger Sherman, signer of the Declaration of Independence. William was born in Boston on February 6, 1818. His father, Jeremiah, died when the boy was thirteen. The son attended the famous Boston Latin School and graduated with honors from Yale in the same class as Samuel Tilden and Morrison R. Waite. In college, he helped found the *Yale Literary Magazine* and, like Hayes, studied law with Greenleaf and Story at Harvard.

Although Evarts' political career is notable, he achieved his greatest renown as a lawyer. He took part in many famous litigations of the nineteenth century including the three most celebrated controversies of the time, and won impressive victories in each. He handled President Andrew Johnson's impeachment trial defense in 1868, served as United States counsel in the Geneva Arbitration of the Alabama Claims in 1871–1872, and appeared as chief counsel for the Republican party before the Electoral Commission in February 1877. This last involvement prevented Hayes from approaching him directly about assuming a place in the cabinet.

Highlights in Evarts' political career embraced service as chairman of the New York delegation to the Republican National Convention in 1860, as Attorney General under Grant (1868–1869), as Secretary of State under Hayes (1877–1881), and as United States Senator from New York (1885–1891). While important, these activites tended further to enhance his eminence at the bar.

On August 30, 1843, Evarts married Helen Minerva Wardner of Windsor, Vermont, who bore him twelve children. She was a handsome woman able to hold her own in Washington social life. At White House receptions, she usually stood, dressed in garnet satin or black velvet, beside Mrs. Hayes. Evarts loved his wife and children dearly, and, however busy, reserved Saturday evenings as a family night or for entertaining in his home.

"Greatest of lawyers and most delightful of men," Evarts numbered many literary figures, including Bryant, Lowell, Holmes, and Henry Adams, among his friends. For the latter, he provided easy access to the government archives, especially State Department documents, and endeavored to make similar arrangements with foreign governments for the historian. Evarts was often in demand as an after-dinner speaker or as an orator for special occasions. His love of storytelling and frequent puns earned him national notice. Evarts became blind toward the end of his life and died in February 1901.

During cabinet meetings, Sherman and Evarts sat opposite one another at the upper end of a conference table to the immediate left and right of the President, thus symbolizing the importance of their departments and their position as close advisers. They shared the latter distinction, however, with another cabinet officer who occupied the chair facing Hayes at the far end of the table. The third member of the triumvirate was the dynamic Carl Schurz, Secretary of the Interior, and by all odds the most interesting and versatile man in the Hayes cabinet.

Carl Schurz made history in a number of important respects.[54] This extraordinarily exciting and gifted man was the foremost German-American of the late nineteenth century and the first United States citizen of German birth in a presidential cabinet, a "refugee of revolution" who became nationally known in America through his outstanding bilingual oratory. A romatic aura surrounded Schurz's life beginning with his birth on March 2, 1829, in a castle in Liblar, near Cologne, Germany. Educated at the Gymnasium of Cologne, he entered the University of Bonn, intending to become a professor of history, but throughout his life two ambitions struggled within him—one tending toward scholarship and the other toward statecraft. Caught up in the ill-fated liberal Revolution of 1848 in Germany, he narrowly escaped death and was compelled to flee his homeland. Voluntarily he returned and engineered the dramatic rescue of a favorite professor from Spandau prison, firing the imagination of liberals around the world. After some journalistic work in Paris and teaching in London, Schurz married Margarethe Meyer, the daughter of a well-to-do Jewish manufacturer in Hamburg, and emigrated with his bride to the United States in 1852. He settled in Philadelphia and then in Watertown, Wisconsin, where he studied law and entered politics. In 1860, he was chairman of the Wisconsin Republican convention delegation and later served as the party's temporary chairman and keynoter of the 1868 convention. Lincoln appointed

him minister to Spain, a post he soon resigned to accept an appointment as a Union brigadier-general of volunteers. Unlike some
"political generals," he displayed real military capacity and
engaged in the dangerous practice of corresponding with President
Lincoln on administrative policy matters. Following the war,
Schurz resumed his newspaper career in Washington, Detroit,
and St. Louis. Shortly after, the Missouri legislature elected him
to the United States Senate, where he served a single term (1869–
1875). Meanwhile Schurz, disgusted with Grant's performance in
the presidency, joined the Liberal Republican revolt of 1872 and
presided over its convention. This defection marked the first of
five changes in party allegiance, which set Schurz apart from ordinary politicians. He freely switched sides if, as he contended,
the sides switched principles. Between 1868 and 1904, he voted
four times for a Republican and six for a Democrat, with his candidate winning in six contests. This record established Schurz
as "the earliest important practitioner of nonpartisanship and
independence in American politics."[55]

Schurz and Hayes became acquainted in 1875 when the man
the *Nation* called "the greatest master of rhetoric in the United
States" visited Ohio to assist Hayes in his third campaign for
the governorship.[56] The two men, utterly different in temperament, background, and early training, struck up an immediate
rapport over fundamental public issues. Shared political views
on the necessity of sound money and civil-service reform ripened
into a sincere friendship and deep mutual respect. Schurz, recently
widowed, visited the White House as much socially as officially.
After his retirement from the Interior Department, he edited the
New York *Evening Post,* to which Hayes subscribed because he
and his wife wished to read everything their friend wrote. A long
correspondence between the two men began in 1875 and ended
only when Hayes died in 1893. Schurz paid appropriate tribute
in the January 28, 1893, issue of *Harper's Weekly.*

Schurz served for only a decade in public office, one full term
as Senator and four years as Secretary of the Interior. There is
a memorandum in the handwriting of Webb C. Hayes which states
that Schurz was his father's first choice for inclusion in the cabinet
although he left the exact position an open matter. Schurz thought
himself best suited for the State Department or Treasury. When
these posts were filled by Evarts and Sherman, Hayes offered "the
red-bearded Teuton" his choice of the Interior or Post Office, and
Schurz quickly accepted the former.

Several reasons had impelled Schurz back into politics. Hayes
professed ideas that he cherished and wished to act upon, and

personal tragedy played a part. Within a twelve-month period, starting in February 1876, Schurz's father, mother, and wife died. Their deaths, "staggering blows from which it was not the easiest thing to rally," caused him to seek relief by throwing himself with renewed vigor into political affairs.[57]

As Secretary of the Interior, Schurz proved to be the most active and resourceful member of the cabinet and certainly one of the best secretaries of a department often called the "great miscellany" because it involved so many assorted activities. At forty-eight years of age, next youngest after McCrary, Schurz had a difficult administrative responsibility, a span-of-control problem in which he was aided only by an assistant secretary and chief clerk, the three of them arrayed against powerful bureau chiefs. In 1877, the four most important of these bureaus within Interior's jurisdiction included the Office of Indian Affairs, the General Land Office, the Pension Office, and the Patent Office. Other activities, such as scientific surveys, control over public buildings, census reports, the Bureau of Education, and supervision of certain welfare institutions, also came within the department's province. Schurz, an able administrator, did not ever fully master this bewildering number of functions, but he managed to initiate new policies important for the future: more enlightened treatment of the American Indian; a merit promotion system with competitive examinations for the department; preservation of the public domain, especially forest resources; and the beginnings of national park development.[58]

Carl Schurz, while thoroughly Americanized in most respects, never lost his foreign appearance. Thick wavy red hair, a moustache and beard, piercing eyes, pince-nez that did not suit his face, and a tall, lanky figure made him stand out in any gathering. Foes called him "Mephistopheles in whiskers" or "that Dutchman."[59] Beneath this exterior was a man of great personal charm, an idealist and free spirit, and a gentleman of purest character. Schurz was devoted to his four children and wife, who started the first American kindergarten in Watertown, Wisconsin. After her death in March 1876, a daughter Agathe Schurz, a young woman in her twenties, became hostess of the large double house on Washington's H Street.

Schurz liked to play the piano and, if disappointed in politics or private life, would seek solace at the keyboard with his favorite composers, Schumann and Chopin. On the night of his wife's death, he reputedly sat until morning at the piano, expressing his grief through music.[60]

Schurz exhibited his scholarly instincts in a number of writings, of which his *Life of Henry Clay* is considered best. Harvard awarded him an honorary degree in June 1876, and, in 1882, he gave the Phi Beta Kappa oration there, one of his proudest achievements. He loved the outdoors and in declining years maintained a summer home on Lake George. Until his death in New York City on May 14, 1906, Carl Schurz waged a constant battle for great causes as a journalist and public-spirited citizen, inspiring other Americans to examine their consciences and to follow his worthy example.

The most surprising appointment of President Hayes to his cabinet was the designation of Richard W. Thompson as twenty-seventh Secretary of the Navy.[61] Thompson (1809–1900), dubbed "the Ancient Mariner of the Wabash" because he hailed from an inland rather than a seaboard state, was not only the first freshwater Secretary of the Navy, but at sixty-seven considerably older than his cabinet colleagues. Hayes selected him partly out of regard for Senator Oliver P. Morton and partly out of the practical necessity of recognizing the pivotal state of Indiana in his administration. Thompson, whose reputation rested upon his ability as an orator, had an uncontroversial record up to this time. More importantly, he represented the Old Whig element in the party and knew the southern Whigs quite well. The President was anxious to have such a person to assist him in his efforts to restore a genuine two-party system in the South. Thompson accompanied Hayes on the southern tour of 1877 and generally used his oratorical skill to promote peace between the sections. He also supported the administration's civil service program, although he was not an ardent reformer of the Schurz variety. He backed the President in his successful contest with Congress over legislative riders to appropriation bills, but he did not fully subscribe to the money views of Sherman and Hayes since the Greenback idea was strong in Indiana and he personally favored bimetallism.

Initially, Thompson received an inquiry through Senator Morton as to his availability for the Interior, War Department, or Post Office positions. He replied that he preferred to be Secretary of War but was notified of his appointment as Navy chief instead. While the position certainly was the most important job Thompson ever held, it was a relatively insignificant and obscure office in the Hayes presidency. A federal navy of 40 vessels in 1861 had expanded to over 600 ships by 1865 only to decline again until, in March 1877, it consisted of 142 ships, many of them unseaworthy or antiquated. At least 4 ships were sixty years old. A limit of 7,500 officers and men, a figure fixed by law, further restricted naval operations. Most deplorable of all, corruption and extravagance in awarding naval contracts, poor management, and congressional indifference to the importance of naval policy plagued the department in the 1870s. Not until 1882 when a modern armored, steam-propelled capital ship navy came into being did these conditions change.[62]

Thompson restored some measure of business and efficiency to naval administration, but he was so unimaginative in policy and strict in interpreting the law that he failed to expend several million dollars appropriated for his department's use. His chief contributions consisted of checking fraudulent contracting, improving personnel, instituting weekly meetings with bureau chiefs, and recruiting more sailors of American birth for United States warships. He was popular with cadets at the Naval Academy and regularly addressed their graduation ceremonies and presented the diplomas.

Richard Thompson, or "Colonel Dick" Thompson as he was generally called in Indiana, lived long enough to see and to be personally acquainted with nearly every American president from Jefferson to McKinley, to serve in Congress with Lincoln, and to vote for McKinley in 1896. His life spanned an era from the candle and the stagecoach to the electric light and the automobile. Born near Culpeper Court House, Virginia, on June 9, 1809, he received a classical education, moved first to Louisville, Kentucky, and then to Lawrence County, Indiana, in 1831. For sixty years he built a record for political oratory outstanding in Indiana's history.

A gentleman of the old school, Thompson stood erect and nearly six feet tall, appeared lithe and sinewy, with white hair, and was known for his courtly and dignified manners. He customarily appeared attired in a long black broadcloth coat, a high collar and black silk stock wound about, and a tall black silk hat. Altogether he resembled Andrew Jackson in face and figure. Hayes habitually called him "Brother Thompson."[63]

Mrs. Thompson, the former Harriet Eliza Gardner of Columbus, Ohio, was the daughter of a Virginia-born editor of the *Ohio State Journal*. She shared the first lady's fondness for flowers and shrubbery and kept house in Washington for her husband and four of their eight children in the southern manner. The Thompsons entertained grandly in Washington; six or seven hundred guests might visit them in an evening during the social season.

Back home in Indiana, Secretary Thompson maintained a handsome country home, "Spring Hill," located amid four hundred acres some four miles southeast of Terre Haute. Fine animals—

blooded horses and pure-bred cattle—distinguished the farm. Thompson took equal pride in his personal library of seven thousand volumes, one of the best private collections of history, biography, and travel literature in the West at the time. Most of his leisure hours were spent with either his family and friends, books, or prize animals.

Thompson remained Secretary of the Navy for three years and nine months until December 21, 1880, when he resigned under presidential pressure because of a conflict of interest created by his injudicious acceptance of a $25,000-a-year position as chairman of the American Committee of the Panama Canal Company.[64] His salary of $8,000 a year as Secretary of the Navy had not been sufficient to pay his living expenses in Washington. A tendency toward carelessness in his personal financial affairs and the near end of the Hayes administration contributed to Thompson's willingness to leave the Navy Department before Hayes went out of office. He did this despite the knowledge that the President preferred him not to lend his name and prestige gained as Secretary of the Navy to further a private and anti-United States policy of a canal company headed by the Frenchman, Ferdinand de Lesseps of Suez Canal fame.[65] The ill-fated venture clouded the remainder of Thompson's life.

Three men—Alexander Ramsey of Minnesota, Horace Maynard of Tennessee, and Nathan Goff, Jr., of West Virginia—became members of the Hayes cabinet through the resignation of original members. Of the new appointees, Ramsey, who assumed the War Department portfolio in place of McCrary on December 15, 1879, was the man of greatest political stature. Born of Presbyterian parents near Harrisburg, Pennsylvania, on September 8, 1815, he attended common schools and Lafayette College. Admitted to the bar in 1839, Ramsey served two terms as a Pennsylvania Whig congressman from 1843 to 1847. President Taylor appointed him territorial governor of Minnesota (1849–1853), which launched Ramsey's second and more important political career. He won election as mayor of St. Paul (1855), governor of Minnesota (1860–1863), and United States Senator (1863–1875). Meantime, Ramsey took a great personal interest in the Minnesota Historical Society, which he helped to organize and to lead as its first president (1849–1863), and again in 1891, until death claimed the state's foremost nineteenth-century citizen on April 22, 1903.[66] Mrs. Ramsey (Elizabeth Jenks), the daughter of one of her husband's former colleagues in the House of Representatives, was very popular in Washington, D.C., social circles.

The "good governor," as Hayes referred to the Minnesota leader, was a large, jovial, friendly man, and a good judge of human nature. He was not a soldier and received his appointment as Secretary of War at least in part because of his popularity with his former Senate associates. The fifteen months Ramsey served in the cabinet were largely spent on such routine matters as attending meetings and visiting various posts and institutions under his authority. In the summer of 1880 he was a member of the presidential party on the Great Western Tour. As the only cabinet officer along, the Secretary of War assisted the President in delivering numerous short speeches stressing prosperity and education.

Following Thompson's forced resignation in December 1880, Ramsey functioned briefly as both Secretary of War and Secretary of the Navy until Hayes could find a permanent official to assume the post.[67] The Chief Executive had hoped at first to appoint the same man President-elect Garfield had in mind as his future Secretary of the Navy. Garfield, however, had not determined his choice so Hayes finally designated Nathan Goff, Jr., for the short-term appointment. A short while later, on March 11, 1881, Ramsey was succeeded at the War Department by Robert T. Lincoln, son of the martyred President.

Since Ramsey served as Secretary of War near the end of the long period of military neglect, which set in after the great Civil War army was disbanded, very little significant action could be expected from his administration of the War Department. He did, nevertheless, give the office his full attention and, by careful reports and recommendations, prepared the way for its future development.

Horace Maynard, who succeeded David M. Key as Postmaster General on June 2, 1880, was born in Westboro, Massachusetts on August 30, 1814. He studied at Millbury Academy and was graduated as valedictorian from Amherst in 1838. He then moved permanently to Tennessee and taught mathematics for five years (1839–1844) at the University of East Tennessee (now the University of Tennessee). In 1840 he married Laura Ann Washburn of Royalton, Vermont, who bore him seven children. Admitted to the bar in 1844, he practiced law in Knoxville and entered politics as a Whig. Later he represented the American party in Congress for three terms (1857–1863). A staunch Unionist, Maynard became attorney general of Tennessee (1863–1865) under the military governorship of Andrew Johnson. Affiliating with the Republican party after the Civil War, Maynard was again elected to Congress five consecutive times and served from 1866 to 1875. Meanwhile he broke his old friendship with President Johnson and aligned himself with the Radical Republicans. Unsuccessful in his bid for the Tennessee governorship in 1874, he accepted an appointment as minister to Turkey (1875–1880), a post he resigned when Hayes named him Postmaster General. Maynard died in Knoxville on May 3, 1882.[68]

Maynard's physical appearance was striking. Over six feet tall, thin, straight, of swarthy complexion, with dark and piercing eyes, and long black hair that fell to his shoulders, he made an unforgettable impression upon political audiences.

Nathan Goff, Jr., of Clarksburg, West Virginia, Secretary of the Navy for the final two months of the Hayes term, earned at least two distinctions in his brief tenure. At thirty-eight years of age, he was by far the youngest member of the Hayes cabinet and the first from his state to hold a cabinet position. The appointment afforded Hayes an opportunity to make another conciliatory gesture toward the South and to pay tribute to Goff's courageous but unsuccessful campaign for governor in 1876.[69]

Goff was born in Clarksburg on February 9, 1843, and educated at Northwestern Academy, Georgetown University, and the University of the City of New York. During the Civil War, he earned a good record as a junior officer on the Union side. After Appomattox, he became the most popular Republican leader in West Virginia, and served in the legislature, and later as United States Attorney for the state, a position he resigned to become Secretary of the Navy, with the understanding that Garfield would reappoint him as United States Attorney after Hayes retired from the presidency.[70] The pledge was honored. Subsequently Goff served his state as a United States Congressman (1883–1889), United States Circuit Judge (1892–1913), and United States Senator (1913–1919). Goff was married twice, first to Laura Ellen Despard on November 7, 1865, and then to Katherine Penney on August 28, 1919.

As Secretary of the Navy, Goff had no opportunity to make a significant contribution, handicapped as he was by such a brief tenure, the weakness and low prestige of the navy, and the unfortunate circumstances of Thompson's departure. Routine business was transacted by experienced subordinates while policy questions remained in the hands of Admiral David D. Porter, a veteran of fifty-one years of navy service. Goff's only chance would have been reappointment by Garfield, a circumstance which neither the West Virginian sought nor the President desired. The young Secretary benefited most by his brief, but close, association with powerful senior members of the Republican party.

With the single exception of Secretary Thompson's eleventh-hour defection, each member of the Hayes cabinet proved loyal to the President, and their collective record in office showed the President to be an excellent judge of merit and fitness in his major appointments. His cabinet fit the situation and worked well under his leadership. Compelled to govern without benefit of support by a majority party in Congress, Hayes concentrated on the day-to-day work of administration and gathered around him able advisers. While not of high rank as a party leader nor as a chief legislator, Hayes did excel as a working chief executive and proved to be the right man for the time. He managed to serve the country well by putting together a strong group of departmental administrators and, while eschewing any desire for a second term himself, contrived to prepare the way for another President of his own party supported by a majority in Congress. Such an achievement depended in no small measure upon the caliber of the Hayes cabinet. Character, experience, and prestige made it the ablest presidential team between the end of the Civil War and the twentieth century.[71]

Notes

1. "White House Secretaries, Messengers, etc., March 4, 1877," manuscript, Hayes Papers, RBHL.

2. "White House, Washington, D.C., List of Employees, December 1, 1880," Hayes Papers, RBHL; *Register of Officers and Agents, Civil, Military, and Naval, in the Service of the United States* (Washington: Government Printing Office, 1878), passim.

3. Gilson Willets, *Inside History of the White House* (New York: The Christian Herald, 1908), 158; "White House Secretaries."

4. Margarita Spalding Gerry, ed., *Through Five Administrations: Reminiscences of Colonel William H. Crook* (New York: Harper and Brothers, 1910), 223.

5. Ibid.

6. Willets, *Inside History*, 180.

7. O. L. Pruden to Hayes, September 27, 1882, Hayes Papers, RBHL; Gerry, *Five Administrations*, 252. It should be noted that the office files of the Hayes presidency are the last ones to be exclusively handwritten. Typed documents appear more regularly from the Garfield administration forward.

8. "White House Secretaries." Charles L. Chapman also served as an executive clerk.

9. C. M. Hendley to Hayes, August 7, 1889, Hayes Papers, RBHL.

10. Willets, *Inside History*, 176.

11. H. C. Morton to E. F. Noyes, October 25, 1875; Morton to Hayes, October 25, 1875, November 17, December 1, 1885, November 26, 1888; Hayes, Diary, October 29, 1884; all in Hayes Papers, RBHL.

12. Gerry, *Five Administrations*, 224.

13. Willets, *Inside History*, 180–181; Margaret Leech, *In the Days of McKinley* (New York: Harper and Brothers, 1959), 126, 232.

14. Emily Platt to Rutherford P. Hayes, October 29, 1877, Hayes Papers, RBHL.

15. Rutherford P. Hayes, "The Age of Innocence in the White House," *Literary Digest* 92 (February 5, 1927): 41.

16. Hayes, Diary, February 19, 1877.

17. Hayes to Schurz, February 2, 1877, Hayes Papers, RBHL.

18. Hayes, Diary, January 17, 1877.

19. Hayes, Diary, March 14, 1877, April 19, 1888; William Henry Smith interview with Hayes, August 9, 1890, Hayes Papers, RBHL.

20. Hayes, Scrapbook, Vol. 113, p. 15; newspaper clipping from Brooklyn *Eagle*, Hayes Papers, RBHL.

21. It has been necessary to use genealogical methods to gather factual information on these men. The author is indebted to Miss Jean Stephenson of Washington, D.C., and the staffs at the Daughters of the American Revolution Library, the National Archives, and the Library of Congress local history division for assistance in tracking the careers of Devens, Key, and McCrary.

22. Thomas C. Donaldson, "Memoirs," April 28, 1877, pp. 14–15, RBHL.

23. For facts concerning Devens, see Arthur Lithgow Devens, ed., *Orations and Addresses of Charles Devens—Civil and Military* (Boston: Little, Brown, and Company, 1891), 1–25; "Charles Devens," *The Dictionary of American Biography* (New York: Charles Scribner's Sons, 1930), V, 260–262; George Frisbie Hoar, *Charles Devens, Henry M. Dexter, Edward I. Thomas* (Worcester: Press of Charles Hamilton, 1891), 7–17; "Charles Devens," *The National Cyclopedia of American Biography* (New York: James T. White & Company, 1893), III, 203.

24. Donaldson, "Memoirs," April 28, 1877, pp. 14–15.

25. Hayes, Diary, January 7, 1891.

26. Ibid., February 17, 1877, April 15, 1891; Hayes to William Henry Smith, January 27, 1881, all in Hayes Papers, RBHL.

27. Albert V. House, "President Hayes' Selection of David M. Key for Postmaster General," *Journal of Southern History* 4 (1938): 87–93; William Henry Smith, *History of the Cabinet of the United States of America* (Baltimore: The Industrial Printing Company, 1925), 386.

28. Dorothy Ganfield Fowler, *The Cabinet Politician: the Postmasters General, 1829–1909* (New York: Columbia University Press, 1943), 165.

29. Smith, *History of the Cabinet*, 387–388.

30. Since this section on David Key was written, a long-needed but disappointing biography has appeared: David M. Abshire, *The South Rejects a Prophet: The Life of Senator D. M. Key, 1824–1900* (New York: Frederick A. Praeger, 1967). Unless otherwise noted, the following works are the basis for Key's biography: Zella Armstrong, *Notable Southern Families* (Chattanooga: The Lookout Publishing Company, 1918), I, 120–123; Confederate Compiled Service Records, Co. K, 43d Tennessee Infantry, Record Group 109, National Archives; "David M. Key," *The Dictionary of American Biography* (New York: Charles Scribner's Sons, 1933), X, 361–362; W. A. Goodspeed, *History of Tennessee from the Earliest Time to the Present* (Nashville: The Goodspeed Publishing Company, 1886), 412–413; Will T. Hale and Dixon L. Merritt, *A History of Tennessee and Tennesseans* (Chicago: The Lewis Publishing Company, 1913), VII, 2051–

2054; John Trotwood Moore, *Tennessee: The Volunteer State, 1769–1923* (Chicago: The S. J. Clarke Publishing Company, 1923), 36–41; Emma M. Wells, *History of Roane County, Tennessee, 1801–1870* (Chattanooga: The Lookout Publishing Company, 1927), 235, 309.

31. Sarah Key Patten Scrapbook, microfilm copy, David M. Key Collection, RBHL.

32. William S. Speer, ed., *Sketches of Prominent Tennesseans* (Nashville: A. B. Tavel, 1888), 444–445.

33. Of all the Hayes cabinet members, McCrary's life is the most difficult one to reconstruct because he has no military service records, no family genealogy has been located, his manuscripts are fugitive or missing, and his name does not appear in the indexes to the *Iowa Magazine of History and Biography*. I have relied upon the following sources of information: *Biographical Directory of the American Congress, 1774–1961* (Washington: U.S. Government Printing Office, 1961), 1290; "George W. McCrary," *The Dictionary of American Biography* (New York: Charles Scribner's Sons, 1933), XII, 2–3; *The History of Lee County, Iowa* (Chicago: Western Historical Company, 1879), 703; "George W. McCrary," *The National Cyclopedia of American Biography* (New York: James T. White and Company, 1893), III, 201–202; Olive K. Porter, comp., "Records from Van Buren County, Iowa," Iowa Daughters of the American Revolution Chapter, 1936, typescript, Daughters of the American Revolution Library, Washington, D.C.; Edward H. Stiles, *Recollections and Sketches of Notable Lawyers and Public Men of Early Iowa* (Des Moines: The Homestead Publishing Company, 1916), 211–215.

34. Smith, *History of the Cabinet*, 298, 346.

35. Obituary, Kansas City *Star*, June 24, 1890.

36. Donaldson, "Memoirs," April 28, 1877, p. 15.

37. "Society Gossip," February 18, 1879, unidentified newspaper clipping; Hayes to H. W. Slocum, January 23, 1884; Hayes to Mrs. George W. McCrary, June 24, 1890, copy of telegram, all in Hayes Papers, RBHL.

38. For many insights into Sherman's career I am indebted to the article by Jeannette P. Nichols, "Rutherford B. Hayes and John Sherman," *Ohio History* 77 (Winter, Spring, Summer 1968): 125–138.

39. See Leonard D. White, *The Republican Era, 1869–1901* (New York: The Macmillan Company, 1958), 111.

40. The carriage, fully restored, is on display in the Museum of the RBHL.

41. Jeannette P. Nichols, "John Sherman," *The Dictionary of American Biography* (New York: Charles Scribner's Sons, 1935), XVII, 84–88.

42. Hayes to Sherman, March 6, 1881, Hayes Papers, RBHL.

43. Ibid., June 27, 1888.

44. Hayes, Diary, January 7, 1892.

45. Donaldson, "Memoirs," April 28, 1877, p. 14.

46. See "The Silver Wedding at the White House," Toledo *Blade*, January 7, 1878.

47. David M. Pletcher, *The Awkward Years: American Foreign Relations Under Garfield and Arthur* (Columbia: University of Missouri Press, 1961), xii.

48. Chester L. Barrows, *William M. Evarts, Lawyer, Diplomat, Statesman* (Chapel Hill: The University of North Carolina Press, 1941), 349.

49. Donaldson, "Memoirs," March 6, 1878, pp. 53–54.

50. Hayes, Diary, March 16, 1878.

51. Donaldson, "Memoirs," April 28, 1877, p. 14, November 8, 1877, p. 35; Barrows, *William M. Evarts*, 338; New York *Tribune*, January 28, 1879.

52. Barrows, *William M. Evarts*, 287–288.

53. For biographies of Evarts other than the Barrows volume already cited, see Brainerd Dyer, *The Public Career of William M. Evarts* (Berkeley: University of California Press, 1933); the sketches in *The Dictionary of American Biography* (New York: Charles Scribner's Sons, 1931), VI, 215–218; Chauncey M. Depew, *My Memories of Eighty Years* (New York: Charles Scribner's Sons, 1922), 101–106, and Walter LaFeber, *The New Empire: An Interpretation of American Expansion, 1860–1898* (Ithaca, New York: Cornell University Press, 1963), 39–46.

54. See Claude Moore Fuess, *Carl Schurz, Reformer* (New York: Dodd, Mead and Company, Inc., 1932) and Carl Wittke, "Carl Schurz and Rutherford B. Hayes," *The Ohio Historical Quarterly* 65 (October 1956): 337–355, and *The Dictionary of American Biography* (New York: Charles Scribner's Sons, 1935), XVI, 466–470.

55. Fuess, *Carl Schurz*, 390.

56. "Glad to know by your dispatch that Mr. Schurz will give us nine speeches. It will be of great importance. I would suggest that you consider Toledo, Sandusky, Akron, and Cleveland as among the points. Here there is still a large defection of Republicans." Hayes to Col. A. T. Wikoff, September 20, 1875, Hayes Papers, RBHL.

57. Fuess, *Carl Schurz*, 218–219. "Schurz began to write to Miss Fanny Chapman of Doylestown, Pa. shortly after the death of his wife, Margarethe, in 1876 & kept it up for 30 years (1700 letters). They did not marry. She was 30 & he 47 in 1876." A. R. Hogue to Carl Wittke, January 5, 1955, RBHL.

58. White, *The Republican Era*, 175–231.

59. Donaldson, "Memoirs," April 28, 1877, p. 15; Wittke, "Schurz and Hayes," 339.

60. Fuess, *Carl Schurz*, 219.

61. The standard biography of Thompson is Charles Roll, *Colonel Dick Thompson* (Indianapolis: Indiana Historical Bureau, 1948). Hayes first endeavored to appoint Eugene Hale of Maine, a Senate authority on naval affairs, as his Secretary of the Navy, but Hale refused the offer. *Biographical Directory of Congress*, 1249.

62. Roll, *Thompson*, 231–233; White, *Republican Era*, 154–174.

63. Donaldson, "Memoirs," April 28, 1877, p. 15.

64. R. W. Thompson to Hayes, December 9, 1880, Hayes to Thompson, December 13, 1880, Hayes Papers, RBHL.

65. "The chief matter, however, is this affair of yours. I assume, that, of course, you will not think of accepting an employment, or connection with the American Syndicate, in the interest of the project of Mr. [de Lesseps] while you continue in the administration, and that your affair refers to the future when you are not a member of the Cabinet." Hayes to Hon. R. W. Thompson, August 28, 1880, Hayes Papers, RBHL. "I am having a peck of your sort of trouble. The resignation of Thompson (a great mistake I fear on his part) sets me to Cab. repairing if not making. If I knew who you would put in the Navy and also that my putting him in my remnant of the term would not embarass you or him, the case would be solved. But I don't ask it." Hayes to Garfield, December 16, 1880, original in Garfield Papers, Library of Congress, copy in RBHL.

66. William James Ryland, *Alexander Ramsey* (Philadelphia: Harris & Partridge Company, 1941), passim.

67. Hayes to Alexander Ramsey, December 13, 1880, Hayes Papers, RBHL.

68. Short sketches of Maynard's life are found in *The Dictionary of American Biography*, XII, 460–461, and *The National Cyclopedia of American Biography*, IX, 286–287.

69. G. Wayne Smith, *Nathan Goff, Jr., A Biography* (Charleston, W. Va.: Education Foundation, Inc., 1959), 104–119.

70. Hayes to James A. Garfield, January 8, 1881, Hayes Papers, RBHL.

71. Arthur N. Holcombe, "John F. Kennedy '40 as Presidential Cabinet-Maker," *Harvard Alumni Bulletin* 63 (May 27, 1961): 641–645.

7

Congressional and Judicial Leadership

The political equilibrium that persisted throughout the 1870s and 1880s made it difficult for either political party to dominate the national legislature, with the Republicans tending to control the Senate and the Democrats holding a majority in the House. This was the situation in 1877 with an upper chamber composed of 39 Republicans, 36 Democrats, and an Independent, Lincoln's friend and executor, Judge David Davis of Illinois. In the House, 153 Democrats opposed 140 Republicans. The Ohio delegation, representing the most populous midwestern state, was one of the most distinguished in either house. John Sherman, the senior Senator, resigned to accept the Treasury portfolio in Hayes' cabinet, and his place was filled by Stanley Matthews, a Kenyon classmate of the President and later Associate Justice of the United States Supreme Court. Ohio's other Senator, Allen G. Thurman, a former chief justice of the state supreme court, served as his party's floor leader in the Senate during the Hayes administration.

Among Ohio Republicans in the lower house, at least five men achieved fame. Jacob D. Cox of Toledo, an ex-governor and cabinet officer, also became a railroad and university president. Two freshman Congressmen, J. Warren Keifer and William McKinley, attained political distinction, the former as an outstanding orator and Speaker of the House and the latter as a two-term governor and President. Charles Foster, a businessman and banker who came from Hayes' home district, served two terms as governor (1880–1884) and two years as Secretary of the Treasury (1891–1893) under Benjamin Harrison. Perhaps the most outstanding Ohioan in the lower chamber was James A. Garfield of Mentor, Ohio, who represented the Nineteenth District continuously from 1863 to 1880, working as a member or chairman of numerous key committees. At Hayes' insistence, he gave up a chance to stand for

Sherman's vacated Senate seat in order to become the administration's minority floor leader in the House. An acknowledged fiscal expert, a good organizer and parliamentarian, Garfield also was one of the party's best stump and platform speakers. In June 1880, as the leader of the Ohio delegation, he attended the Republican National Convention in Chicago for the purpose of nominating the administration's candidate, John Sherman, only to witness, after the convention was unable to agree upon either Grant, Blaine, or Sherman, his own dramatic selection as a dark-horse candidate on the thirty-sixth ballot.[1]

The Maine Senators and Representatives also comprised a notable group. Hannibal Hamlin, ex-governor and Lincoln's first-term Vice President, and James G. Blaine, just promoted from the House, held the state's two Senate seats. Among Maine's five representatives were Thomas B. Reed, future Speaker of the House, and William P. Frye and Eugene Hale, who both served ten years in the House and thirty years in the Senate.

Other powerful figures in the Congress at the opening of the Hayes administration included Joseph G. Cannon of Illinois and John G. Carlisle, both future Speakers; Roger Q. Mills of Texas; Alexander Stephens of Georgia; and S. S. Cox of New York. Fernando Wood of New York, chairman of the Ways and Means Committee, and Samuel J. Randall of Pennsylvania served respectively as majority floor leader and Speaker of the House during all four years of the Hayes presidency.

Had he lived, Senator Oliver P. Morton of Indiana, whom Hayes had admired for over a decade, would have been the administration's majority leader in the Senate. Morton had helped Hayes campaign for the Ohio governorship and was the controlling power within his party in the settlement arrived at by the Electoral Commission.[2] Hayes thought of him as "the great statesman at Washington . . . a strong, logical debater, who has the faculty of putting an argument in a way that is satisfactory to the best minds, and at the same [time] is understood and appreciated by the most ignorant."[3] Unfortunately Morton became ill in August 1877 and died on November 1, 1877, without ever taking part in the forty-fifth Congress.

Morton's expected role was filled instead by Vermont's flinty senior Senator, George F. Edmunds, chairman of the Judiciary Committee and a favorite of the Mugwump, or reform, element in the Republican party. Constitutional law was his specialty. Hayes had mixed feelings about him. "Senator Edmunds tells good anecdotes, and is *both* witty and humorous—a rare combination," but alluding to the Senator's known fondness for spirits, the President characterized him as a "confirmed—well, hard, drinker."[4]

Justin S. Morrill, Vermont's other venerable Senator and head of the Finance Committee, achieved fame as the author of the Land-Grant College Act of 1862 and for his unusually long House and Senate career extending from 1855 to 1898. Both Thomas W. Ferry of Michigan and William Windom of Minnesota entered the Senate in 1871 and, by their reelection to a second term in 1877, held key posts as chairmen of the Committees on Rules and Appropriations. Meanwhile in 1873 William Boyd Allison of Iowa launched an unbroken thirty-five-year Senate career.

Among key Senators on the Democratic side of the aisle were the future Associate Supreme Court Justice, Lucius Q. C. Lamar of Mississippi; Thomas F. Bayard of Delaware, later Secretary of State; and Georgia's two leaders, John B. Gordon and Benjamin H. Hill.

The President disapproved of only two members of the Congress, Roscoe Conkling in the Senate and Benjamin F. Butler in the House. He thought Conkling had betrayed the Republican party on three occasions: by failing to work for the ticket in 1876; by sulking during the electoral count of 1877; and by intriguing with the Potter Committee in its attack upon the presidential title in 1878.[5] Hayes attributed no significant measures or speeches to Conkling's credit and termed him a victim of "monomania on the subject of his own importance."[6] Butler he saw as "unscrupulous, able, rich, untiring . . . the most dangerous and wicked demagogue we have ever had."[7] In summing up his opinion of both rivals he was able to boast, "If there are any two men in the country whose opposition and hatred are a certificate of good character and sound statesmanship, they are Conkling and Butler. I enjoy the satisfaction of being fully endorsed by the hatred and opposition of both these men."[8]

During the Hayes presidency, the Supreme Court continued to meet in a chamber originally occupied by the United States Senate until the Senators moved in 1859 to their present quarters in the new Senate wing of the Capitol. The following year, the Court took over the remodeled Old Senate Chamber (from which the principal overhead gallery had been removed) and remained there for three-quarters of a century (1860–1935). This same room also served, early in 1877, as the meeting place of the special Electoral Commission, which declared Hayes the victor in the contested presidential election of 1876.[9]

With the death of Salmon P. Chase in 1873, President Grant acquired the distinction of designating a new Chief Justice, an honor shared by only four earlier Presidents. After five or six men in public and private life declined or caused too much opposition, Grant finally decided to select a solid lawyer for the post. The lot fell to Morrison R. Waite, a Toledoan and a leader of the Ohio bar, whose father had been chief justice of the Connecticut Supreme Court.[10] Waite was willing to give up $25,000 a year he received for representing various business firms to accept $10,500 as Chief Justice, a sacrifice that prevented him from gaining financial security; he left a relatively small estate to his wife at his death in 1888.

The new Chief Justice, while not brilliant, possessed solid legal competence, and despite rather pedestrian opinions lacking in the literary style of his brethren on the high tribunal, he rendered a valuable service by the tactful manner in which he presided over a group of strong-minded jurists and administered the court routine. Of seventy-two key decisions between 1874 and 1881, Waite sided with the majority in sixty-six and thus had the authority to decide who should write the opinion in these cases.[11] His assignments proved both wise and practical.

Waite was a native of Connecticut and a graduate of Yale (1837) in the same class with William M. Evarts and Samuel J. Tilden. While a young man, he moved to Ohio to establish his practice and meantime served a single term in the state senate (1849–1850). Among his early Ohio friends were Sardis Birchard and Allen G. Thurman, who later helped to get him confirmed as Chief Justice. Hayes knew of Waite through his uncle, but they did not really become close friends until Hayes was elected President. Thereafter the Chief Justice and his family were frequent social visitors at the White House. The two men shared common interests.[12]

Waite's most famous opinion, *Munn* v. *Illinois* (1877), was handed down just a few days before Hayes took the presidential oath of office. The Chief Justice, despite his background as a businessman's lawyer, upheld the Granger legislation (which substituted restraints for laissez-faire), and thereby laid the legal groundwork for most of the federal and state regulatory agencies we know today.[13] In matters of race relations, Waite took a more conservative stance and failed to involve the court in civil-rights issues. With the exception of Justice Harlan, the Waite court took the position that the high tribunal should remain aloof on questions of civil rights, postponing the problem to our own day. In general, Chief Justice Waite belongs to the tradition of judicial self-restraint. Upon his death, Hayes characterized him as "great-hearted, warm-hearted, and of generous nature. . . . He had a saving common sense, undying industry, and great energy. He was always cheer-

ful, easily made happy by others and with amazing powers and
a never-failing disposition to make others happy."[14]

When Waite was sworn in as Chief Justice on March 4, 1874,
the Associate Justices included three Democrats and five Republicans. Nathan Clifford, the senior jurist, had been appointed by
President Buchanan in 1858 and was the last of the pre-Civil War
judges still serving on the bench.[15] A states' rights Democrat of
the old school, Clifford wrote ponderous opinions largely dealing
with commerical and admiralty law. He had served as a Con-
gresman from Maine (1839–1843) and as Attorney General in President Polk's cabinet. He also helped to negotiate the treaty ending
the Mexican War. A large man of enormous appetite who seldom
took any exercise, he liked to relax by fishing. Originally a Con-
gregationalist, Clifford took up the practice of attending different
churches each Sunday and eventually became a Unitarian sym-
pathizer. By 1877, after nearly twenty years on the bench, Clifford
had grown obstinate and at seventy-four years of age was near
the end of his effectiveness. He looked upon Waite as an interloper,
and the Chief Justice had to handle him very tactfully. Clifford
presided over the Electoral Commission in 1877, his last significant
duty. As a life-long Democrat, he felt Tilden had been cheated
out of the presidency and refused for a while even to enter the
White House during the Hayes administration.[16] His mental powers began to fail in 1879. The next year, his health failed utterly,
and he suffered a stroke which so affected his speech that he
never again resumed the bench. He died in Maine on July 25,
1881.

The outstanding Democrat on the Waite court was Stephen J.
Field of California. Like Clifford he thought Tilden should have
been President.[17] Neither man attended the Hayes inauguration
or accepted a White House invitation for several years. Stephen
Field remained on the high court for nearly thirty-five years, longer
than anyone else in the court's history. Starting out as a spokesman
for rugged individualism and laissez-faire, this first representative
from the Pacific Coast on the bench slowly altered his legal
philosophy, gradually putting property rights above individual
rights. His court opinions reflect the gospel of wealth more than
they do humane values.

A member of a distinguished Connecticut family, Field, with
his flowing beard, looked the part of a judge. A belligerent, cantan-
kerous, and colorful personality, he had graduated with highest
honors from Williams College in 1837, practiced law in New York
City several years, and then joined the Gold Rush in 1849. He
quickly acquired considerable knowledge of California's legal and

political affairs and served in the state legislature before he was elevated to the California Supreme Court in 1857. Two years later he became the state's Chief Justice. During the Civil War he supported the Union and was rewarded when Lincoln named him an Associate Justice in 1863. In 1890 he was a principal in the dramatic *In re Neagle* case.[18]

David Davis of Illinois, Lincoln's manager at the 1860 Republican National Convention, became a Supreme Court Justice in 1862 but resigned his seat early in 1877 in circumstances which virtually assured the victory of Hayes over Tilden. As something of a political independent, Davis had been expected to hold the decisive vote on the fifteen-member Electoral Commission. At the critical juncture, however, the Illinois legislature elected him to the United States Senate. Even so, three of his Supreme Court colleagues still favored his selection for the commission, and he was offered the place but declined to serve; since Clifford and Field, both already members of the commission, were the only other Democrats on the Court, the position intended for Davis went to Joseph P. Bradley. In his Senate career, Davis continued to follow independent inclinations. A massive man, he proved to be more of a politician than a judge.[19]

The real strength of the Waite court in 1877 rested with three able Republican appointees: Samuel Freeman Miller of Iowa, Joseph P. Bradley of New Jersey, and William Strong of Pennsylvania. Miller, who was born in Kentucky, had pursued successive careers as a rural doctor and country lawyer before moving to Iowa in 1850, where he helped to organize the Republican party. Although he had little formal legal training and had never previously held a public office, Miller attained such distinction on the bench that today he ranks as one of the great Justices in the entire history of the court and is certainly the most outstanding jurist appointed by President Lincoln. When Chief Justice Chase died in 1873, the Iowan hoped to succeed him and was endorsed by the legal profession for the post. Disappointed and embittered by his failure to achieve his ambition, he never held Waite in high regard as the leader of the Court. Miller was the first Supreme Court Justice from west of the Mississippi. Blunt, self-confident, and prone to vanity, he nevertheless evidenced an independent and logical intellect in his many court opinions. Generally speaking, he was a strong nationalist and defender of personal liberties as opposed to corporate and financial wealth.[20]

Joseph P. Bradley, a self-made New Jersey railroad attorney named to the bench along with William Strong in 1870, ranks with the best legal minds in the Court's history. He also figured in the speculation for promotion to Chief Justice in 1874 although he did not seek the honor. A graduate of Rutgers University, he was admitted to the New Jersey bar in 1839 and began to specialize in patent, commercial, and corporate cases. On the Supreme Court bench for twenty-two years, he became known as a nationalist and a great interpreter of the commerce clause. Despite his background as a corporation lawyer, Bradley assumed an independent posture as a judge and upheld economic regulation. In addition, his circuit court duties took him into the deep South, extending from Georgia to Texas, where he presided over many of the most difficult Reconstruction cases arising out of the new federal rights defined in the 1870s. Bradley possessed strong scholarly instincts, and for diversion read widely in history and literature, besides preparing a genealogical history of his family. His personal library contained six thousand general books and ten thousand law books. He ranks with Justices Miller and Field as one of the three most prominent members of the court during the 1870s and 1880s. Bradley worked very closely with Morrison Waite who collaborated with him more often than with any other Justice.[21]

William Strong also had excellent relations with his chief. He had served with distinction for eleven years on the Pennsylvania Supreme Court, and, while a very capable judge, he is practically unknown today because of his relatively short tenure as an Associate Justice. Generally sympathetic to corporations, he usually voted with Field on economic questions. Strong had received both a bachelor's and master's degree from Yale University. An active Presbyterian layman, he served for many years as vice president of the American Bible Society, president of the American Tract Society, and president of the American Sunday School Union. He was an erstwhile law teacher in Washington, D.C., and fond of outdoor sports. Shortly after his retirement from the bench in 1880, President Hayes offered the Navy Department portfolio to him, but Strong declined, preferring to live out his remaining years quietly. He died in 1895.[22]

The two other Republicans on the Court, Noah H. Swayne of Ohio and Ward Hunt of New York, were its least distinguished members in 1877. Swayne, a successful Ohio lawyer for over thirty years, but lacking in prior judicial experience or a national reputation, came to the Supreme Court largely because he was a close friend of retiring Justice John McLean who recommended him highly to President Lincoln.[23] One of Swayne's early law students had been Allen G. Thurman, later so prominent in Democratic party circles. Swayne proved to be the weakest of Lincoln's nominees to the Court. Despite his advancing years, he aspired

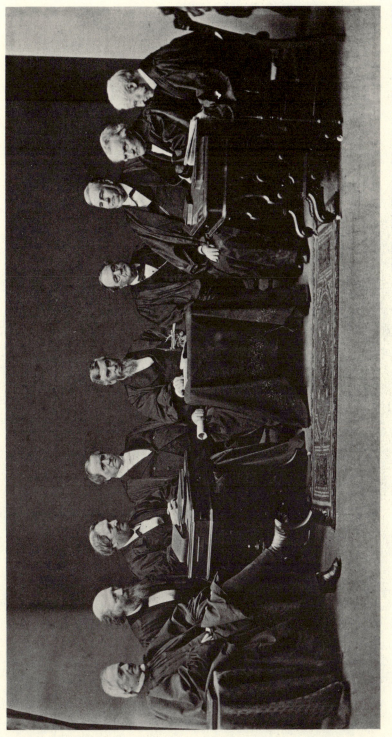

*The United States Supreme Court, 1876. Left to right: Joseph P. Bradley, Stephen J. Field,
Samuel Freeman Miller, Nathan Clifford, Morrison R. Waite, Noah H. Swayne, David Davis,
William Strong, and Ward Hunt. John Marshall Harlan replaced Justice Davis in 1877.*

Office seekers in the White House *lobby waiting for an interview with President Hayes.*
From Frank Leslie's Illustrated Newspaper, *1877.*

Secretary of
the Treasury John Sherman,
hero of specie resumption.

to succeed Chase as Chief Justice in 1874 and became the principal opponent of Justice Miller on the Court for the possible promotion. The end result of this rivalry was a tragic and lasting enmity between the two Associate Justices, which Waite had to overcome by adroit and tactful administration.[24] Swayne eventually retired because of age in January 1881. He lived on in Washington for a year and then moved to New York City.

Ward Hunt, appointed by Grant in 1873, was a Conkling follower with respectable credentials. He had graduated with honors from Union College in 1828 and had later studied at Hamilton College. Originally a Jacksonian Democrat in the New York Assembly and later mayor of Utica, Hunt joined the Free Soil party in 1848 and from there found his way into the new Republican party, which he helped to organize in New York State. After the Civil War, Hunt was elected to the Court of Appeals and became its chief judge in 1868. As a member of the United States Supreme Court (1873–1882), he was not a conspicuous judge nor associated with any outstanding decisions or doctrines, although he did write 149 opinions and 4 dissents. In January 1879, Justice Hunt suffered a paralytic stroke on the right side rendering him a permanent invalid. He steadfastly refused to resign despite his grave disability, in part because he expected Congress to pass a special bill providing him with a pension, and because he felt obligated to Roscoe Conkling who wished to deny President Hayes, his self-proclaimed political enemy, the privilege of filling a high court vacancy. Hunt finally left the Court in 1882 after his pension was authorized by special act of Congress, and President Arthur, himself a Conkling ally, named a successor.[25]

President Hayes made three appointments to the Supreme Court. John Marshall Harlan of Kentucky gained the seat vacated early in 1877 by the surprise election of David Davis to the Senate. Justice William Strong of Pennsylvania retired in December 1880, after ten years of service, and William B. Woods of Alabama took his place on December 21. Shortly afterward, on January 25, 1881, Judge Noah H. Swayne of Ohio resigned because of age. The very next day Hayes named his old friend and college classmate, Stanley Matthews of Cincinnati, to succeed Swayne. When Matthews was not confirmed before the Congress adjourned and the Hayes administration left office, the ex-President prevailed upon his good friend and fellow Ohioan, President Garfield, to renominate Matthews. Once more strong opposition manifested itself because of the nominee's long career as a railroad and corporation lawyer. Garfield remained steadfast and refused to recall his nomination, and after two months Matthews finally won confirmation by a single vote, 24 to 23. Journalist, lawyer, judge, soldier, politician, and legislator, Matthews served on the Supreme Court nearly eight years until his death in 1889. Like Strong and Harlan he was an active Presbyterian layman.[26]

The choice of Harlan for the Supreme Court proved to be one of Hayes' most important presidential acts. Only forty-four years of age in 1877, the Kentuckian served for nearly thirty-four years and became one of the great dissenters in the history of the Court. At the time of his appointment, however, he was not nationally known nor considered judicial timber. Some anticipated Harlan would become Attorney General in the new President's cabinet (a position he would have accepted) since he had served his state in that capacity for four years. Moreover, he had played a key role in the presidential nomination of Hayes by delivering the Kentucky delegation at a crucial moment in the balloting, and had further aided the Hayes cause as a member of the Louisiana Commission in November 1876. But since political complications in other states obviated a cabinet appointment, Harlan was offered a foreign mission instead, which he promptly declined, preferring not to leave the legal profession.[27]

Meanwhile the President considered possible candidates for the Supreme Court vacancy, and in keeping with his desire to placate the South, looked for a native southern Whig. By late September 1877, he asked his old political adviser W. H. Smith, "Confidentially and on the whole is not Harlan the man? Of the right age—able—of whole character—industrious—fine manners, temper and appearance. Who leads him?"[28] Smith concurred a few days later:

> Is Harlan the man? I think so. His age, vigor—mental and physical—his agreeable manners and personal magnetism are strongly for him. I think him [a] very much better man every way than Bristow, and if a Southern man is to be taken, he is the man. The appointment will offend a good many people of both parties of this section, who believe the selection would be made from this state [Illinois]. They will complain at first but in time if the Administration continues in well doing, they will forget about it or overlook it. This remark applies *to the people,* not to a *few* politicians who sympathize with Conkling and swear you have destroyed the party by breaking the machine. I hope, however, the appointment of a judge will not be made at a date earlier than November. The more time you get, the surer of victory.[29]

Hayes sent Harlan's name to the Senate on October 17, 1877, but confirmation was delayed for forty-one days. The nominee had held public office for just five years, only one of them as a judge. Typical of the opposition to Harlan was the sentiment of James F. Wilson of Iowa who wrote to Senator Allison: "I hope you will not vote to confirm Harlan (John M.) for the Supreme Court. He is unfit for the place. He is not a first class lawyer and is a mere politician. For God's sake give us no more of that kind of cattle on the Supreme Bench. If he is confirmed we will all live to regret it. Tell Kirkwood so."[30]

Bristow's friends, of course, thought he, rather than Harlan, merited the Supreme Court post. Samuel Bowles, a Bristow backer and editor of the influential Springfield *Republican,* expressed his thorough disgust with the Harlan nomination. The real cause for the Senate's delay, however, lay elsewhere. Two Senators, Timothy Howe of Wisconsin and Isaac Christiancy of Michigan, both thought they deserved the appointment, and other Senators supported their claims.[31]

While Harlan never achieved his ambition to become Chief Justice, especially after the death of Melville W. Fuller in 1910, and missed exceeding by less than nine months Stephen Field's record tenure of thirty-four years and eight months, he did create a remarkable judicial career, moving through every chair from junior to senior Associate Justice and even functioning temporarily as acting Chief Justice after Fuller's death.[32] More important he became the lone dissenter to a number of prominent civil-rights opinions, which, like the "separate but equal" doctrine, he opposed as discriminatory rulings. He wrote a thirty-four page dissent in the famous civil-rights cases of 1883 in which the majority held that the Fourteenth Amendment did not compel a private citizen to refrain from discrimination. This stance was all the more unusual because Harlan, originally a slave owner opposed to abolition, so transformed his social philosophy that he became one of the most vigorous champions of Negro rights.

Harlan was a native of Kentucky whose father, a prominent Whig and lawyer, owned a dozen slaves. Young Harlan graduated from Centre College, where he acquired a lifelong devotion to Presbyterianism, the Sabbath, and Bible study. He subsequently studied law at Transylvania, another Kentucky institution known as "the Harvard of the West." Harlan served a year (1858) as a Franklin County judge, his only judicial experience before joining the Supreme Court. During the Civil War, he remained loyal to the Union and fought in the federal army. After the war Harlan gave his support to the Fifteenth Amendment and joined the Republican party, becoming its unsuccessful standard-bearer for governor in 1871 and 1875, though he polled a substantial vote each time. An able orator who stood six feet two inches tall, he made an impressive leader, and was a natural choice to head the Kentucky delegation to the Cincinnati convention of 1876 in behalf of the presidential ambitions of his law partner and former Secretary of the Treasury, Benjamin H. Bristow.

Harlan developed into an aggressive and courageous judge with a mind of his own. He possessed both wit and humor and had a knack for leaving his differences in the conference room. During his exceptionally long tenure (1877–1911) he participated in 14,226 cases and wrote the opinion of the court in 745 of them, to which he added 380 dissents.[33]

Off the bench, Harlan was close socially to Chief Justice Waite, and the two jurists, in company with their families, were the most frequent social callers at the White House during the Hayes era of all their judicial brethren. Harlan was especially good at anecdotes and very fond of Kentucky bourbon, which he dispensed freely to his friends.[34]

After Strong resigned in 1880, Hayes appointed Circuit Judge William Burnham Woods, a former Ohioan, who had settled in Alabama as a carpetbagger after Union Army service. Woods had been highly recommended to Hayes for the David Davis vacancy as early as May 1877 by Associate Justice Joseph P. Bradley, who became acquainted with Woods while presiding with him during circuit court duty in the deep South. Later Bradley again endorsed Woods as "one whose general constitutional views coincide with your own."[35]

Woods was born in Newark, Ohio (1824), and educated at Western Reserve College and Yale, where he graduated as valedictorian in 1845. Admitted to the bar two years later, Woods gradually entered politics, changed from a Whig to a Democrat, and became successively mayor of Newark, Speaker of the Ohio General Assembly, and finally minority floor leader. Initially, he opposed Lincoln's policies, but in the end supported the Union and brought his party with him. His war record was creditable, and he left the service as a brigadier-general.

By 1866, Woods had settled in Alabama, resumed his practice in Mobile, become a cotton planter, and joined the Republican party. When Grant appointed him judge of the United States Circuit Court, Woods moved to Atlanta.[36] In elevating him to the Supreme Court, Hayes honored the sitting judges of the lower federal courts and also gave the South another seat on the high court. Though a transplanted northerner, the new judge supported restrictions upon the Negro. Woods served six years and wrote 218 opinions. While a jurist of only average abilities, Waite liked his capacity for work and told Hayes, "You have made the best possible choice under the circumstances."[37]

Notes

1. See the excellent sketch of Garfield in the introduction to Harry J. Brown and Frederick D. Williams, *The Diary of James A. Garfield* (East Lansing: Michigan State University Press, 1967), I, ix–lxx. Hayes to Garfield, March 10, 1877, Hayes Papers, RBHL.

2. Indianapolis *News*, January 18, 1893, Burgoon Collection, Box 6, RBHL.

3. Hayes, Diary, July 1, 1870, Hayes Papers, RBHL.

4. Ibid., December 17, 1880; H. Wayne Morgan, *From Hayes to McKinley* (Syracuse: Syracuse University Press, 1969), 73–74.

5. Hayes, Diary, March 26, 1879.

6. Ibid., April 19, 1888.

7. Ibid., November 6, 1878.

8. Ibid., January 16, 1881.

9. For a good illustration of the Old Senate Chamber, see Stefan Lorant, *The Glorious Burden* (New York: Harper & Row, 1968), 336–337. The historic chamber was described in graphic detail by a contemporary observer: "The hall is small but one of the handsomest in the Capitol. It is semicircular in form, is seventy-five feet long, forty-five feet high, and forty-five feet wide in the centre, which is the widest part. A row of handsome green pillars of Potomac marble extends across the eastern, or rear side of the hall, and the wall which sweeps around the western side, is ornamented with pilasters of the same material. The ceiling is in the form of a dome, is very beautiful, and is ornamented with square caissons of stucco. A large skylight in the centre of the room lights the chamber. A handsome white marble clock is placed over the main door which is on the western side. Opposite, from the eastern wall, a large gilded eagle spreads his wings above a raised platform, railed in, and tastefully draped, along which are arranged the comfortable armchairs of the Chief Justice and his associates, the former being in the centre. Above them is still the old 'eastern gallery of the Senate,' so famous in the history of the country. The desks and seats of the lawyers are ranged in front of the Court, and enclosed by a tasteful railing. The floor is covered with soft, heavy carpets; cushioned benches for spectators are placed along the semicircular wall, and busts of John Jay, John Rutledge, Oliver Ellsworth, and John Marshall, former Chief Justices, adorn the hall." Carl Brent Swisher, *Stephen J. Field: Craftsman of the Law* (Washington: The Brookings Institution, 1930), 126–127.

10. The sketch of Waite is based largely upon an excellent biography of the Justice: Peter Magrath, *Morrison R. Waite: The Triumph of Character* (New York: The Macmillan Company, 1963).

11. Ibid., 263.

12. "Morrison Remick Waite," *The National Cyclopedia of American Biography* (New York: James T. White & Company, 1891), I, 30. Hayes and Waite both received honorary doctorates from Kenyon College, and each served on the board of trustees of the Peabody Fund. Both, incidentally, also liked to eat oysters.

13. Magrath, *Waite*, 173–191.

14. Hayes, Diary, March 23, 1888.

15. The best biography is Philip Greely Clifford, *Nathan Clifford, Democrat (1803–1881)* (New York: G. P. Putnam's Sons, 1922).

16. Magrath, *Waite*, 260.

17. The best life of Field is Swisher, *Stephen J. Field.*

18. *In re Neagle*, 135 U.S. 1. Neagle was a deputy United States Marshal assigned as a bodyguard to Justice Field during the latter's duty in holding circuit court. Field's life had been threatened by David S. Terry who had been imprisoned on a sentence imposed by Justice Field. Terry attacked Field, whereupon Neagle shot and killed him. Neagle was arrested by local authorities for murder but was released by the federal circuit court on a writ of habeas corpus. See Gary L. Roberts, "In Pursuit of Duty," *The American West* 7 (September 1970): 26–33, 62–63.

19. See Magrath, *Waite*, 101, 292–94, and Willard L. King, *Lincoln's Manager, David Davis* (Cambridge: Harvard University Press, 1960), 289–293.

20. The standard biography is by Charles Fairman, *Mr. Justice Miller and the Supreme Court, 1862–1890* (Cambridge: Harvard University Press, 1939).

21. See the sketch by Charles Fairman, "Joseph P. Bradley," in Allison Dunham and Philip B. Kurland, eds., *Mr. Justice* (Chicago: University of Chicago Press, 1956), 65–89.

22. Francis S. Philbrick, "William Strong," *The Dictionary of American Biography* (New York: Charles Scribner's Sons, 1936), XVIII, 153–155.

23. "Mr. Justice Swayne," May 1, 1881, pamphlet, RBHL.

24. Magrath, *Waite*, 7–8, 100, 265–66.

25. Ibid., 101, 268–69.

26. The controversial appointment of Matthews is treated in Magrath, *Waite*, 243–246. Magrath suggests that Jay Gould, rather than Hayes, "held" Garfield to Matthews' renomination.

27. See the sketch by Alan F. Westin, "Mr. Justice Harlan," in Durham and Kurland, eds., *Mr. Justice*, 93–128; and an earlier article by Westin, "John Marshall Harlan and the Constitutional Rights of Negroes: The Transformation of a Southerner," *Yale Law Journal* 66 (1957): 637–710.

28. Hayes to William Henry Smith, September 29, 1877, Smith Papers, Indiana Historical Society, Indianapolis.

29. Smith to Hayes, October 3, 1877, Hayes Papers, RBHL.

30. James F. Wilson to William Boyd Allison, Box 231, Allison Mss., Iowa State Department of History and Archives, Des Moines.

31. Cortez A. M. Ewing, *The Judges of the Supreme Court, 1789–1937* (Minneapolis: The University of Minnesota Press, 1938), 23–24.

32. Charles Henry Butler, *A Century at the Bar of the Supreme Court of the United States* (New York: G. P. Putnam's Sons, 1942), 173.

33. Westin, "Mr. Justice Harlan," 117.

34. Magrath, *Waite*, 300–301; "White House Social Register," passim, Hayes Papers, RBHL.

35. Magrath, *Waite*, 120; Joseph P. Bradley to Hayes, May 9, 1877, December 31, 1880, Hayes Papers, RBHL.

36. Alonzo H. Tuttle, "William Burnham Woods," *Dictionary of American Biography* (New York: Charles Scribner's Sons, 1936), XX, 505–506.

37. Waite to Hayes, January 4, 1881, cited in Magrath, *Waite*, 269.

Part III

PROBLEMS AND
POLICIES

8

The Southern Issue

Among the domestic issues Republican administrations from
Hayes to McKinley faced, none proved more difficult to solve than
the southern question. Presidents Hayes, Garfield, Arthur, and Harrison all attempted to win back the southern states for their party,
yet each met with conspicuous failure. In the twentieth century,
other Republican leaders—Theodore Roosevelt, Taft, Hoover,
Eisenhower, and Nixon—have also sought to break the solid South
through a variety of methods, but without lasting success. The
effort has been largely an exercise in futility, a futility born chiefly
of the failure of Reconstruction.[1]

The secession of the South from the Union in 1860–1861 and the
departure of southern Democrats from Congress gave the Republicans unchallenged control of all three branches of the federal
government for more than a decade. The election after the Civil
War of additional Republican representatives from an occupied
South further entrenched the party in power. By 1872, the peak of
their strength, the Republicans dominated North, West, and South
and seemed destined to be the nation's majority party indefi-
nitely. But the congressional elections of 1874 shattered this
prospect as the Republicans lost control of the House and the
resurgent Democrats gained ten seats in the Senate. The new
alignment came about partly because of closer party competition
in the eastern and central states—Connecticut, New York, New
Jersey, Ohio, Indiana, and Illinois— and partly because Democratic
supremacy became synonymous with white supremacy in the
New South.

In an effort to restore their former ascendancy, the Republicans
evolved several strategies. To win the doubtful states, they put
together presidential tickets representing the central states and
New York like the 1876 slate of Hayes and Wheeler. To break
the Democratic South, Republican leaders tried three distinct and

contradictory techniques from 1877 to 1892. One, pursued by Hayes, aimed at winning white southerners to Republicanism by cooperation and conciliation. A second tactic, followed by Chester Arthur, concentrated on making common cause with splinter groups acting independently of the Democratic organization. A third policy, identified with Benjamin Harrison, involved a return to military control. None of these approaches worked for the Republicans, and, without representation from the South, they could not keep control of the House of Representatives. Their strength in northern and western states, however, gave them reasonable expectations of organizing the Senate and winning the presidency.

The policy of Rutherford Hayes toward the South departed significantly from the Reconstruction program of enforcing the Fourteenth and Fifteenth amendments. Hayes replaced coercion with conciliation. Although he admired President Grant as a soldier and supported the Reconstruction measures as a fledgling Congressman in the late 1860s, Hayes gradually grew disillusioned with the Radical Republican policy and favored reunion of the sections and races. Whereas the party of Grant had maintained its control in the southern states by military force, systematic disfranchisement of southern whites, and the strength of carpetbagger and Negro votes, Hayes tried to follow a different tack. He felt that the policy of military interference frustrated Republican chances of permanent success in the South. His new policy was called a "total departure from the principles, traditions, and wishes of the party."[2] Convinced that the country and most white southerners would welcome a policy of moderation, he issued orders to transfer to the nearest army barracks the few remaining federal officers and soldiers still stationed in South Carolina and Louisiana for the purpose of upholding carpetbag governments.

This so-called withdrawal of the troops by Hayes in April 1877 is usually cited as the formal ending of Reconstruction and has given him a reputation as a "statesman of reunion" and "healer of strife." Actually the Grant administration had already abandoned "bayonet rule" by reassigning most of the troops protecting carpetbag governments before Hayes ever took office. Furthermore the idea of withdrawal is somewhat misleading, since the troops did not leave the state in which they were stationed but simply returned to their regular barracks nearby. Some of them did receive transfers in early and mid-1877 but for reasons other than the disappearance of military rule in the South.

The entire United States Army, plus Indian scouts, chaplains, medical personnel, ordinance, quartermaster sergeants, and West

Point cadets, totaled only about 25,000 men in 1876–1877, and
most of them were either engaged in fighting Indians on the Plains
or protecting the Mexican and Indian frontier of Texas. Omitting
Texas, just 3,280 officers and men were on duty in the South at
the end of fiscal 1876, and most of these were there primarily
to assist revenue officers or to guard seacoast fortifications. In
Louisiana troops were widely scattered in sixty-two places. Hayes'
order to remove the troops from the capitols at Columbia and
New Orleans did not cause a single soldier to leave the South.
It is true that some left later in the year because railroad strikes
or Indian raids and wars urgently required their presence
elsewhere.[3]

The real objective of the Hayes southern policy was neither
removal of the troops nor restoration of home rule but rather a
change in the base of Republican support to make it a truly national
party. By 1877, most northerners agreed with southerners that
the Negro was not prepared for equality and that the South should
be allowed to deal with the situation in its own way. Hayes therefore reluctantly decided largely to bypass Negro and carpetbagger
leadership in the Republican party of the South and to cultivate
instead the friendship of white southern conservatives in the
expectation of winning them to the Republican side. In other
words, rather than relying upon black votes for the main strength
of the Republican party, the new President thought he might shift
the emphasis away from the race question by splitting the southern
white vote along economic lines through a program of national
aid for internal improvements. This would appeal to southern
Whigs, whose party had sponsored this policy, and also to discontented southern Democrats, who believed that northern Democrats
had forsaken them on the issue of federal aid for state projects.
A former Whig himself, Hayes hoped that by using conciliation
in place of coercion he could win erstwhile southern Whigs to
the Republican party, take the race issue out of politics, and create
a national Republican coalition based on economic rather than
on sectional issues. Hayes also believed that the goodwill of southern whites would provide far better protection for the freedmen
than federal bayonets. If such a shift could be effected, Hayes
thought the Republicans could win in North Carolina and have
a fair chance in Maryland, Virginia, Tennessee, and Arkansas.
The solid South would be broken, and two-party politics would
once more flourish in the region. At the same time, he hoped
to retain the support of southern blacks.

In this context, Hayes proceeded to implement his southern
strategy. David M. Key, a southern Democrat, was chosen to be

Postmaster General, a politically potent position for its power over patronage. The transfer of the troops then became imperative. Hayes could scarcely do otherwise if he wished to command the respect of southern whites. Besides, northern Republicans and the business community favored the idea and the southern Republican governments were steadily weakening anyway. Nor could additional troops be brought in to bolster the tottering carpetbag governments. Congress had reduced the size of the army and further crippled effective action by failing to make normal army appropriations to pay the officers and men.

At first Hayes, lending his support to the Texas and Pacific Railroad project in particular, spoke favorably of national aid for internal improvements in the South. Meanwhile he broke with party tradition by using his patronage power to appoint numerous southern Democrats to federal offices. In this direct way, he hoped to win over Douglas Democrats and ex-Whigs. The President also took two trips into the South to meet the southerners on their home ground and to see at close range how well his policy was working. Generally speaking, he was enthusiastically received, and he misinterpreted the warm welcome and prolonged cheering as proof that he could restore the party balance.

Part of the trouble arose from the difficulty the southerners, however hospitable to Hayes, had in breaking their traditional party allegiance and racial prejudices. They admired Hayes and his sentiments, but desired greater assurance of his sincerity toward them. The President also made some unwise appointments. In Louisiana, forty-seven ousted Negro members of the legislature received federal jobs. The ex-carpetbag governor of Louisiana, S. B. Packard, secured the Liverpool consulship, one of the most lucrative of all appointments in the President's power to bestow. Then too, all of the members of the controversial Louisiana Returning Board, which had helped Hayes become President, and some of their relatives and secretaries received government positions. Hayes later acknowledged he had erred: "In my anxiety to complete the great work of pacification, I have neglected to give due attention to the civil service—to the appointments and removals. The result is, some bad appointments have been made. Some removals have been mistakes. There have been delays in action. All this, I must now try to correct."[4]

Some Republicans saw a possibility of strengthening their southern wing by embracing the Independent Democratic movement led so successfully in Virginia by William Mahone whose party swept the state offices in the 1879 election. But Hayes studiously avoided a coalition with "the Readjusters" since their doctrine of repudiation of the state debt did not square with his concept of orthodox Republicanism and southern conservatism. To make such an alliance would give only a temporary advantage and hurt his cause in the long run. Neither did he attempt to establish a new party or revive the old Whig party in the South. Rather his appointment policy emphasized character and ability, and he strove above all else to enlist civil servants who would command respect in their communities. To this end, he resolved to name to office native whites only if of conservative temper, blacks only if qualified, and no carpetbaggers. If no Republicans could meet these standards, then he was willing to appoint Douglas Democrats or ex-Whigs.

Stalwarts and carpetbaggers naturally opposed the Hayes policy because it meant their doom. Besides they were also unhappy over the President's independence in making cabinet appointments without consulting the Senate, and they did not like his civil-service reform either. To them Hayes seemed a traitor, undoing the Civil War victory won by their hero General Grant and the Grand Army of the Republic. The Hayes program also seemed to abandon the Negro to his prewar status.

The most curious response to Hayes' new departure policy came from the Negro Republicans of the South. Although they were placed at the mercy of state governments controlled by their white rivals, they still went along with the Hayes plan, partly because they thought of it as an experiment, which would be quickly ended if it resulted in curtailment of their rights, and partly because they had no other place to go. Many blacks also believed Grant would succeed Hayes as President and resume military protection of their rights.

Meantime, a few Negro leaders, notably John M. Langston and Frederick Douglass, received personal recognition from Hayes in the form of presidential appointments respectively as minister to Haiti and marshal for the District of Columbia. But the President steadfastly refused to give control of patronage in the southern states to Negro politicians even when they were of the prestige of Blanche K. Bruce in Mississippi or Robert B. Elliott in South Carolina.

Hayes undoubtedly believed southern whites when they told him during his tour of the South that they would honor full civil and political rights for black citizens. He also became thoroughly convinced that the price of such recognition was no further interference in the affairs of southern state governments by the national administration. As a Victorian gentleman of humanitarian instincts, Hayes sincerely hoped Negroes would think of him as their friend and protector, and nothing upset him more than repeated allegations that he was hurting their cause. He failed to understand that two-and-one-half centuries of bondage could not be altered by a few sentiments of goodwill uttered in pleasant circumstances.

A bad omen occurred in October 1877 when the southern Democrats refused to desert their party in sufficient numbers to make James A. Garfield, the Hayes floor leader, Speaker of the House. A bigger political blow to the Hayes southern policy came with the midyear congressional elections of 1878 when Hayes eagerly awaited vindication of his program. To his surprise and chagrin, the referendum went badly. The Republican party, instead of reviving, all but disappeared in the South. No Republican governors were elected, and only three Congressmen were sent to the House. In 1876, there had been nine. The party suffered considerable loss of support in both white and black counties. Even so confirmed an idealist as Hayes confessed to a reporter, "I am reluctantly forced to admit that the experiment was a failure."[5] Still, he remained faithful to his policy, convinced that history would bear him out, but the presidential election of 1880 again confirmed the inability of his strategy to produce Republican votes in the South: Garfield failed to carry a single southern state. Undaunted, impervious to election results and attacks by Stalwarts and carpetbaggers alike, Hayes remained true to his policy to the end of his term. Without an army adequate to police the South or majority control over both houses of the legislature, Hayes took a long view of the southern question and concluded he could best serve his party and country by making a clean break with the past and giving a new tone to party government. History has confirmed his wisdom, but the problem of racial adjustment has proved to be more complicated and far less easy of solution than he envisaged.

Two years after leaving the White House, Hayes penned an optimistic footnote to his handling of the southern question:

> In 1877 I believed that a radical change of policy with respect to the South would bring ultimate safety and prosperity to the colored people and restore good feeling between the hostile sections. This change could be most successfully made by one who represented the victors in the Civil War. Many were disappointed because in the South there were those who did not accept the olive branch. I am *not* of the number. The change did its work. Not instantly, but slowly and surely. The anticipated progress is still going on. . . . Certain it is, the people of the North have not in the last six years made a greater progress in getting away from barbarism in the treatment of the colored man than the people of the South have

made in the same period. But I do not wish to institute comparisons. We are all to blame in this matter. How few can say sincerely with Dr. Haygood, "our *brother* in black."[6]

The usual interpretation of the Hayes southern policy is to say that when he removed the troops as part of his overall program to reconcile North and South, conciliate southern whites, and ingratiate the Republican party with the white South, he also abandoned the Negro in the South. Given the hindsight afforded by subsequent history it is hard to see how he might have done differently in the situation he faced in March 1877. The Grant administration, for all practical purposes, had already ended military occupation. Public opinion also favored the demise of Reconstruction. And, even if military force had been reinstituted as federal policy in the South, it would have been rendered meaningless by the lack of an army to enforce it. The situation on the Indian frontier demanded that all available soldiers be sent there. Besides Congress did not have any inclination to enlarge the army, let alone authorize appropriations for paying men already in the service.

Neither could Hayes support the carpetbag govenments on merit when they had not commanded the respect of the rest of the country. In a perceptive passage, a leading student of the situation has said of these carpetbagger regimes:

> They had not represented the Negro struggling for rights, security, and material progress. Neither had they reflected a Republican sentiment based on a political conviction and sympathy growing among southern whites. In the main, they had portrayed political shrewdness, skill in manipulating political machinery, and personal greediness. Grant's course, instead of alleviating this condition, had increased the antagonism of southern whites toward the Republican party. Hayes, Garfield, Arthur, and Harrison were fully aware that only through the addition of a sizable number of whites to the party in the South could they hope to strengthen it and make it more respectable. Each in his own way sought to attain this end. Each failed because his policy was unable to allay the fear of Negro-carpetbagger rule.[7]

Hayes' policy, however well conceived and intentioned, ran in the face of other serious obstacles. Factionalism among southern Republicans—carpetbaggers, native whites, and Negro leaders—created confusion and prevented mounting a united front against the resurgent Democrats. The Democrats, by effectively keeping black and white Republicans in the South from the polls or nullifying their votes, sharply reduced Republican strength in all the southern states. Hayes complained bitterly, "By state legislation, by frauds, by intimidation, and by violence of the most atrocious character, colored citizens have been deprived of the right of suffrage—a right guaranteed by the Constitution, and to the protection of which the people of those states have been solemnly pledged."[8]

Hayes had hoped that his policy of conciliation would encourage southern whites to allow Negroes to vote, but where white men had come to divide solely on the race question, it proved impossible to entice them away from the party identified with white supremacy no matter how attractive the alternative might be.

In a sense, Hayes was a victim of his own antebellum education and inherited beliefs. He had a passion for social harmony at a time when fierce regional, partisan, religious, ethnic, class, and racial tensions bitterly divided Americans. A conciliator by nature, a statesman who made national unity the aim of his presidency, a man suspicious of any group condoning violence as a way to achieve ends, Hayes put his confidence in the power of education, religion, and a direct appeal to the minds and hearts of individuals. To Guy Bryan, his southern friend and classmate at Kenyon, he wrote, "My theory of the Southern situation is this. Let the rights of the colored people be secured and the laws enforced only by the usual peaceful methods—by the action of the civil tribunals and wait for the healing influences of time and reflection to solve and remove the remaining difficulties. This will be a slow process, but the world moves faster than formerly, and it is plain that the politicians on both sides who seek to thrive by agitation and bitterness are losing rapidly their hold."[9] Thus, his intellectual heritage, especially a skepticism toward force and legislation, and a fear of an oppressive government, left Hayes without enthusiasm for a creative, positive state.[10]

Notes

1. For the major portion of my discussion of the southern problem, I am heavily indebted to the research findings of Professor Vincent P. De Santis, a keen student of the period and subject. See especially his monograph, *Republicans Face the Southern Question: The New Departure Years, 1877–1897* (Baltimore: The Johns Hopkins Press, 1959) and a series of five articles by De Santis, which treat the same topic in slightly different form: "Negro Dissatisfaction with Republican Policy in the South, 1882–1884," *The Journal of Negro History* 36, no. 2 (April 1951): 148–159; "Republican Efforts to 'Crack' the Democratic South," *Review of Politics* 14 (April 1952): 244–264; "President Hayes's Southern Policy," *The Journal of Southern History* 21, no. 4 (November 1955): 476–494; "President Garfield and the Solid South," *The North Carolina Historical Review* 36, no. 4 (October 1959): 442–465; "The Republican Party and the Southern Negro,

1877–1897," *The Journal of Negro History* 45, no. 2 (April 1960): 71–87. Also useful is James M. McPherson, "Coercion or Conciliation? Abolitionists Debate President Hayes's Southern Policy," *The New England Quarterly* 39 (December 1966): 474–497. An excellent retrospective article is George B. Tindall, "Southern Strategy: A Historical Perspective," *The North Carolina Historical Review* 48 (Spring 1971): 126–141, which maintains that President Eisenhower achieved a measure of success in practicing Hayes' southern policy. President Nixon's difficulty, however, in either extending or consolidating Eisenhower's example is analyzed in Reg Murphy and Hal Gulliver, *The Southern Strategy* (New York: Charles Scribner's Sons, 1971).

2. Hayes, Diary, October 24, 1877, Hayes Papers, RBHL.

3. Clarence C. Clendenen, "President Hayes' 'Withdrawal' of the Troops—An Enduring Myth," *South Carolina Historical Magazine* (October 1969): 240–250.

4. Hayes, Diary, October 24, 1877.

5. Washington *National Republican*, November 23, 1878, cited in De Santis, "President Hayes's Southern Policy," 492.

6. Hayes to B. T. Tanner, February 20, 1883, Hayes Papers, RBHL.

7. De Santis, "Republican Efforts to 'Crack' the Democratic South," 255–256.

8. Hayes, Diary, November 12, 1878.

9. Hayes to Guy M. Bryan, January 10, 1879, Hayes Papers, RBHL.

10. For an excellent discussion of Hayes' social thought, see David P. Thelen, "Rutherford B. Hayes and the Reform Tradition in the Gilded Age," *American Quarterly* 22, no. 2, pt. 1 (Summer 1970): 150–165.

9

The Great Railway
Strike

A major crisis leading to a fundamental change in the functioning of American government occurred during the summer of 1877, when the Hayes administration had been in office less than five months. For the first time, America experienced a strike of national emergency proportions involving its largest single business enterprise, the railroads.[1]

Beginning at Martinsburg, West Virginia, the strike spread immediately to other states, including Maryland, Pennsylvania, New York, Ohio, Kentucky, and Illinois. Only New England and the Old South escaped completely. Violence was commonplace, especially in Baltimore, Pittsburgh, and Chicago. At Pittsburgh, the Pennsylvania Railroad roundhouse was set on fire, and other railroad properties, comprising over 125 locomotives, more than 2,000 freight cars, and a depot, were burned with a total loss of several million dollars. Railroad strikers did not create such havoc by themselves; tramps, unemployed persons, women, and some children joined them in the massive destruction. State militiamen, privately sympathetic to the strikers, proved highly unreliable in stopping the rioting. Lacking the discipline of regular troops, they fired shots at a good many people and killed a number of innocent bystanders.

While the strike lasted only a few weeks, it caught government officials, businessmen, and the general public by surprise. Governor John Hartranft of Pennsylvania, whose state was the scene of some of the worst disorders, had just left on a western trip, satisfied that he was going away at a time "when the peace of the Commonwealth seemed assured," only to be frantically recalled by state officials.[2] Although the nation seemed totally unprepared for the calamity and lacked viable precedents for handling its first major confrontation between labor and capital, ample evidence existed to forewarn the country of impending danger. A business depression following the panic of 1873 had been particularly hard on the railroads. Competitive rate wars further lowered rail revenues. Then, to compensate for their loss of income, the railroads cut wages paid to their workers—but maintained salaries of management and paid 8 percent dividends to stockholders.

The brakemen, despite their hazardous work, received the lowest pay, averaging in the spring of 1877 about $1.75 for a twelve-hour day. The typical conductor made $2.78 per day, while firemen earned approximately $1.90 a day on most roads. Engineers might make $3.25. In contrast, Erie Railroad President Hugh J. Jewett had a contract (1874–1884) calling for a ten-year guarantee of $40,000 a year, of which $150,000 was paid in advance. These figures illustrate only part of the rail workers' predicament. At the end of a run, the train crew had to lay over, at their own expense, or ride back on their own time, paying full fare like other passengers. Even at home, unpaid time was common; the workers had to be in constant readiness for work, and in 1877, idle days increased as companies attempted to spread the available work among their employees. Meanwhile a series of wage cuts began. As it was, with temporary layoffs, brakemen and firemen made only $30 a month. After meeting board bills, as little as $10 a month remained to support their families.[3] The resistance point was reached when an additional 10 percent wage reduction was put into effect in the summer of 1877.

Thus on July 16, 1877, the day when the latest wage cut went into effect, strikes started at the B&O Camden Station in Baltimore and at Martinsburg, West Virginia. Police promptly arrested the Maryland strike leaders but, in Martinsburg, as a result of pro-worker sympathy among the townspeople and the inadequacy of the local police force, a similar attempt by the police failed. State militia, quickly ordered to the scene, were equally ineffective as strikebreakers. The state lacked an adequate police force and the legislature, not in session, could not be convened soon enough to deal with the emergency. Alarmed, President John W. Garrett of the B&O urgently requested Governor Henry M. Mathews to call upon President Hayes for federal troops. Hayes cautiously requested more information. How many insurgents were there? Why was West Virginia unable to cope with the crisis? Mathews replied that eight hundred rioters were too many for the mere forty volunteers he could depend upon to give effective resistance. Hayes consequently ordered to Martinsburg two small detachments from Fort McHenry and from the Washington arsenal with instructions to wait for a presidential proclamation. Within a day,

260 troops converged on Martinsburg; a proclamation warning against further disorder was duly circulated; and peace was restored without bloodshed.

Hayes had acted within the context of prior administrative experience. In 1876, while governor of Ohio, he had sent state militia to quell rioting in the coal mining area around Massillon, in circumstances strikingly similar to those he faced while President. When Ohio mine operators asked the local sheriff to protect their property, the sheriff, unable to succeed without help, petitioned Governor Hayes for state troopers. Hayes responded with a proclamation warning strikers against any further lawless action and sent his adjutant general to inspect the situation. Only after he received corroborating evidence did he dispatch the militia to Massillon.[4]

Shortly after the Martinsburg episode, striking trainmen walked off the job in several other states and began rioting, burning, and plundering. State militia were called out to aid local police forces. In Baltimore, after ten persons died in a pitched battle, Governor John Lee Carroll asked for help. Hayes replied with a second proclamation backed by troops under the command of General W. S. Hancock. As in West Virginia, respect for law and order resumed the moment United States troops appeared. General Hancock went next to his own state of Pennsylvania where the use of state militia had intensified rather than stopped the violence, and had caused at Pittsburgh nearly one hundred deaths and scores of injuries. President Hayes, aware of the deteriorating situation, anxiously awaited a requisition for troops from Governor Hartranft. An appeal did reach him on July 22, but it came from subordinates in Harrisburg and not from the absent governor. The next day Hayes received the first of four frantic telegrams from Hartranft, each one more specific in requesting aid, until the exact constitutional language Hayes insisted upon appeared: "Domestic insurrection exists in Pennsylvania which the State authorities are unable to suppress and the legislature is not in session and cannot be convened in time."[5]

Thereupon Hayes issued his third proclamation against domestic violence in a specific state and gave General Hancock full authority to act as necessary in restoring order. In concert with Hartranft, this was speedily accomplished without further bloodshed. By this time, Ohio, Indiana, and Illinois were also strikebound. Governor Thomas L. Young of Ohio asked for arms from the federal arsenal in Columbus instead of troops. His request was honored.

Indiana posed a somewhat different problem. A small number of federal troops guarded a large federal arsenal in Indianapolis.

When local authorities sensed the need for reinforcements, Governor James D. Williams asked Hayes for help from the federal detachment guarding the arsenal. He was refused on the ground that federal forces could be used only to protect United States property or to enforce processes of federal courts. Actually many of the state's railroads were in receivership over which United States marshals held responsibility. While denying the direct request of Governor Williams, Hayes did send troops to Indiana but made them responsible to federal authorities. Henceforth persons arrested for obstructing trains of companies in the hands of receivers were convicted of contempt by federal courts.

United States troops, numbering 650, also went to Chicago at the request of Governor Shelby M. Cullom, again with instructions simply to protect government property and enforce federal court orders. No further trouble ensued. Downstate, at East St. Louis, federal troops were employed to protect railroads operating under receivers appointed by federal judges. Once more the policy worked to settle the dispute without further property damage.

Meanwhile Hayes issued special executive orders to the armed forces to secure all federal buildings—arsenals, customhouses, subtreasuries—for the duration of the strikes. "In the New York City area, for example, Army regulars and Marines were used to supplement the already armed treasury clerks who were guarding $100 million in the vaults of the subtreasury, armed forces were dispatched to protect government property in Brooklyn, and a Navy monitor was stationed in New York harbor to protect the United States custom-house."[6]

Elsewhere the governors of Michigan, Wisconsin, and California requested federal assistance, which was not forthcoming, and, as later events proved, unnecessary. A total of fourteen states experienced varying degrees of disorder, and most states suffered from the tieup of rail transport and passenger service. It should be observed that federal troops saw little or no action against mobs during the 1877 strikes. Either they arrived after the most serious trouble had passed or their presence inspired a return to law and order and won the respect of all citizens. They did their job so well that not a single soldier or civilian lost his life.

The total response of President Hayes to telegrams from nine governors requesting help in restoring domestic tranquillity, so violently disrupted by the nation's first great industrial strike, is highly significant in several respects. First, his action marks the beginning of a federal strike policy and a move away from laissez-faire government. Prior to 1877, the state and local governments were primarily responsible for maintaining law and order.

Second, the railway crisis illustrates the manner in which President Hayes created important policy precedents by administrative decisions that did not require approval of a Congress in which his party lacked a majority. As Congress was not in session during the railway strike, the federal courts and the chief executive had to deal with the immediate problem. Furthermore, Congress completely abrogated its primary responsibility by failing to enact any labor reform legislation once order was restored. Third, the entire sequence of events demonstrates the exercise of "prudence and care" by the President in the use of his powers.[7] He was not stampeded into hasty or ill-advised action, nor did he overcommit himself and lose control of the situation. What is more, he achieved his objective and gained added respect and prestige for presidential authority.

Once the initial shock wave of the first general strike in America[8] awakened the populace to the very serious nature of the struggle between capital and labor, President Hayes became a symbol of hope to all those who felt that their lives or their property were in danger. Businessmen, government officials, and labor leaders alike sent him a flood of messages urging federal intervention to avert chaos. At the peak of the turmoil, all five trunk railroad lines from the Midwest to the East were closed, freight traffic stopped, and passenger and mail trains were delayed for many hours. Food supplies, especially perishables, quickly disappeared since, even under the best of conditions, a lack of refrigeration kept provisions low in the hot summer months. Unemployment rose swiftly and loss of income mounted as various industries and businesses dependent upon the railroads ceased normal operations.

Faced with such a sudden and unexpected turn of events, the chief executive quickly weighed his alternatives. To act without reflection could be disastrous. Since his very title to the presidency was still under a cloud of suspicion and distrust, any use of troops against American citizens was a risky business not calculated to enhance his popularity. To do nothing was out of the question, if for no other reason than the statutory requirement of some response to Governor Mathew's request for aid.[9] No really comparable federal precedent existed for the President's guidance. The army, after surpassing one million men in 1865, steadily declined in strength under congressional directive to a mere 25,000 men, and most of these soldiers were stationed in the West to guard the Mexican border or keep the Indians in check. Relatively few officers and men who could be reassigned to emergency patrol duty in eastern cities remained. Another handicap was the failure of Congress to vote an army appropriation bill before adjournment, so that wages were in arrears after July 1. The President wished to act upon accurate intelligence. As one who knew from observation and experience the shortcomings of newspaper accounts and the tendency of letter writers to partisan exaggeration, he sought a reliable and independent news media.

Hayes worked out a neat solution to his dilemma. Beginning on July 21, he met daily with his cabinet until the crisis subsided.[10] As a method of ascertaining facts, he relied upon cryptic messages transmitted by the army Signal Corps from officers and trusted confidants in the field. To avoid any technical or legal possibility of constitutional questions arising over his intervention, he determined to send troops only upon the call of a governor seeking to suppress domestic violence or a federal judge endeavoring to protect federal property or to enforce a court order. The Hayes administration made no effort to justify federal intervention as a protection of the uninterrupted flow of United States mails or interstate commerce. Hayes also issued carefully phrased presidential proclamations and instructions before authorizing any use of United States troops. Hayes and his cabinet considered, but rejected, more extreme measures, such as declaring martial law or sending troops without a request from state officials. In general the administration assumed a posture of relative neutrality in the conflict between labor and capital, used troops only sparingly, and achieved order without more bloodshed.

Certain other aspects of the strikes deserve notice, especially the blockage of mail and the conviction of strikers for obstructing railroads operated by receivers.[11] Mail delays grew most acute during the week of July 22 to 28 and came up as a matter for cabinet discussion. Strikers had tried to avoid any interference with the mail service by offering to pass mail trains freely through their lines or to permit specials composed only of mail cars to run past their barricades; but, in practice, the mail was delayed because it was blocked by freight-choked yards or by railroad companies that refused to operate at a loss trains carrying just mail and no passengers.

Postal officials attempted to negotiate a compromise in which the railroads would carry the mail on regular passenger trains as far as possible and then transfer it to special cars at trouble spots. The railroad executives flatly refused to cooperate. Ultimately the Hayes administration declared that any passenger train carrying mail was a mail train and that persons who interfered would be prosecuted. This decision immediately ended any further threat to the mails in the Chicago area, but actually benefited the companies more than the strikers by providing federal courts with a way to convict strikers. At several trials in Indianapolis, Philadelphia, and Portland, Maine, strikers were found guilty in this fashion.

Another technique of evolving federal strike policy developed from the decisions of certain federal judges in the Midwest where a number of nearly bankrupt railroads were operated by receivers under court protection, free from the demands of stockholders and creditors. The legal concept that any railroad in receivership could be protected against strikers gained wide acceptance through the opinions of Thomas S. Drummond, Walter Q. Gresham, and Samuel H. Treat, all judges of the Seventh Circuit, which included Illinois, Indiana, and Wisconsin. In effect these judges authorized United States marshals to safeguard all railroad property under court custody and to summon military aid if needed. The Hayes cabinet endorsed this policy and suggested it be used elsewhere by federal judges to stop strikes. Judge Drummond became the first federal judge to apply the new procedure, sentencing two dozen railway strikers for contempt of court. As he reasoned, by interfering with a railroad, strikers disrupted the transportation of persons, property, and the mails, which was a quasipublic function.

In retrospect, the President's handling of the emergency had both positive and negative features. On the positive side, he exercised considerable restraint while under great pressure and developed a calm and deliberate policy firmly based in constitutional and statute law. It must be remembered he governed at a time when presidential authority was far more limited than today, with little federal experience to guide him, and a pitifully small army to enforce his decisions. By issuing exact orders and employing a few well-disciplined troops, he surmounted the crisis. Throughout an anxious fortnight, he kept himself accurately informed and met regularly with his chief advisers. That his policy worked so well may be attributed to the long experience of the President and his cabinet officers in war and politics. Each was a man with a strong background of leadership. Together they hammered out a more reasoned response than any of them might have evolved alone. They understood the art of the possible, reckoned with the limited enforcement power at their disposal, and appraised the immediate issues on the basis of thoroughly reliable reports from the scenes of violence.

On the less favorable side, Hayes understood only too well that restoration of order did not solve the larger issue at hand between labor and capital. "The strikes have been put down by force," he wrote in his diary, "but now for the *real* remedy. Can't something [be] done by education of the strikers, by judicious control of the capitalists, by wise general policy to end or diminish the evil? The railroad strikers, as a rule, are good men, sober, intelligent, and industrious." He also quickly countered the claim of some newspapers that the strikes were anarchist-inspired and an assault upon the national government: "Prevailing disorders give no evidence of a spirit of communism because the attacks of the mob have not been directed against the property of the general public, but against the corporations with which the laboring element is at war."[12]

More seriously, however, the President's policy amounted to strikebreaking in the effort to restore normal railway service. It did not send the workers and management to a bargaining table or alleviate the plight of the railroaders. The attitude of the courts left much to be desired. Why should a railroad in the hands of receivers have a special status? "Rights and protections," one prominent jurist declared, "ought to be the same everywhere; the property which the receiver manages for its owners is no more sacred than that which the owners manage in person; it ought to have the same protection and no more." The contempt proceedings against the strikers also were open to question. To punish as judicial contempts, without a jury trial, acts not committed in the presence of the court, stretched the meaning of fairness and justice to absurd ends.

What then of the overall impact of the 1877 railway strikes? In many ways, they created unfortunate precedents for the future. Labor reform, the real need, did not follow the restoration of law and order. Capital still held the upper hand. Courts and lawyers remained business-oriented, looking upon corporations as privileged "persons," and unions, still lacking in leadership and planning, as suspect organizations whose members might be prosecuted individually as conspirators if disputes arose between employers and employees. The public showed little sympathy for or understanding of the basic problem. The strikes did not last long enough to compel a change in public attitude or congressional reform. Meanwhile the executive and judiciary, acting in the heat of crisis, did not evolve a long-term policy in a realm not really their responsibility in 1877.

But all was not lost. Gains were registered as some roads rescinded their wage cuts. Indeed the Great Strike of 1877 came very close to success as the private correspondence of management reveals.[13] *The New York Times* called it "a drawn battle." Robert V. Bruce, who has made the most thorough study of the 1877 strikes, concludes:

> Even on the roads where pay was not raised, what had the men lost? The universality of the strike prevented reprisals against more

than a small fraction of strikers. The rest lost only one or two weeks' wages. But since they were paid by the trip or the mile, most made up at least part of those wages in the subsequent rush of business. . . . If the railroad wage-cutting experiment had succeeded, it would probably have been repeated as pitilessly as among the miners. The Great Strike put a stop to that, not only on railroads but elsewhere. And in so doing (as *Iron Age* duly and gratefully noted) it also put a floor under prices, thus helping to break the spiral of deflation and depression. . . . In October the [New York] Central restored half of the July cut, and in February 1880 it restored the rest. Other roads followed suit, including the Pennsylvania.[14]

The B&O remedied many grievances. Its men received passes home during layovers, regular runs with full-time work, and a quarter-day's pay whether the train left or not. The Michigan Central increased wages by 4 to 12 percent. Back wages and full pay for July were honored by other railroads. Employee morale became a matter of concern in management's labor policy, and companies began to consider written contracts, relief funds, and insurance plans. It took another decade for these reforms to materialize, but the tide changed perceptively in the aftermath of the 1877 violence.

Moreover the great strike marked a decided shift in the responsibility of the federal government in labor disputes and launched the first real governmental effort to regulate strikes in the public interest. That Hayes represented this newer attitude is reflected in a postpresidential diary entry for May 2, 1886: "It may be truly said that for twenty-five years, at least, railroad workingmen have had too little, and railroad capitalists and managers, those who have controlled and manipulated railroads, have had too much of their earnings—or too much of the money made out of them. The public has been neglected; its rights and interests disregarded. Not enough men employed—not paid enough—etc., etc. The railroads should be under a wise, watchful, and powerful supervision of the Government."[15] It is also worthy to note that, despite his own ties and those of his cabinet to the railroads, President Hayes did not allow the companies to dictate policy.[16] He acted consistently according to his own concept of the public good.

Notes

1. I have relied upon the following sources in preparing this chapter: Robert V. Bruce, *1877: Year of Violence* (Indianapolis: The Bobbs-Merrill Company, Inc., 1959); Gerald T. Eggert, *Railroad Labor Disputes: The Beginnings of Federal Strike Policy* (Ann Arbor: The University of Michigan Press, 1967); Bennett Milton Rich, *The Presidents and Civil Disorder* (Washington: The Brookings Institution, 1941).

2. Cited in Rich, *Presidents and Civil Disorder*, 74.

3. Ibid., 72; Bruce, *1877: Year of Violence*, 44–47, 53.

4. Eggert, *Railroad Labor Disputes*, 29.

5. Rich, *Presidents and Civil Disorder*, 76.

6. Eggert, *Railroad Labor Disputes*, 34.

7. Washington *National Republican*, editorial, July 28, 1877.

8. See David T. Burbank, *Reign of the Rabble: The St. Louis General Strike of 1877* (New York: Augustus M. Kelley, 1966).

9. Eggert, *Railroad Labor Disputes*, 27.

10. See George Frederick Howe, "President Hayes's Notes of Four Cabinet Meetings," *American Historical Review* 37 (January 1932): 286–289.

11. Eggert, *Railroad Labor Disputes*, 35–47.

12. Hayes, Diary, April 5, 1877, Hayes Papers, RBHL.

13. Bruce, *1877: Year of Violence*, 283–284.

14. Ibid., 301–302.

15. Hayes, Diary, May 2, 1886.

16. Eggert, *Railroad Labor Disputes*, 27–29. Thomas A. Scott, president of the Pennsylvania Railroad, was prominent in the negotiations settling the disputed election of 1876 in Hayes' favor. Hayes also used two of Scott's private railway cars in traveling to his inauguration. Hayes, Diary March 14, 1877.

10

The Use of Executive Power

Few persons recognize the contribution of Rutherford Hayes to the office of the presidency. At the time he assumed office, the federal administrative machinery badly needly a major reorganization. While he did not fully succeed in revitalizing the bureaucracy, he did effectively terminate the erosion of executive authority into the hands of the legislative branch. In four major struggles with the Congress, he emerged triumphant and went a long way toward rejuvenating the powers of the presidency.[1]

Growing administrative weaknesses and inefficiency had characterized the federal government for the dozen years before Hayes became President. Morality and morale among government workers hit bottom. The amount of business imposed upon the Washington bureaucracy doubled during the 1870s and grew further complicated as the number of truly competent and experienced persons in the civil service steadily dwindled under the operation of the spoils system and the principal of rotation in office. Nor did better methods of handling the increased work load materialize quickly enough. Technology applied to the art of government seemed virtually unknown. Low-salaried clerks laboriously copied everything by hand, and executive orders from one government official to another were still transmitted by messengers. Typewriters did not become important until the 1880s, and it was considered quite a marvel when Secretary of Navy Thompson installed a telephone between his office and the navy yard three miles away.[2] Edison had not yet patented his various office machines or improved on the work of other inventors. Executive talent also appeared sadly lacking as qualified persons preferred positions in private employment. Hayes suffered under this very handicap in constituting his executive office staff. After General Manning F. Force declined the appointment of private secretary as beneath his dignity, and William Henry Smith did not think it worth accepting, the President named his improvident college chum, William K. Rogers, to the position and then partly redeemed the unsatisfactory situation by asking his second son, Webb C. Hayes, to serve as his confidential secretary.

Beneath such obvious bureaucratic shortcomings lurked the forces of party patronage and powerful pressure groups, like the Grand Army of the Republic, not to mention the constant meddling of congressional leaders in administrative affairs. James A. Garfield neatly summarized the first of these administrative handicaps in 1877: "During the last twenty-five years, it has been understood, by the Congress and the people, that offices are to be obtained by the aid of senators and representatives, who thus become the dispensers, sometimes the brokers of patronage.... The usurpation, by the senate, of a large share of the appointing power... has resulted in seriously crippling the just powers of the executive, and has placed in the hands of senators and representatives a power most corrupting and dangerous."[3] The GAR, like veteran groups of all wars, expected government largesse in peacetime. To the usual demand for preference in government employment, the Union soldiers added a potent argument, which colored the constituency of the federal departments: the loyalty issue. No ex-Confederate should be appointed to a job in a government he had fought to overthrow. A Rebel simply could not be trusted with political power. Conversely, those who struggled to preserve the Union ought to be rewarded for their patriotism.

As for the authority of the presidency in 1877, the Lincoln model of strong executive leadership lay in shambles, shattered by the near conviction of Andrew Johnson on impeachment charges, and the many unwise appointments by President Grant of his old army friends and cronies to offices they were either incompetent to fill or ready to betray by corrupt behavior.

Thus, when President Hayes came to the White House, he inherited an office greatly weakened by a steady erosion of power and prestige during the administrations of his two immediate predecessors and an inept bureaucracy based upon the twin vices of party patronage and assessment of officeholders for political contributions, instead of upon virtues like fitness for duty and dedication to the general welfare. A clear challenge confronted the President. He would have to reassert presidential prerogatives in a forceful manner and supplant the spoils system with the merit principle of office-holding.

Hayes is generally classified with those Presidents who have subscribed to the Whig theory of executive authority, which limits a President to the passive role of administering policy formulated by Congress. His recorded statements and actions in office, however, suggest that he believed in a more vigorous concept of executive power. To a publicist who in 1889 applied for information on the subject, he carefully distinguished between theory and practice, maintaining that few writers or public persons understood the real power of the American executive. Practically, he said, the President had the nation in his hand. He was Commander-in-Chief of the army and navy and had control of foreign affairs. He could at any time force Congress into war with foreign powers. "The executive power is large because not defined in the Constitution. The real test has never come," Hayes asserted, "because the Presidents have, down to the present, been conservative, or what might be called conscientious, men, and have kept within limited range. And there is an unwritten law of usage that has come to regulate an average administration. But if a Napoleon ever became President, he could make the executive almost what he wished to make it. The war power of President Lincoln went to lengths which could scarcely be surpassed in despotic principle." Hayes further observed "that much of the legislation of Congress was ordinarily initiated by the President. The Constitution did not provide for this, but in practice it was done. A large part of legislation was first considered in Cabinet, and then started in Congress by contact privately between the secretaries and the committees of Congress."[4]

In his own presidential experience, Hayes stoutly resisted the Senate oligarchy in choosing the members of his cabinet and gaining confirmation for them; asserted anew his power of removal and appointment by reforming the New York Custom House; protested congressional efforts to dictate the executive decision-making process by successfully vetoing no less than seven badly needed appropriation bills because of coercive legislative riders attached to them; and last, but equally important, effectively withstood the ill-fated Potter Investigation, a Democratic congressional attempt to unseat him by reopening the disputed election controversy. By winning four such decisive victories over the Congress, Hayes not only defended the separation-of-powers principle but also turned the tide against any further legislative encroachment on executive prerogatives. In so doing, he prepared the way for President Garfield's convincing triumph over the New York Senators, Roscoe Conkling and Thomas C. Platt.

One of the more curious aspects about Hayes' theory of presidential power was his advocacy of a single term, which he believed should be amended to six years instead of being limited to four years. As early as his letter of acceptance of July 8, 1876, Hayes indicated his "inflexible purpose," if elected, to serve only one term and then to retire voluntarily from the political scene. He believed that "restoration of the civil service to the system established by Washington and followed by the early Presidents" could best be accomplished by an executive who was "under no temptation to use the patronage of his office to promote his own reelection."[5] Although his devotion and sincerity in openly espousing such a policy is admirable, it was politically unwise for Hayes to reveal his sentiments so far in advance. He would have done better to wait until out of office, or at least until the next presidential nominating convention, to make such a self-denying pledge. A distinct disadvantage accrued to him by his premature announcement: he needlessly sacrificed political power and prestige. Once it is known that a President has no intention of seeking a second term, his party leadership evaporates rapidly, and every politician down the line begins to transfer his allegiance to possible heirs apparent. Hayes surely knew this; then why did he do it? One explanation is that he allowed his idealism for a cause to get the better of his political judgment. A more plausible possibility is that he simply was not interested in a second term. He apparently believed a President ought to be able to achieve his major goals within one term or not at all. If so, history seems to bear him out, as most American presidents who have served more than four years have discovered. Their political fortunes tend to go downhill after one term. Furthermore, Hayes never really sought public office very assiduously. He was always the reluctant candidate, but once in the fight he warmed to the campaign struggle like an old war-horse. Hayes basically looked upon office-holding as a public trust to be dutifully discharged and was never so corrupted by possession of political power as to seek longevity in office. Content to stand on his record, he retired gracefully, without remorse and with few political enmities. Only Roscoe Conkling and Benjamin A. Butler seem to have really annoyed him. He even came to accept James G. Blaine and Chester A. Arthur, whose careers were so different from his own.[6]

To assist him in making decisions, Hayes relied heavily upon his cabinet, which normally met twice a week when the President was in Washington. Firmly believing that "Presidents were masters of the situation, not only by law, but by the fact that Cabinet officers were appointed by and dependent upon the executive," however, he at times acted independently of the advice of his cabinet officers. Like Lincoln, Hayes felt justified in bypassing his cabinet when necessary. If he knew them to be opposed to a measure he had decided upon, he did not ask their views but simply announced his own policy and carried it out. In departmental matters, he gave greater weight to the opinion of the secretary of that department, if the secretary opposed his own views; but at least twice he carried out matters against the expressed wishes of a department head. He even differed in this respect with perhaps his most valued adviser, Treasury Secretary John Sherman. As to cabinet business, if a cabinet officer wished to introduce a measure, he usually consulted the President privately ahead of time. "In fact, no measures could succeed except by the President's own act in either introducing them or approving them."[7]

A consideration of Hayes' philosophy of executive authority would be incomplete without some reference to his policy of appointments and removals and his use of the presidential power to pardon and to veto. Hayes tried to limit his appointments to the filling of vacancies and the dismissal of government workers only for the good of the service. He boasted of fewer removals than under any other administration in its first year since John Quincy Adams.[8] The Post Office Department is an excellent illustration. Not since complete records had been kept had there been so few changes. Only sixty-seven presidential postmasters were removed during Hayes' four years. Although the President considered eight years a reasonable time for one individual to hold the same job, in actual practice most postmasters were reappointed during his presidency when their commissions expired.[9] He held to one strict rule: he prohibited the appointment of any person connected to him by blood or marriage. He thoroughly discouraged job applications to him or to other members of the first family. Appointments in the various departments were left largely to cabinet heads. Recommendations from Congressmen, while still important, lost much of their previous influence.[10]

All this does not mean that President Hayes completely ignored political considerations in his exercise of the patronage. He kept loyalty to his party ever in mind to the extent of even appointing Stalwarts whenever it would harmonize or strengthen the party —"my own personal preference notwithstanding." To this policy he partly attributed the Republican victory of 1880, in which the party recaptured control of the House and Senate and kept the presidency.[11] Other qualifications being equal, Hayes tended to appoint Union veterans.[12] He also rewarded many delegates to the 1876 Republican National Convention who were prominent in helping him secure the party's nomination.[13] He made mistakes. In an effort to placate the South, he appointed numerous Democrats, perhaps as many as one-third of all southern appointments during his first five months in office going to the opposition party. He also assumed a major risk by giving office to Republican members of the election and returning boards of the disputed states in 1876.[14] He frankly admitted errors of judgment: "In my anxiety to complete the great work of pacification, I have neglected to give due attention to the civil service—to the appointments and removals. The result is, some bad appointments have been made. . . . There have been delays in action." Alluding to the Post Office, he confided to his diary: "I grow more conservative every day on the question of removals. On ex-parte statements, I have made mistakes in removing men, who, perhaps, ought to have been retained, and in appointing wrong men."[15]

Fundamentally, he disliked the spoils system. "All appointments *hurt*. Five friends are made cold or hostile for every appointment; no *new* friends are made. All *patronage* is perilous to men of real ability or merit. It aids only those who lack other claims to public support."[16]

While some unsavory persons undoubtedly received offices under Hayes, the great majority of his appointees represented the best available Republicans in each section of the country. Among them were John Marshall Harlan, destined to have a long and distinguished career on the Supreme Court, and James Russell Lowell, who became minister to Spain in 1877 and to Great Britain in 1879.

President Hayes took an unusual interest in the exercise of the pardoning power. "This is a wide power," as noted later by William Howard Taft, "and enables the President to pardon any one guilty of an offense against the United States before indictment, after indictment and before conviction, or after conviction."[17] Moreover, Congress may not restrict the President in the exercise of his power of pardon. While governor of Ohio, Hayes emphasized the great importance of more humane and scientific methods in the administration of justice. For years he studied penology and corresponded with prominent leaders of the prison reform movement. In 1870 he presided when the first National Prison Congress convened in Cincinnati. As governor he believed more in trying to rehabilitate prisoners than to extract retribution from them, and he was particularly lenient toward first offenders. Gradually he evolved several working principles for his guidance in exercising the power of pardon:

1. Grant no pardon and make no promises on the first presentation of a case. Take time before deciding, or even encouraging the party.
2. If two or more are concerned in the crime, consider the cases of all together. One is often called the dupe until he is pardoned; then the other becomes dupe, and the pardoned man the leader.

3. Pardon no man who is not provided with employment or the means of subsistence.
4. Pardon no man unless some friend is ready to receive him as he comes from the prison.
5. Of course, the judge, the prosecuting attorney, and some intelligent citizen of sound sense should be heard from in all cases. These rules may be departed from in cases requiring it, but let them always be considered before the pardon is granted or any committal had.[18]

When in doubt Hayes inclined to the side of mercy.

Typical of his approach and policy while President were two celebrated cases involving obscenity and the use of the mails. He pardoned Ezra Hervey Heywood, a feminist, pacifist, socialist, freethinker, and one of the founders of the Free Love League, who was arrested in 1877 at the instigation of Anthony Comstock (reformer and secretary of the New York Society for the Suppression of Vice) and convicted in Boston, June 1878, for circulating through the mail a tract advocating the abolition of marriage. The penalty imposed consisted of a $100 fine and two years of hard labor at Dedham Jail. Hayes released him after six months in December 1878. During the prisoner's incarceration, his family was forced to depend on the charity of friends. The President, much abused by the public and the press for his reprieve of so controversial a figure as Heywood, based his decision on "unassailable" grounds:

1. Imprisonment imperilled his health as shown by the certificate of respectable medical authority.
2. There was no intention to violate the law.
3. In my judgment the law was not in fact violated—the pamphlet was not obscene matter.

Hayes asserted his firm policy of opposing books "intended or calculated to corrupt the young," but he maintained that Heywood's real difficulty was not "that he discussed a question in an objectionable manner, but that [in advocating free love] he was on the wrong side of the [marriage] question.... But it is no crime by the laws of the United States to advocate the abolition of marriage.... In this case the writings were objectionable but were not obscene, lascivious, lewd, or corrupting in the criminal sense."[19]

Approximately six months later, Hayes was petitioned by Robert S. Ingersoll and Thaddeus B. Wakeman to pardon another freethinker, D. M. Bennett, who, like Heywood, was pursued and convicted largely through the efforts of Anthony Comstock. Bennett's specific offense was to send through the mail a book opposing marriage and in favor of free-love practices titled *Cupid's Yoke: or, The Binding Forces of Conjugal Life.* He was fined $300 and sentenced to thirteen months in jail. Hayes pondered the case for several weeks before denying a pardon. Again, he felt the accused ought not to have been convicted but hesitated to interfere with the province of the legislature or the judiciary. "The pardoning power must not be used to nullify or repeal Statutes," he insisted, "not to overrule the judgments of the Courts. Palpable mistakes, hasty decisions, newly discovered facts may all furnish occasions for pardons." The fact that a book or pamphlet is "aesthetic, or infidel, or immoral in doctrine, does not make it obscene." What finally persuaded Hayes not to grant a pardon for Bennett was that the author used "many passages not required for the argument—in language and sentiment indecent, which enable the seller to advertise it as 'spicy,' as 'rich, rare, and racy,' and which add greatly to the demand for it. In short, obscenity to make money, may be truthfully alleged of it."[20] He was also strongly influenced by the great criticism of his pardon for Heywood and the fact that denominational leaders and most of their followers strongly opposed both men.

The Bennett case is chiefly important in Hayes' career as another episode that offered him an opportunity to express his philosophy of presidential power: "While I maintain inflexibly the authority of the Executive department against all attempts to cripple it by other departments, I must not magnify it at the expense of the just prerogatives of either the judicial or legislative departments." In the last year of his life, Hayes admitted that he had failed to pardon Bennett largely because the main current of judicial opinion in 1879 held that *Cupid's Yoke* was obscene and that he simply followed the opinion of the judges. He was never satisfied, however, with the correctness of this view. The publication was a "pamphlet of bad principles, and in bad taste, but Colonel Ingersoll had abundant reason for his argument that it was not, in the legal sense, 'an obscene publication.' "[21]

President Hayes used the veto power thirteen times, or more often in a single term than any other previous chief executive except Andrew Johnson and Ulysses S. Grant.[22] Altogether 1,396 acts and joint resolutions passed Congress during Hayes' administration. Only one of these measures, the Bland-Allison Act, lacked his signature and became law over his veto. Each of his twelve remaining veto messages, all but one involving public bills, were sustained. A key statement concerned Chinese immigration policy and the Burlingame Treaty, while perhaps the most significant group consisted of seven successive defenses of executive authority against attempted congressional intimidation through legislative riders attached to mandatory appropriation bills. Hayes took this challenge to his authority very seriously and branded the effort as "the first attempt in our history to break down the functions of the Executive by coercion."[23] The immediate controversy concerned enforcement of the federal election laws. In order to prevent fraud, Hayes believed it was perfectly proper for the federal government to protect federal elections just as it was for a state to protect state elections. Democrats and Liberal Republicans, however, sought to abolish a system which they felt was a bad legacy from the Civil War era. After his first five vetoes in this struggle were sustained, it seemed as if the President had won a total victory. But in the next session, the fight was renewed two more times before he finally triumphed. His steadfastness greatly enhanced presidential authority and recovered some of the important ground lost to Congress under Johnson and Grant. In safeguarding the independence of the executive department, Hayes revived the attitude of Jackson and Lincoln, and handed on a much stronger and respected presidency to his successors than he had received from his predecessor.[24]

It should be observed, too, that in the contest over legislative riders, Hayes used the veto power in a positive fashion designed to uphold and restore the separation of powers principle. In addition, he employed during the struggle the rather rare administrative technique of a presidential protest against the failure of Congress to provide for the payment of United States marshals.[25]

In comparison with twentieth-century practice, the Hayes method of preparing veto messages and other state documents was highly individualistic. Gradually jotting down a few notes or key ideas in his diary, he generally mulled over an issue in his mind for several weeks before reaching a decision. Then, after oral consultations with friends and opponents, he composed his own state paper. Hayes drafted all of his veto messages in this manner, except the one concerning the Chinese Exclusion Bill. On this occasion he accepted a version written by Secretary of State Evarts, which paralleled his own draft.[26] "Probably few public men have done so large a part of the writing of official papers, correspondence and the like as I have. The notion that others wrote my papers is a total mistake," he informed a publicist in 1890. "Mr. Crook, Mr. Pruden and others at the White House now will tell you that I was one of the rapid and voluminous writers, and that, especially, my messages were written by myself."[27]

When Hayes delivered his inaugural address on March 5, 1877, the United States Senate stood at the zenith of its power and mastery over the executive.[28] Senators even claimed a place at the dinner table above the President's cabinet whose members had hitherto outranked them at social functions. The new President proceeded immediately to challenge successfully this state of affairs by naming his own cabinet without deferring to the Senate oligarchy. The Senate leaders had fully expected to nominate whom they wished for the department portfolios. Patronage-conscious Roscoe Conkling wanted to make his colleague Thomas C. Platt Postmaster General, and Simon Cameron wanted his son Don to remain Secretary of War. Meanwhile James G. Blaine promoted the cause of William P. Frye of Maine. The Senators belatedly awoke to the realization that the new President had some ideas of his own on the subject.

Not only did Hayes completely ignore the promptings of the party professionals by choosing his cabinet independently, but he further aroused their ire by deliberately picking persons antithetical to the Republican leadership. Secretary of State William M. Evarts, although from New York State, belonged to the Republican faction opposed to Conkling. Carl Schurz, Interior Department designate, was much too independent and progressive in his politics to be accepted by party regulars. The nomination of David M. Key, a Democrat and ex-Confederate officer, as Postmaster General in a Republican administration aroused much bitterness. What could not be missed by any impartial observer, however, was the nominees' sheer fitness for duty. Nevertheless, the Senate sought to deny confirmation by referring the entire list to committees for examination and report. Not even their fellow Senator, John Sherman, escaped this legislative harassment. Public opinion rallied to the side of the President, however, and within seventy hours the Senate was forced to capitulate before a flood of protest —telegrams, letters, editorial comment, and mass meetings. Each of the nominees won confirmation. A President had decisively defeated the Senate in a major power struggle for the first time since the Civil War.

Hayes soon found another opportunity to challenge the will of the Senators. In taking office, he had publicly pledged himself to reform the civil service, but first he had to pacify the South and reassign the remaining federal troops. This accomplished, he directed his attention to the New York Custom House as the cynosure of the spoils system. Here Senator Conkling had entrenched his henchmen. A citizens' investigating committee headed by John Jay quickly uncovered considerable waste and corruption. When Alonzo B. Cornell, naval officer of the port, violated a presidential executive order forbidding federal office-holders from participating in party management, the President requested his resignation along with that of the two other principal officers of the port. Although each man refused to quit, Hayes nominated replacements and sent new names to the special session of the Senate for action, where they were at once referred to a committee of which none other than Senator Conkling was chairman. The Hayes nominees were rejected by a vote of 31 to 25, but the contest was far from over. Once the regular session convened, Hayes again sent his nominations to the Senate, with the same result as before. This time, the President's power of dismissal seemed completely checked, but Hayes absolutely refused to accept defeat. During the summer, while Congress was not in session, he fired the three top officials of the Custom House, and made recess appointments to fill the new vacancies. In December, for the third successive time, he presented his appointees for confirmation.

Thereupon Conkling lost his composure and made an angry attack upon the Hayes administration, deeply offending, in the process, influential Senate colleagues by quoting private correspondence of cabinet officials.[29] Simultaneously John Sherman put his prestige with the Senate on the line by threatening to resign the Treasury post if all of the President's nominations were not approved. Enough Senators now deserted Conkling to give Hayes his long-sought victory over senatorial patronage. The President noted the significance of the protracted struggle in his diary: "I have had great success. No member of either House now attempts even to dictate appointments. My sole right to make appointments is tacitly conceded."[30] Conkling's total defeat came in 1881 when he tried to reestablish his control over New York patronage by blocking Garfield's nomination of William H. Robertson, an anti-Conkling man, for Collector of the Port of New York. But Garfield parried the thrust skillfully, and Conkling and Platt both resigned their Senate seats, expecting the New York legislature triumphantly to reelect them and thereby strengthen their power. To their surprise, the legislature repudiated them, and the presidency emerged far stronger than when it had first entered the patronage fray. Hayes took great pride in the result: "If the boss system is to go down, I can say I struck the first and most difficult blows. . . . The principle steps have been 1) The appointment of the Cabinet in 1877, 2) The defeat of Conkling in the Custom House conflict which made a business house institution of the New York Custom House, 3) The defeat of Conkling and Platt and their dismissal from Public Life in 1881."[31]

In the summer of 1878, President Hayes' authority came under congressional assault in yet another way. The Democrats, aided by some Republican malcontents, reopened the 1876 presidential election controversy by launching an investigation into the election

returns of the disputed southern states. Congressman Clarkson
N. Potter of New York headed the committee. Throughout the
committee's proceedings, Hayes remained completely calm,
assured of his legal title to hold office, and convinced that the
investigation would damage its authors more than the Republican
cause. He was perfectly correct. The whole affair ended in disaster
for the Democrats when certain secret dispatches, sent in code
by friends of Samuel J. Tilden to his New York address, were
uncovered and deciphered. Portions published by the New York
Tribune proved beyond doubt that the Democrats had engaged
in corrupt bargaining with the returning boards of South Carolina
and Florida.

Instead of embarrassing the administration by raising the fraud
issue anew in 1878, the Democrats unwittingly implicated themselves, dashed Tilden's chances of running again in 1880, and
effectively removed much of the original opprobrium attached to
Hayes as the alleged fraudulent victor in 1876–1877. Near the end
of his life, Hayes penned a final judgment on the disputed election
circumstances. After first citing the effect of failure to observe
the Fifteenth Amendment in depriving the Republicans of many
Negro votes in the southern states, he went on to more conclusive
evidence: "In 1880 the Democratic National Convention quietly
ignored Tilden, thereby admitting the whole case against him,
and nominated General Hancock, one of the few Democrats of
note who publicly accepted the decision in 1876, and was among
the first to call and congratulate me on the result. In addition
to this, *the people at the election of 1880 elected General Garfield,
who was more fully identified with the result in 1876–77 than any
other* PUBLIC MAN . . . . On the whole, I have every reason to be
content with the public treatment of me and of my public conduct."[32]

Four events occurred in the normal course of business during
the Hayes administration, which must be mentioned briefly
because of their later significance. The first was a fire in the Patent
Office of the Interior Department in September 1877, which
destroyed numerous models and documents. The episode
prompted the President to issue an executive order providing for
a thorough inspection of all other government office buildings
in Washington to determine their safety against fire and to recom-
mend other measures for the protection of government property
and records. Hayes suggested a Hall of Records to house government documents of enduring value. Although his idea went
unheeded, it provided an important precedent for the eventual
erection of the National Archives building a half century later.
Hayes' concern for public records began at the time he was in

Congress when, while chairman of the Joint Committee on the Library, he helped to obtain manuscripts for the Library of Congress. While governor of Ohio, he demonstrated his interest further by soliciting and collecting letters and manuscript materials relating to Ohio history for the fireproof state library.[33] Through his efforts the papers of Arthur St. Clair, Return Jonathan Meigs, Thomas Worthington, and Ethan Allen Brown, plus a packet of miscellaneous papers from William Allen, all former governors, were obtained.[34] Finding portraits of each of Ohio's governors also occupied Hayes' attention.[35] When he became President, he adapted his archival habits to the federal government's needs and completed the White House collection of presidential portraits of which eight were lacking when he became President.[36] He also spent his declining years in part by carefully organizing his private and public papers and memorabilia since it was his intention "that a history of my Administration, containing good portraits and sketches of Lucy and myself, may be written and I place the materials where they will be found together."[37]

The President lent his vigorous support to another activity: the revival of the Washington Monument project. He argued for no change in the original plan, and to him is due the credit for continuing the obelisk. There had been a discussion among rival engineers lasting several months as to whether the foundations of the monument were strong enough to justify continuation of the shaft.[38] Some maintained the foundation would not support an average warehouse and to patch it would be folly; others objected to its design—"a tall and awkward smokestack at the best." It was even proposed to tear down the completed portion and build an arch or museum filled with statues in its place. "For some months," wrote Hayes, "I made it a study—a hobby. General [Thomas L.] Casey commissioner of Public Buildings and Grounds skillfully prepared a plan to strengthen the foundation. Mr. Spofford [Librarian of Congress] furnished the heights of other tall structures . . . gradually all opposition was overcome. We decided that the monument should overtop all other tall structures, and fixed its height therefore at five hundred and fifty feet. . . . General Casey is entitled to special and honorable mention. He solved the difficult problem presented by the defective foundation."[39] On August 7, 1880, in a simple ceremony, the first stone was laid in the continuance of the monument. To commemorate the occasion Hayes placed a half-dollar, marked on one side "R. B. H." and on the other "1880," beneath the new cornerstone.[40]

The President's responsibility as Commander-in-Chief led to his involvement near the end of his term in the serious case of Johnson C. Whittaker of South Carolina, one of the first black cadets at the United States Military Academy. Whittaker had arrived at West Point in 1876. After the graduation of his roommate, Henry O. Flipper of Georgia in 1877, Whittaker was the sole black cadet enrolled at the academy. One of the customary diversions, which filled the place of extracurricular activities for the cadets, was hazing. After 1865 this usually took the form of exhausting physical exercises and the forced eating of unpalatable items. West Point superintendents generally opposed such activities, but were powerless to cope with the situation; whenever they dismissed cadets for hazing, the War Department promptly reinstated the troublemakers.

The superintendent of West Point from 1876 to 1880 was General John M. Schofield, an outstanding Union general in the Civil War. Schofield never liked his West Point assignment and considered the post beneath his dignity. Furthermore, he sincerely believed it was unreasonable to expect black cadets to compete successfully with their white classmen at the academy.

In 1879 Whittaker was declared deficient in his studies by the academic board. Schofield recommended that he be dropped back a class but not dismissed. On the morning of April 6, 1880, Whittaker failed to answer reveille and was later found battered and bleeding, trussed to his barracks bed. Whittaker claimed three masked men had attacked him during the night, but an investigation led to the conclusion that Whittaker's injuries were self-inflicted, and the result of his fear that he would fail a test he was about to take. When the black cadet refused to admit his guilt, Schofield attempted to expel him on disciplinary grounds. President Hayes, who was drawn into the controversy by the public clamor over the case, ruled that Whittaker might be discharged only for academic failure.

On August 17, 1880, Schofield came to the White House to discuss the case with the chief executive. In the aftermath the President cashiered Schofield, who, although he did not like being stationed at West Point, resented even more his dismissal and reassignment to a newly created post as commander of the Department of the Border, on what he considered to be unjust political charges against the academy for its treatment of black cadets. Schofield's replacement was General Oliver O. Howard, a founder and president of Howard University, and former head of the Freedman's Bureau, who had an excellent record of friendship for black citizens.

Throughout the whole proceedings, General Sherman, an old army friend of Hayes, stoutly defended General Schofield and West Point against the charges of prejudice. Schofield's dismissal infuriated Sherman and caused his temporary estrangement from the President. When Hayes realized that the Chief of Staff was piqued, he went to see Sherman and offered his apology. "The Entente Cordiale is completely restored," Sherman wrote. "I simply stood off until he came of his own volition."[41]

A final questionable sequence of events occurred during the Hayes administration which did not come fully to either the President's attention or public knowledge until he had retired from the White House.[42] The case concerned certain operations in the Post Office Department later called the "Star-Route Frauds." The Star Routes involved contracts for carrying mail, mostly in the sparsely settled region west of the Mississippi River. Low bidders who won a franchise also received additional compensation for "expediting the service." Large sums of money were paid for carrying relatively small quantities of mail, and certain favored persons, notably Stephen W. Dorsey, Secretary of the Republican National Committee in 1880, received extremely lucrative contracts. A thorough investigation by Garfield's reform-minded Postmaster General, Thomas L. James, led to the implication of Second Assistant Postmaster General Thomas J. Brady, a Grant appointee who was removed from office pending results of the inquiry. Appropriations were also cut sharply, and both Brady and Dorsey were brought to trial, but surprisingly acquitted. No evidence linking David M. Key or Horace Maynard, Postmaster Generals under Hayes, with these crimes came to light during the course of two separate trials. Nor did President Hayes grasp the extent of wrongdoing.

> The only presentation of the present prevailing opinion ever made to me in a way to attract attention was by General Hawley. I immediately had Rogers (private secretary) see the Postmaster General (I am uncertain whether it was you or Maynard) and Tyner. He soon reported to me that both were confident that Brady was perfectly honest in the matter. On personal inquiry the same thing was reported to me. The matter was then under investigation by Congress. . . . It was proper to postpone a decision until the results of their work were reached. But in the meantime . . . the further progress of the course of things complained of was stopped by my directions.[43]

To William Henry Smith, Hayes asserted, "One thing you may be sure of, I was not a party to covering up anything. Brady and his set of Stalwarts were always my enemies as you know.[44]

Privately the President believed "Key was honest but inexperienced and too confiding." To his own share of responsibility for the postal scandal Hayes took exception: "Enemies blame me for not discovering the fraud and putting a stop to it. When I took office the Post-Office Department was believed to be well conducted, with honesty and efficiency. . . . I did not wish to change what was in good condition." He alluded to a basic difference over policy as a contributing factor. The West naturally favored generous mail service; the older states preferred a more economical and restricted delivery in the sparsely settled West. Key and Hayes subscribed to the western viewpoint. "Beyond this I had nothing to do with it," Hayes concluded. Congressmen who favored restriction assailed the Star Route system; those who favored a liberal policy sustained it. "I called the attention of both Key and Tyner to the subject repeatedly. They both regarded the controversy as due not to mismanagement or fraud but to a difference of opinion on an important question of policy. The investigation was in the hands of Congress. They sustained Brady. But in the course of it I became satisfied that a more careful supervision of post-office contracts ought to be had. I directed that no more liabilities should be incurred or increased by contract without a full consideration by the Postmaster General, and that the question after such consideration by him should be presented to the Cabinet and [the] President. This undoubtedly was sufficient to stop all crooked or even inconsiderate action by the head of the bureau [Brady] on contracts of this class."[45]

Finally Hayes excused himself: "I shall not ultimately suffer for doing the right thing as it then appeared. Enemies will talk, but the outcome will not hurt. For me and my friends the course is to let the matter go on.[46] Altogether the President felt that Congress was in a better position to investigate than the executive. "Their means are ample and their powers great. I had no means to take testimony or compel witnesses to testify.... I directed them [Key and Tyner] to afford every possible facility to the congressional committee of investigation.... But I was satisfied that this business required a supervision which it had not had. To secure this, I directed that hereafter no contract should be made or altered involving any considerable expense or liability unless it was submitted to the Postmaster General and by him brought before the President and Cabinet. This no doubt would have prevented the frauds now complained of."[47]

Other than Richard W. Thompson's indiscretion in accepting a lucrative private post as American agent of the Panama Canal Company while he was still Secretary of the Navy, the Star Route episode was the only blot on the otherwise high standard of public service maintained throughout the Hayes administration.

Notes

1. For an excellent analysis of the staggering management problems confronting the federal government in the late nineteenth century, see

Leonard D. White, *The Republican Era: 1869–1901* (New York: The Macmillan Company, 1958).

2. "The first commercial exchange was installed in 1878, the year in which Congress appropriated $150 to the Public Printer to connect his office with the Capitol." Ibid., 3*n*.3.

3. James A. Garfield, "A Century of Progress," *Atlantic Monthly* 40 (1877): 61.

4. "Notes of Conversation of the Author with President Hayes, September 30, 1889" cited in C. Ellis Stevens, *Sources of the Constitution of the United States* (New York: Macmillan and Company, 1894), 167–170 *n*.2.

5. Charles Richard Williams, *The Life of Rutherford Birchard Hayes* (Boston: Houghton Mifflin Company, 1914), I, 461.

6. "I have throughout regarded Mr. Blaine as a gentleman with whom I would like to be on good terms. . . . I do not feel that the past stands in the way of good relations." Hayes to William Walter Phelps, December 4, 1879, Hayes Papers, RBHL. Hayes and Arthur shared a private carriage in the Grant funeral procession. "President Arthur proved an excellent companion for such a drive—five hours." Hayes, Diary, August 9, 1885, Hayes Papers, RBHL. Hayes later attended Arthur's funeral and was requested by the Arthur family to be a pallbearer. Hayes to Fanny Hayes, November 19, 1886, Hayes Papers, RBHL. Actually he and President Cleveland rode with the mourners. Hayes, Diary, November 21, 1886.

7. "Notes of Conversation of the Author with President Hayes, September 30, 1889."

8. Hayes, Diary, March 12, 1878.

9. Dorothy Ganfield Fowler, *The Cabinet Politician: The Postmasters General, 1829–1909* (New York: Columbia University Press, 1943), 165.

10. Hayes, Diary, March 24, 1877, March 12, 1878.

11. Ibid., September 12, 1889.

12. "Last night I took up the papers in the Lebanon, Ohio, case. There were eight competitors. Three women—two, widows of officers. Three or four of the men were well qualified and well supported by the people. I appointed a crippled private soldier. He was getting a smaller pension than the ladies received—poor, honest, moral, and religious, with requisite business qualifications." Hayes, Diary, December 17, 1878.

13. For example, John Marshall Harlan, who swung the Kentucky delegation to Hayes, was named Associate Justice of the United States Supreme Court, and Governor William A. Howard of Michigan, who delivered his state to Hayes at a critical juncture, became governor of the Dakota Territory. Ex-Governor Edward F. Noyes, chairman of the Ohio delegation who placed Hayes' name in nomination, became minister to France.

14. C. Vann Woodward, *Reunion and Reaction* (Garden City, New York: Doubleday & Company, 1956), 245–246.

15. Hayes, Diary, October 24, August 5, 1877.

16. Hayes to William McKinley, December 27, 1892, Hayes Papers, RBHL.

17. William Howard Taft, *The President and His Powers* (New York: Columbia University Press, 1967), 118–119, originally published as *Our Chief Magistrate and His Powers* (New York: Columbia University Press, 1916).

18. Hayes, Diary, April 11, 1876.

19. Hayes to Rev. Dr. R. M. Hatfield, February 21, 1879, Hayes Papers, RBHL; Hayes, Diary, January 10, 1879.

20. Hayes, Diary, July 1, 10, 11, 19, 1879.

21. Hayes, Diary, July 19, 1879, March 27, 1892.

22. Two excellent studies of the veto power upon which I have relied are Edward Campbell Mason, *The Veto Power* (Boston: Ginn & Company, 1890) and Carlton Jackson, *Presidential Vetoes, 1792–1945* (Athens: University of Georgia Press, 1967).

23. Hayes, Diary, March 21, 1879.

24. Jackson, *Presidential Vetoes,* 141–144, contains a good discussion of these legislative rider vetoes, as does White, *Republican Era,* 35–38.

25. Mason, *The Veto Power,* 177, 209.

26. Hayes, Diary, December 20, 1885; Williams, *Life of Hayes,* 213–217.

27. Hayes to F. G. Carpenter, December 11, 1890. Lloyd W. Smith Collection, Morristown Historical Park Collections, microfilm reel 22, copy in RBHL.

28. Wilfred E. Binkley, *President and Congress* (New York: Alfred A. Knopf, 1947), 151*ff.,* discusses the hegemony of the Senate, an account I have followed closely.

29. Venila Lovina Shores, "The Hayes-Conkling Controversy, 1877–79," *Smith College Studies in History* 4 (July 1919): 262–263.

30. Hayes, Diary, July 14, 1880.

31. Ibid., May 17, 1881.

32. Ibid., February 16, 1892.

33. Hayes to Hon. William Allen, October 27, 1870, William Allen Papers, Library of Congress.

34. *American Archivist* 25 (July 1962): 330*n.*

35. Hayes to Hon. William Bebb, January 20, 1870, RBHL.

36. Hayes to A. R. Spofford, January 12, 1881, A. R. Spofford Papers, Library of Congress.

37. Hayes, Diary, March 30, 1892.

38. Thomas C. Donaldson, "Memoirs," 103–104, transcribed copy in RBHL.

39. Hayes to J. Edward Clarke, December 24, 1886, Hayes Papers, RBHL.

40. Hayes, Diary, August 8, 1880.

41. Cited in James M. Merrill, *William Tecumseh Sherman* (Chicago: Rand McNally & Company, 1971), 385. For other accounts of the celebrated Whittaker case, see two general histories of the academy by Thomas J. Fleming, *West Point: The Men and Times of the United States Military Academy* (New York: William Morrow & Company, Inc., 1969) and Stephen E. Ambrose, *Duty, Honor, Country: A History of West Point* (Baltimore: The Johns Hopkins Press, 1966). For an important dissenting viewpoint, much more favorable to Whittaker, consult John F. Marszalek, Jr., "A Black Cadet at West Point," *American Heritage* 22 (August 1971): 30–37, 104–106, which is based upon a forthcoming book detailing the entire affair and its aftermath. Marszalek has made an exhaustive study of the court of inquiry and court-martial records in the National Archives.

42. Fowler, *The Cabinet Politician,* 178. The most recent study is Earl J. Leland, "The Post Office and Politics, 1876–1884: The Star Route Frauds" (Ph.D. diss., University of Chicago, 1964).

43. Hayes to D. M. Key, November 5, 1881, Hayes Papers, RBHL.

44. Hayes to William Henry Smith, October 26, 1881, Hayes Papers, RBHL.

45. "Is it not true that under Tyner the P. O. Department was General Grant's best Department except Governor Fish's?" [State Department].

Hayes to My Dear Sir (unidentified), May 3, 1881, Hayes Papers, RBHL. See also Hayes, Diary, May 3, 1881.

46. Hayes to My Dear Sir (unidentified), May 3, 1881.
47. Hayes, Diary, April 28, 1881.

11

The Money Question

Historical interpretations of the Reconstruction era and the Gilded Age have undergone intensive revision in the last dozen years. Among the many issues bridging these two periods, none is more pervasive or significant than the debate over monetary policy. After many decades of relative neglect, the money question of the late nineteenth century has recently received abundant attention from a vigorous coterie of young historians and economists. The result has been a wholesale shift in our understanding of a very complex issue, which deeply divided Americans in its day and has defeated for a long time the efforts of modern scholars essaying a trustworthy explanation of exactly what happened. Now at last the mystery seems to be clearing up.

For the Hayes period, Jeannette P. Nichols, starting in 1934 and continuing for over three decades, led a small vanguard of investigators into new paths of research by her painstaking articles on John Sherman. Together, they constitute the first modern scholarship on a key personality who figured prominently in American financial history through nearly half a century. For years, Sherman served as chairman of the Senate's Committee on Finance and reached perhaps the pinnacle of personal success when, while Secretary of the Treasury in the Hayes administration, he accomplished the resumption of specie payment without causing a public run on the banks to convert paper money into gold dollars.[1]

More recently, scholars like Robert P. Sharkey, Irwin Unger, Allen Weinstein, and Walter T. K. Nugent have brilliantly challenged older assumptions.[2] Nugent's contribution is particularly helpful because he documents a dominant trend toward gold monometallism and the general failure of efforts toward international bimetallism, especially in relating American monetary affairs to similar trends in Great Britain, France, and Germany. Sharkey,

Unger, and Weinstein trace in great detail the political and financial history of the money question during the 1860s and 1870s.

The net effect of this recent scholarship is to contradict the older interpretations of Charles Beard and Howard K. Beale, who had pictured Reconstruction as a postlude to the Civil War years in which a triumphant northern capitalism greatly strengthened its economic grip over a "prostrate South and a preadolescent West." In the new formulation since 1959, the Reconstruction era appears more as a prelude to the late nineteenth and early twentieth centuries. Furthermore, the idea of a single business point of view on basic issues like the tariff or currency policies, as opposed to an agrarian or labor position, has been exposed as a myth. The facts prove conclusively that wide differences of opinion existed among bankers, merchants, transporters, and manufacturers, depending on numerous factors—such as rhetoric, ideology, and political expediency—rather than just on economic interests alone. The Specie Resumption Act of 1875 now appears to be John Sherman's practical way of uniting his party on monetary policy lest continued disagreement within Republican ranks contribute toward political defeat in the 1876 national election.

The experience of the twentieth century in monetary affairs led scholars to approach the intensive currency debate of the late nineteenth century from a different perspective. The gold standard argument with its implied assumption of "sound money" no longer seems quite so safe or sacrosanct. Domestic specie payments were, after all, abandoned in the 1930s in favor of inconvertible paper currency. Not only gold, but also silver, which had triumphed over the greenbacks in the late 1870s, eventually lost out to paper money. Whereas the single gold standard advocates of the 1870s had opposed free silver or unlimited bimetallism as the main threat, it turned out that both sides ultimately succumbed to paper currency, the real rival to gold and silver bullionism.[3] In turn, the rise of bank check money became more important than either hard or paper currency.

While Rutherford Hayes was President, the money debate revolved around two primary issues: the coinage of silver dollars and the resumption of specie payments. A short sketch of the economic background will help to put each issue in focus.[4]

From 1792 to 1873 the United States theoretically operated on a bimetallic standard. Put another way, both gold and silver dollars circulated as legal tender in payment of debt. Since gold was more precious than silver, however, the Mint defined exactly how much gold should go into a gold dollar and how much silver should go into a silver dollar. The ratio between silver and gold was set at approximately sixteen to one, meaning that one grain of gold was worth about sixteen grains of silver. The idea was to keep both metals circulating simultaneously by maintaining a constant balance between them. Actually, in practice this theory proved impossible. A modest scarcity of silver began as early as the 1830s and became more pronounced after 1849. This scarcity caused silver to be undervalued at the Mint. Thereupon silver miners sold their product commercially rather than to the government in order to get the best price. This practice finally drove silver dollars out of circulation so that a whole generation of Americans grew up unaccustomed to thinking of silver dollars as legal tender.

Then in 1873 the Congress passed a law officially abolishing the silver coinage, an action commonly called the demonetization of silver. Evidence now indicates that as far back as the late 1860s several officials of the government, including Grant's Secretary of the Treasury George Boutwell, Senator John Sherman, and Henry R. Linderman, director of the Mint, had anticipated a drop in the price of silver. Since they thought this would jeopardize a stable currency and the public credit, they bent all their efforts toward achieving a single and reliable gold standard.[5] But the debtors, many of them farmers, argued that the demonetization of silver amounted to a "crime," because it contracted the currency, created a scarcity of money in circulation, and compelled them to pay debts in dollars worth more than when they had borrowed the money. The fact that the price of farm crops fell from 1873 to 1878 only helped to confirm agrarian suspicions concerning the new monetary policy. This sentiment gradually gained strength until a bill sponsored by Richard Bland of Missouri calling for free and unlimited coinage of silver passed the House of Representatives in November 1877. Subsequently the Allison amendment in the Senate modified it by limiting coinage of silver to a minimum of 2 million and a maximum of 4 million silver dollars per month. President Hayes vetoed this measure in February 1878. Promptly repassed over his veto, it is the only bill ever to become law without his signature in his four-year term.

The other issue, specie payments, involved the ability and practice of banks and the Treasury to exchange gold and silver coins for bank notes or greenbacks (paper currency issued during the Civil War supported only by the credit of the United States) at the customer's demand. This was the practice in the United States before 1862, but during the Civil War it was stopped. Nor was it resumed in 1865. Eventually the Congress passed the Specie Resumption Act of 1875, which called for the redemption of legal tender notes in specie at full value by January 1, 1879, a process designed to retire the greenbacks from circulation. The Hayes administration inherited this obligation, and it was left to Treasury Secretary John Sherman to plan the details of the resumption of specie payments, something Congress had neglected to spell out.

President Hayes favored a single gold standard and the resumption of specie payments as the surest way of restoring confidence in the economy and upholding the nation's financial honor. He strongly believed that it was the responsibility of government to maintain the value of the currency and that the Treasury must be prepared at all times to redeem currency at face value in gold. Hence he enthusiastically supported John Sherman's efforts to build up the gold reserve against the expected demand for specie when resumption day would arrive on January 2, 1879. What he did not seem to realize was that such a policy favored some persons and created injustices for the debtor class.

John Sherman was superbly equipped by long experience and thorough knowledge to carry out the Hayes financial program. The President could not have had a more "faithful servitor."[6]

Sherman had entered the House of Representatives in 1855 and had served three full terms before resigning to accept a seat in the Senate. His reputation as a keen student of finance prompted President Lincoln to ask him not to leave the upper chamber for an army post, and instead, he became intimately involved in the wartime establishment of the greenback currency and the national banking system and gained sixteen years experience in these complicated financial matters before Hayes appointed him Secretary of the Treasury. Sherman readily assumed his assignment of protecting the nation's credit by making the greenbacks redeemable in gold and by avoiding unlimited coinage of cheap dollars.[7]

Unlike Hayes, he was willing to accept the compromise Bland-Allison Act that permitted a limited issue of silver dollars, and he cautioned the President against a veto since he expected Congress could override the veto anyway, as it promptly did. The congressional concession to inflationary sentiment and the fact that, two weeks before January 1879, greenbacks became worth their face value in gold, lessened opposition to the resumption of specie payment and helped kill the greenback cause. Improving business trends and his own careful management of Treasury bond issues and other government resources also enabled the Secretary to resume specie payment on schedule. Sherman took great pride in the result and felt it justified his hope for the Republican presidential nomination in 1880. As Irwin Unger has concluded: "John Sherman, the supple master of accommodation ... subordinated the ideal to the workable and succeeded where men more righteous, perhaps, had failed."[8]

Hayes' handling of the silver question enabled him to satisfy his own conscience concerning monetary policy, afforded Sherman enough latitude to insure the success of resumption, and forestalled campaign use of the issue in the state elections of 1878.

For many weeks the President and his Secretary adroitly kept politicians and businessmen guessing about the administration's silver policy. Together they tried to prevent the party from splintering too badly over the money question and also to keep the confidence of a large domestic and international banking syndicate, which would buy American public securities only if assured that government bonds would be redeemed in gold alone.

Persons familiar with the President's public career ought to have known what his final position would be. While a Congressman, he had supported a resolution declaring the sacredness of the public debt and denouncing repudiation. He won his third gubernatorial election in 1875 on an antiinflation plank and endorsement of the party's January 1875 Resumption Act.[9] In this campaign, he welcomed John Sherman's support: "I am glad *exceedingly* that you will go to Lawrence County [to open the campaign with me]. There are many reasons for this. It would please me and aid me greatly if you could go with me to the other early meetings in that region. The tariff and finances are controlling subjects in that region. You can deal with them better than any other man."[10]

By the time of the 1876 presidential contest, the controversy over remonetization was gaining momentum across the country, but both parties, badly divided internally on the issue, wisely avoided it in their platforms, and neither Hayes nor Tilden mentioned it in their letters of acceptance.[11] Hayes also avoided the silver issue in his inaugural address, simply restating his letter of acceptance stance in which he expressed opposition to an "irredeemable paper currency" and asserting "the only safe paper money is one which rests upon a coin basis, and is at all times and promptly convertible into coin."[12] Just what he meant by "coin" remained undefined. Hayes was careful not to say anything on the silver question before Congress had disposed of the issue. Besides he had no wish to alienate midwestern Republican bimetallists prior to the local and state elections later in the year. The President's refusal to commit himself led to much speculation among politicians and the press as to his ultimate decision on the silver question. Bankers were especially restive.

Sherman also avoided positive declarations on the remonetization issue until the financiers he had interested in buying govern-

ment bonds demanded to know if the Hayes administration would
honor these _____ _____ _____ pal or interest, in anything
_____ _____ _____ cial since Sherman intended
_____ reserve to sustain resump-
_____ avoid an open declaration
_____ ntil after the fall elections,
_____ ty of facilitating bond sales
19, 1877, Sherman wrote
now in force, there is no
principle of the Four per
st payable except the gold

_____ nited remonetization—'the
extent that it can be main-
most bimetallists for the
gold repayment of govern-
sts in the Eastern invest-

_____ Hayes and Sherman again
_____ d on the silver question,
_____ Bland silver bill by more
_____ er 5. This action had the
_____ es below par on the New
_____ and European purchases
_____ e President's annual mes-
_____ etary of the Treasury in
_____ ared their opposition to
_____ ern over the sharp decline
_____ of the Bland bill, more
_____ ecision to oppose the bill

_____ nate Finance Committee
_____ to draft changes in the
_____ financial question and
_____ rs produced an amended
_____ age of silver. This easily
_____ the House on February

_____ bill as it made its way
_____ to silver coinage if the
_____ I cannot consent to a
_____ keep that untainted.''[15]
_____ etween the government
_____ l not legally be broken

without the consent of both parties. Since Eastern and foreign bondholders demanded gold redemption, he felt it would be a repudiation of the public debt to do otherwise. In his veto message of February 28 he argued that in the previous year the market value of silver had ranged from ninety to ninety-two cents as compared with the standard gold dollar: "Thus the silver dollar authorized by this bill is worth 8 to 10 per cent less than it purports to be worth, and is made a legal tender for debts contracted when the law did not recognize such coins as lawful money."[16] He could not approve a measure to repay debts with a money cheaper than that borrowed. The country's indebtedness was based on gold; it should be paid in gold. "If the country is to be benefitted by a silver coinage it can be done only by the issue of silver dollars of full value, which will defraud no man."[17]

Although later attributed by *Harper's Weekly* to Sherman, the veto message was personally written by the President.[18] Before issuing it, however, he did consult with the cabinet. Only Navy Secretary Thompson opposed it outright. Sherman and McCrary expressed some misgivings while the rest—Evarts, Key, Schurz, and Devens—supported the President fully.[19]

With undue haste, the Congress, after only one day, repassed the bill over the President's veto, in the House by a vote of 196 to 73 and in the Senate by 46 to 19. Hayes accepted the defeat philosophically: "I am content to abide the judgment—the sober second thought—of the people."[20]

Events seemed to bear him out. Both friends and foes of the Bland-Allison Act were disappointed. It did not depress the price of American securities in the world bond markets as Hayes had anticipated nor did it fulfill silverite expectations by turning "the wheels of trade" and reviving industry. The government, month after month, bought silver in a falling market, and the price of silver continued to decline as less of the metal was used in Europe. Meanwhile more gold came in from abroad, crop prices improved, and the five-year depression ended in 1879.

Notes

1. Dr. Nichols has traced Sherman's varying money policies in six excellent articles: "John Sherman: A Study in Inflation," *Mississippi Valley Historical Review* 21(September 1934): 181–194; "The Politics and Personalities of Silver Repeal in the United States Senate," *American Historical Review* 41(October 1935): 26–53; "John Sherman and the Silver Drive of 1877–78: The Origins of the Gigantic Subsidy," *Ohio State Archaeological and Historical Quarterly* 46 (April 1937): 148–165; "The Monetary Problems of William McKinley," *Ohio History* 72 (October 1963): 263–292; "Rutherford B. Hayes

and John Sherman," *Ohio History* 77 (Winter, Spring, Summer 1968): 125–138; and "John Sherman" in *For the Union: Ohio Leaders in the Civil War,* ed. Kenneth W. Wheeler (Columbus: The Ohio State University Press, 1968), 377–438.

2. See Robert P. Sharkey, *Money, Class, and Party* (Baltimore: The Johns Hopkins Press, 1959); Irwin Unger, *The Greenback Era, A Social and Political History of American Finance, 1865–1879* (Princeton: Princeton University Press, 1964); Allen Weinstein, *Prelude to Populism: Origins of the Silver Issue, 1867–1878* (New Haven: Yale University Press, 1970); and two volumes by Walter T. K. Nugent: *Money and American Society, 1865–1880* (New York: The Free Press, 1968) and *The Money Question During Reconstruction* (New York: W. W. Norton & Company, Inc., 1967).

3. For an excellent bibliographical review of changing interpretations, see the critical essay in Nugent, *The Money Question,* 107–121, upon which I have based my own brief historiographical résumé.

4. Ibid., 6–13.

5. Ibid., 162–171; Allen Weinstein, "Was There a 'Crime of 1873'?: The Case of the Demonetized Dollar," *The Journal of American History* 59 (September 1967): 307–326.

6. Nichols, "Rutherford B. Hayes and John Sherman," 125–126, describes the long friendship between the two men.

7. Ibid., 126–127, 136–137.

8. Unger, *The Greenback Era,* 403.

9. Irwin Unger, "Business and Currency in the Ohio Gubernatorial Campaign of 1875," *Mid-America* 41, no. 1 (January 1959): 27–39.

10. Hayes to Sherman, June 29, 1875, Hayes Papers, RBHL.

11. My discussion of the remonetization issue relies partly upon an excellent manuscript prepared by Allen Weinstein, "Hayes and the Silver Question: The History of a Presidential Veto" (1968), 1–29, RBHL.

12. Ibid., 10, citing Edward McPherson, *Tribune Almanac for 1877* (New York, 1877), 28–30, and "Interview with Carl Schurz," Chicago *Inter-Ocean,* January 2, 1877.

13. Sherman to F. O. French, June 19, 1877, Sherman Papers, Library of Congress.

14. Weinstein, "Hayes and the Silver Question," 15.

15. Hayes, Diary, February 3, 1878, Hayes Papers, RBHL.

16. James D. Richardson, ed., *A Compilation of the Messages and Papers of the Presidents* (New York: Bureau of National Literature, Inc., 1897), IX, 4439.

17. Ibid., 4440.

18. Hayes, Diary, December 20, 1885.

19. Ibid., February 26, 1878. Sherman changed his mind on the bill after the Senate amendment was added to it. He felt that the limited coinage would not have any adverse effects. Since the silver bill was widely supported by the American public, he thought it wise to make no strong objections to its passage. Carlton Jackson, *Presidential Vetoes, 1792–1945* (Athens: University of Georgia Press, 1967), 232*n*.51.

20. Hayes, Diary, March 1, 1878.

12

A New Era in Indian Policy

The closing of the frontier by the white man's unbridled expansion into the trans-Mississippi West during the post–Civil War years created the most critical period of Indian–white relations in American history. No longer could the Indians simply retreat or be removed to lands farther west beyond the pale of white culture. A majority of "Uncle Sam's 300,000 step-children" lived directly in the path of two advancing white settler lines from East and West, which steadily compressed the Indian tribes into ever smaller corridors of freedom. Alarmed and menaced by the constant diminishing of their lands and buffalo, the red men gamely resisted white penetration of their reservations and hunting grounds. Meanwhile the government in Washington found itself compelled to resolve two urgent questions: what to do about the Indian, and what agency should handle the coming crisis, the Department of the Interior or the War Department?[1]

For sixty years prior to the creation of the Interior Department in 1849, Indian affairs were under the complete jurisdiction of the War Department. Thereafter, a confusing system of divided responsibility evolved, caused by the transfer of the Indian Bureau, along with various other burdensome agencies from the Treasury, War, and Navy departments, to the newly created Department of the Interior. Under the system of dual control, a skeleton frontier army shared authority over Indian affairs with a host of civilian agents. In general, the army sought to protect frontier settlements and overland routes, suppress warlike tribes, discipline reservation Indians, and safeguard the Indians from the white men. The Interior Department's Indian service, meanwhile, attempted to fulfill treaty commitments, to provide for the Indian's welfare, and to educate and Christianize the tribes. Although the policy of neither department operated by unanimous consent, the army tended to favor pacification by force, while the Interior program promoted conciliation of the tribes.

Mixed with government inertia, inefficiency, and indifference, this system had many drawbacks and proved impossible to administer with full justice to the Indians. Attempts to define authority more carefully failed, and much confusion and recrimination over failures of policy resulted. The army regularly agitated for the return of the Indian Bureau to the War Department, arguing that this would be a more efficient, honest, and economical way of handling the Indian problem. With equal vigor, the Interior Department, arguing that the army's policy really meant extermination of the Indian tribes, stoutly resisted any transfer of Indian affairs back to the War Department.

In practice both departments were open to criticism. Reports of fraud and mismanagement long plagued the Indian Bureau, and recurrent Indian uprisings seemed to disprove the validity of its policy of conciliating the tribes. The army, on the other hand, dealt harshly with Indian prisoners and was responsible for a number of unwarranted frontier massacres.

Other conditions complicated the problem of divided jurisdiction. The Interior Department suffered under the burden of the sheer breadth of its administrative responsibilities and a continual shortage of funds. The undermanned army could scarcely wage a major Indian war if required. Fortunately, only a few of the 943 engagements against the Indians from 1865 to 1898 necessitated masses of three or four thousand men. Faced with an enemy using hit-and-run tactics, the army's dilemma was to balance adequate strength with adequate mobility. To do that, it broke up into several columns, but this method posed the danger of defeat, as Custer's annihilation in June 1876 so horribly demonstrated.[2]

To the lack of organic unity in the administration of Indian affairs must be added the constant turnover of leadership in the Interior and War Departments. Between 1865 and 1887, no fewer than ten Secretaries of the Interior, twelve Commissioners of Indian Affairs, thirteen Secretaries of War (three ad interim), and three generals-in-chief of the army supervised Indian policy, making any kind of continuity and improvement in the quality of Indian life difficult to attain.

When the Hayes administration took office, it inherited the unsolved Indian question and all of its ramifications. At first, conditions seemed not to improve, but by 1879 a new era in Indian policy began to emerge, and by the time President Hayes and Secretary of the Interior Carl Schurz left office in March 1881, a decided change in Indian–white relations had occurred. Several factors contributed to the new departure.

First, the last of the major Indian wars was fought.[3] No longer was there any danger of a general Indian uprising against the American government. The Sioux War of 1876–1877 was the high-water mark of Indian resistance on the Great Plains, and Custer's defeat, just a few days after Hayes was nominated for President, proved to be the last great Indian victory over the United States Army in the West. Sitting Bull's isolated band of Sioux escaped to Canada, but at length, hungry and destitute, recrossed the border and surrendered at Fort Buford, North Dakota, in July 1881.

Meantime, one of the most remarkable Indian leaders and a superb military strategist, Chief Joseph of the Nez Perce tribe, conducted a brilliant retreat of more than a thousand miles across Montana, Idaho, and Yellowstone Park between June and October 1877. He managed to elude one United States expedition under General O. O. Howard and to defeat elements of the Seventh Infantry under General John Gibbon at Big Hole, Montana, before he was compelled to surrender to Howard in the Bear Paw Mountains just thirty or forty miles away from Canadian sanctuary.[4]

In the spring of 1878, the Bannocks of Idaho left the Fort Hall Reservation and began plundering white settlements and ranches. General Howard eventually defeated them in July at Birch Creek, Oregon, and they returned to the reservation.

One final Indian uprising, the Meeker Massacre by Utes at the White River Agency in northwestern Colorado, occurred during the Hayes presidency. Considered one of "the most violent expressions of Indian resentment of the reservation system,"[5] the nomadic Utes burned the agency buildings, killed agent N. C. Meeker and some of his employees, and took the white women captive. The revolt was suppressed in October, but only after cavalry troops sent south from Fort Fred Steele in Wyoming were ambushed and besieged at Mill Creek, Colorado, on September 29, 1879. On October 5, reinforcements arrived and lifted the siege. With the collapse of the revolt, several Ute leaders were sent to prison, and the tribe was relocated on a new reservation in Utah.

With the ending of the Ute and Bannock troubles, lasting peace prevailed on the northern and southern Plains and in the Northwest. Only the Apaches of the Southwest remained openly hostile, a problem solved by the surrender of Geronimo in 1886.

A second major event of the Hayes presidency affecting the government's Indian policy was the final defeat of the "transfer issue" in February 1879 after "one of the most heated polemic arguments in the history of Congress."[6] Two major efforts were conducted after the Civil War (1867–1871 and 1876–1879) to transfer the Indian Bureau back to the War Department. The advocates of transfer tended to be military leaders or westerners, while the defenders of the status quo were largely Indian service employees or easterners. Another generalization to note is that the Democrats, who controlled the House, voted for transfer, and the Republicans, who held a majority in the Senate, opposed transfer. During the second great debate, Generals W. T. Sherman and George Crook, both friends of the President, testified in favor of transfer, while Senator William Windom of Minnesota, Secretary Schurz, and Indian Commissioner Ezra Hayt led the forces opposing it. The proposal finally was rejected by Congress for a variety of reasons: abatement of the Indian wars; effective lobbying by friends of the Indians; and a rather general feeling that the military was unsuited to govern the Indian tribes. The significance of the defeat of the transfer movement is that for the first time the Indian Bureau did not have to be constantly on the defensive but could now turn its attention to much-needed reform activities.

A third event making the Hayes Indian policy unusual was the appointment of Carl Schurz, a well-known reformer of independent proclivities, as Secretary of the Interior.[7] Schurz held the post for four full years, the first Interior head to do so since before the Civil War. He not only provided greater continuity and stability for the department but also worked harder at the job than any of his six predecessors appointed by Johnson or Grant. Furthermore, Schurz, of all the Hayes cabinet officers, most nearly conducted his department in the spirit of the civil-service reform crusade. He purified the Indian service and led the critical fight to preserve civilian control over Indian affairs.

Schurz, as Secretary of the Interior, headed a department involving probably more work and care than any other under the government in 1877. In his charge were the Indian service with its many officers, over a quarter of a million Indians, and millions of acres of reservations; the public lands; hundreds of thousands of government pensioners; the Patent Bureau; all business dealings of the government with the land-grant railroads; the Bureau of the Census; the Geological and Geographical Surveys; the charitable institutions of the capital; and many of the public grounds and parks.

As a student of politics suddenly thrust into high executive office, Schurz was not expected to be a very practical administrator let alone one up to the standards of his immediate predecessor, Zachariah Chandler, the Secretary of the Interior considered the best official among the practical politicians who had held the post up to that time.[8] But Schurz confounded his critics. Whereas Chandler adhered to a regular office schedule of ten in the morning until four in the afternoon, Schurz, even though he had a quicker and better-trained mind, established a nine-to-six routine in order to acquaint himself better with the personnel and problems of his department. Probably no executive officer since the close of John Quincy Adams' administration found so much time to devote to the real business of government as did Carl Schurz.

Since the Indian Bureau of all the agencies under his control seemed most in need of attention, he began by appointing a three-man commission to investigate it. The commission, which gathered evidence from June 1877 to January 1878, unearthed many kinds of irregularities: poor supervision, inadequate accounting by Indian agents, improper inspection of agencies, concealment of vital documents from superiors, and, in particular, widespread cheating of Indians by unscrupulous agents and traders. Once he had the facts, Schurz moved swiftly to correct abuses. Some employees, including S. A. Galpin, the chief clerk of the Indian Bureau, and John Q. Smith, commissioner of Indian affairs, were dismissed.[9] A code of regulations for the guidance of Indian agents appeared for the first time, and the system of keeping accounts was revised. Agents were now required to file regular reports and might be inspected at any time without forewarning. By licensing and bonding all Indian traders, Schurz also checked the swindling of Indians. Further, to increase his knowledge of Indian affairs, the Secretary made an extended western trip during August and September 1879, in company with Webb Hayes, the President's son.

Schurz thus became the first Secretary of the Interior to deal with the Indian problem in a scientific spirit. He visited Indians on the reservations, met them in Washington, sympathetically considered their problems, and studied their character. Instead of adopting toward the Indians the view of either naive eastern philanthropists or vengeful frontiersmen, Schurz took a middle stance, treating the Indians as he found them, a capable race in need of government aid and assistance. He concluded that the rapid and irresistible spread of settlements in the interior of the continent, the building of Pacific railways, and the consequent disappearance of the buffalo and wild horse, with all the larger game, spelled the end of Indian subsistence by hunting. Indians, he felt, must be taught agriculture, herding, and freight hauling.[10]

He sought to give dignity to each Indian as an individual. The new book of regulations for the bureau specified that annuities and supplies should go directly to heads of families rather than to the tribal chieftains. An Indian police force became a reality, and tribal ownership of land began to give way to the principle of severalty. The general application of business methods to government and the improvement in moral tone and efficiency of the Indian service won for Schurz the respect of Indian tribes and white reformers alike.[11]

A fourth development in the Hayes era contributing to a change in Indian relations was a new system of Indian education associated with a Presbyterian army officer, Captain Richard Henry Pratt.[12] Before Hayes' time, the native tribesmen were quite commonly regarded as incapable of being civilized. In April 1878, Pratt and General Samuel Chapman Armstrong, head of Hampton Institute, a Virginia school for blacks, began an experiment at Hampton in Indian education by overseeing the training of seventeen Indian ex-prisoners of war. Armstrong then got Schurz's consent to train an additional fifty Indian pupils. Meanwhile, Pratt, who preferred to educate Indians separately from Negroes, requested permission to open an Indian school in the deserted army barracks at Carlisle, Pennsylvania, a proposal endorsed by both Schurz and Secretary of War George W. McCrary.[13] Pratt opened the Carlisle Indian School in October 1879 with eighty-two Sioux students. Enrollment climbed steadily, until Congress, faced with a successful experiment, formally authorized the school and voted it financial support in May 1882.

The progress of Indians at Hampton and Carlisle had three immediate effects: first, it led to the establishment of a third boarding school for Indians of the Pacific region at Forest Grove, Oregon; second, by demonstrating that Indian children were "as bright and teachable as average white children of the same ages," it helped to arouse a strong interest in Indian assimilation among benevolent people; and third, it produced the most vituperative attack upon advocates of Indian education that western sponsors of the inferior-race concept could deliver.[14]

The hostile view of the West had prevailed throughout the 1870s because public opinion could not be aroused in favor of an undefeated people. The passing of the major Indian wars, the decline of the transfer issue, and the reforms of Schurz and Pratt brought about a new attitude by the end of the decade. The time for healing the wounds inflicted on the Indian by the nation had arrived.

The new crusade for Indian reform was sparked by two influential books published in 1879 and 1881. First came *Our Indian Wards* written by George W. Manypenny, commissioner of Indian affairs under President Pierce, whose knowledgeable treatise called attention to the foolish jurisdictional discord between the Department of the Interior and the army, and arraigned the latter for sharing the worst prejudices of the frontier against the Indians.[15]

Far more powerful in its impact on public opinion and the Congress was Helen Hunt Jackson's *A Century of Dishonor*, which indicted the civil arm of the government and, in particular, Secretary Schurz for the wrongs and neglect of Indians. The irony in this situation was strange indeed. Schurz, the very epitome of sympathetic reform, a man who devoted himself to improving the lot of the helpless tribes, became the target of a vicious and unrelenting attack by an obscure magazine writer who made literary warfare on behalf of the Indians into a personal crusade. Her book consisted of a series of powerful vignettes documenting the relations of twelve important tribes with the federal and state governments. It showed clearly how the Indian had been obviously victimized by white civilization. Each member of Congress received a copy as part of the author's campaign to get the nation to correct its record of Indian mistreatment. In a period of four years prior to her death in 1885, Mrs. Jackson aroused the country to the Indian's plight through extensive travel, magazine articles, and a highly sentimental second book called *Ramona* (1884), a tour de force novel depicting the decline of California's Spanish culture and its dependent Indian society.[16]

Another event that shook the Hayes administration almost from start to finish concerned removal of a minor tribe, the Poncas, from their reserve in southeastern Dakota to Indian territory (Oklahoma) during the spring and summer of 1877.[17] It was through her protest of the government's treatment of the Poncas that Helen Hunt Jackson first gained prominence as a defender of Indian rights. Public furor over the plight of the Poncas gradually mounted and finally reached such a pitch that President Hayes appointed a special commission to deal with the problem.

Hayes and Schurz actually inherited the Ponca question from the Grant administration. A peaceful tribe of about eight hundred farming people, the Poncas were caught in a congressional blunder that gave away their lands to the warlike Sioux. Just a day before Schurz assumed office, Congress attempted to rectify its error by transferring the Poncas far to the south. When the tribe protested moving to Indian territory, the army forcibly removed them in a pitiful two-month trek complicated by storms, flooding, and epidemic malaria; many died. Upon arrival, the new reservation proved to have poor soil and bad water. With their farm implements and most of their cattle gone, the Poncas wanted to return to their Dakota homes, which by then were in Sioux hands. Schurz could not allow this, but he did give them new and more fertile lands in Indian territory, necessitating still another costly removal attended by more sickness and death. In the spring of 1879, unable to bear the heat and dust of the Oklahoma plains, some of the

Poncas, led by Chief Standing Bear, attempted to flee to Dakota, but when they stopped for supplies at the Omaha Reservation, soldiers blocked their path and endeavored to make them go back south. Standing Bear resisted and was promptly cast into prison.

A violent controversy led by Omaha citizens ensued. Mrs. Jackson entered the fray and raised a fund to defend Standing Bear in the courts. On January 9, 1880, she wrote to Schurz demanding that he aid the Poncas by bringing suit to recover their original reservation. Schurz declined, saying the Supreme Court would not permit an Indian tribe to sue in a federal court anyway, and pointed out that the Poncas had already built new homes and planted their crops. He recommended that the funds raised by Mrs. Jackson be used instead to help the Indians get individual titles to their new farms.

Mrs. Jackson refused to be placated, however, and others rallied to her side. Meantime, Standing Bear and an Indian girl, Bright Eyes, went on a lecture tour, under the tutelage of a missionary named Thomas H. Tibbles, to plead their case. Large crowds came out to hear the pair in Chicago, Philadelphia, New York, and Boston, where the orator Wendell Phillips added his eloquence to the cause.

President Hayes quite frankly admitted a grievous wrong had been inflicted upon the Poncas but decided to make restitution by better treatment rather than by removal of the Poncas for still a third time.[18] He appointed a presidential commission in December 1880, composed of Brigadier Generals George Crook and Nelson A. Miles; William Stickney, a member of the Board of Indian Commissioners; and Walter Allen, who represented a Boston citizens' committee, to visit the Ponca tribe, ascertain facts, and make recommendations.[19]

As an aftermath, in a message to Congress on February 1, 1881, Hayes reported that the 521 Poncas living in the Indian territory were satisfied with their new homes, were healthy, comfortable, and contented, and did not wish to return to Dakota. Another group of about 150 Poncas, still in Dakota and Nebraska, preferred to remain on their old reservation. Given this situation, the President urged that the wishes of both branches of the tribe be recognized. He then outlined a four-point Indian policy for the future: (1) a program of industrial and general education for Indian boys and girls to prepare them for citizenship; (2) land allotments in severalty, inalienable for a certain period; (3) fair compensation for Indian lands; and (4) Indian citizenship. These proposals clearly foreshadowed events of the 1880s, especially the Dawes Severalty Act of 1887.

The Sioux were also to be compensated for relinquishing land to the Poncas. Hayes avoided assessing blame among the executive branch, Congress, or the public for the injustices done to the Poncas. He simply asserted, "As the Chief Executive at the time when the wrong was consummated, I am deeply sensible that enough of the responsibility for that wrong justly attaches to me to make it my particular duty and earnest desire to do all I can to give to these injured people that measure of redress which is required alike by justice and humanity."[20] In response to his message, Congress quickly appropriated $165,000 to indemify the Poncas. This action seemed wholly to satisfy them.[21]

Hayes issued several other presidential decrees affecting Indian rights, which met with much less success than his Ponca message. He was unable to prevent a series of unlawful white invasions of Indian territory despite presidential proclamations containing stern warnings and the threat of imprisonment.[22]

What had been accomplished in the improvement of Indian rights and status by the Hayes administration, however, far outweighed any failures of omission or commission. As the 1880s opened, a new approach to the Indian question was evident in government policy and public opinion. The idea of Indians being "aliens" or "wards" was passing. The reservation system was yielding to the movement for severalty legislation. The success of Carlisle and other early schools discounted the belief that the Indian was incapable of civilization and gave impetus to the drive for full opportunity and political equality. It was also obvious that civilians, and not the military, would shape the future of the American Indian.

The Ponca episode was the one great tragic error of the Hayes administration in its Indian relations. Otherwise the President and Secretary Schurz worked to create a new national policy on the Indian question which was not, however, fully implemented until after they had left office. Both statesmen desired a more enlightened program toward the native Americans, and both freely admitted the government's responsibility for breaking treaty obligations. Hayes steadfastly supported Schurz's Indian reforms in his messages to Congress in which he stressed the necessity of honesty and humanity in Indian affairs. Hayes consistently advocated a new policy which would encourage Indians to own land as individuals, educate Indian children at government expense in the pursuits of agriculture, herding, and freighting, and give the red men citizenship. He also successfully instituted on the reservations a police force manned by Indians.

By study of the Indian question, by visits to Indian reservations and schools, by discussion with Indian leaders in the White House, and by presidential pronouncements, Hayes demonstrated his deep concern for the American Indian. His personal library also contained many books on Indian history and culture. In his first Annual Message of December 3, 1877, Hayes proclaimed:

> The Indians are certainly entitled to our sympathy and to a conscientious respect on our part for their claims upon our sense of justice.... Many, if not most, of our Indian wars have had their origin in broken promises and acts of injustice upon our part.... We can not expect them to improve and to follow our guidance unless we keep faith with them in respecting the rights they possess, and unless, instead of depriving them of their opportunities, we lend them a helping hand.... The faithful performance of our promises is the first condition of a good understanding with the Indians. I can not too urgently recommend to Congress that prompt and liberal provision be made for the conscientious fulfillment of all engagements entered into by the Government with the Indian tribes.[23]

In July 1878, while preparing some notes for a speech commemorating the centennial of the Wyoming Valley massacre, Hayes confided to his diary that the matter of how the white man should deal with the Indian was a problem that for three centuries had remained almost unsolved. Taking a cue from William Penn's philosophy on the subject, he concluded: "If by reason of the intrigues of the whites or from any cause Indian wars come, then let us correct the errors of the past. Always the numbers and prowess of the Indians have been underrated."[24]

Near the end of his term, the President enumerated the points in which he felt his administration had been successful to a marked degree. One of his proudest boasts was "an Indian policy [of] justice and fidelity to engagements, *and placing the Indians on the footing of citizens.*"[25] It was a rightful claim to fame.

Notes

1. Important studies of the Indian question that have helped in the preparation of this chapter include Loring B. Priest, *Uncle Sam's Stepchildren: The Reformation of United States Indian Policy, 1865–1887* (New Brunswick: Rutgers University Press, 1942); Henry E. Fritz, *The Movement for Indian Assimilation, 1860–1890* (Philadelphia: University of Pennsylvania, 1963); and Henry G. Waltmann, "The Interior Department, War Department and Indian Policy, 1865–1887" (Ph.D. diss., The University of Nebraska, 1962). See also Donald J. D'Elia, "The Argument Over Civilian or Military Indian Control, 1865–1880," *The Historian* 24, no. 2 (February 1962): 207–225.
2. Russell F. Weigley, *History of the United States Army* (New York: The Macmillan Company, 1967), 267–268.

3. An excellent brief résumé of the Indian wars may be found in U.S., National Park Service, *Soldier and Brave: Indian and Military Affairs in the Trans-Mississippi West, Including a Guide to Historic Sites and Landmarks* (New York: Harper & Row, Publishers, 1963), Part I, 1–89. For details of Sitting Bull's surrender, see Gary Pennanen, "Sitting Bull: Indian Without a Country," *The Canadian Historical Review* 51, no. 2 (June 1970): 123–140.

4. Merrill D. Beal, *"I Will Fight No More Forever": Chief Joseph and the Nez Perce War* (Seattle: University of Washington Press, 1963), and Mark H. Brown, *The Flight of the Nez Perce* (New York: G. P. Putnam's Sons, 1967), are two recent accounts of this episode.

5. U.S., National Park Service, *Soldier and Brave*, 63.

6. Waltmann, "The Interior Department," 304.

7. A very good contemporary analysis of Schurz as Secretary of Interior is Henry L. Nelson, "Schurz's Administration of the Interior Department," *The International Review* 10 (April 1881): 380–396. Other details are provided by Claude Moore Fuess, *Carl Schurz, Reformer (1829–1906)*, (Port Washington, New York: Kennikatt Press, 1963), chaps. 19 and 20.

8. Nelson, "Schurz's Administration," 381. A recent appraisal of Secretary Chandler may be found in Sister Mary Karl George, R.S.M., *Zachariah Chandler: A Political Biography* (East Lansing: Michigan State University Press, 1969), 241–248.

9. When Smith's successor, Ezra A. Hayt, commissioner of Indian affairs, 1877–1880, got in trouble over a shady transaction to acquire a silver mine near the San Carlos Agency, Schurz after due inquiry cashiered him also.

10. See, "A Century of Dishonor," *The Nation* 22, no. 818 (March 3, 1881): 152.

11. When Schurz paid an official visit to Hampton Institute at its commencement in 1880, he was greeted by the Indian pupils as their "wise and kind friend." Cited in Fuess, *Carl Schurz*, 264n.1. A good summary of Schurz's outlook on Indian affairs is contained in his article "Present Aspects of the Indian Problem," *North American Review* 133 (July 1881): 1–24.

12. The contributions of Pratt are detailed in Priest, *Uncle Sam's Stepchildren*, chap. 11; Elaine Goodale Eastman, *Pratt: The Red Man's Moses* (Norman: The University of Oklahoma Press, 1935); Everett Arthur Gilcreast, "Richard Henry Pratt and American Indian Policy, 1877–1906: A Study of the Assimilation Movement" (Ph.D. diss., Yale University, 1967); and Daniel T. Chapman, "The Great White Father's Little Red Indian School," *American Heritage* 22, no. 1 (December 1970): 48–53, 102.

13. Both Secretary of War McCrary (1877–1879) and his successor, Alexander Ramsey (1879–1881), had prior experience with Indian affairs. As a Congressman from Iowa, McCrary had served with the House Committee on Indian Affairs and Ramsey, as a former governor of both the Territory and State of Minnesota, had firsthand knowledge of red men on the warpath.

14. Fritz, *Movement for Indian Assimilation*, 166.

15. A Democrat in politics and for many years editor of an Ohio paper, Manypenny had retired from active participation in public affairs until he was invited by President Hayes to take the chairmanship of the committee appointed under Act of Congress to treat with the Sioux.

16. Allan Nevins, "Helen Hunt Jackson, Sentimentalist *vs.* Realist," *The American Scholar* 10, no. 3 (Summer 1941): 269–285.

17. Earl W. Hayter, "The Ponca Removal," *North Dakota Historical Quarterly* 6, no. 4 (July 1932): 262–275, is sympathetic to the Indians. Stanley Clark, "Ponca Publicity," *Mississippi Valley Historical Review* 29, no. 4 (March 1943): 495–516, tends to belittle the evicted Poncas.

18. Hayes, Diary, December 8, 1880; Hayes to George F. Hoar, December 16, 1880, both Hayes Papers, RBHL.

19. *Annual Report of the Secretary of the Interior for the Year Ended June 30, 1881*, II, 275.

20. James D. Richardson, ed., *A Compilation of the Messages and Papers of the Presidents* (New York: Bureau of National Literature, Inc., 1897), X, 4582–4586.

21. Fuess, *Carl Schurz*, 263.

22. Richardson, *Messages and Papers*, IX, 4499–4500, X, 4550–4551.

23. Fred L. Israel, ed., *The State of the Union Messages of the Presidents, 1790–1966* (New York: Chelsea House, 1966), II, 1350–1351.

24. Hayes, Diary, July 1, 1878.

25. Ibid., April 11, 1880.

13

The Hayes–Evarts Foreign Policy

Scholars have bestowed very little attention upon the study of American foreign policy in the 1870s and 1880s. The Hayes years, once termed the nadir in the history of American foreign relations from 1865 to 1898, are now best understood as a time of preparation for the later so-called Large Policy.[1] During the tenure of Hayes' Secretary of State, William M. Evarts, able career officers were retained or promoted to higher posts within the department. Meanwhile men of wide experience in business were recruited for the consular service. Diplomatic appointments, while still evidencing political overtones, also showed marked improvement over those of the Grant administration, so that Evarts had a far easier time working with American representatives abroad than had Grant's long-suffering Secretary of State, Hamilton Fish, who had excelled as an administrator of the State Department.[2] When he turned over his office to Evarts on March 12, 1877, the new Secretary inherited a smooth and efficiently run department based upon a major reorganization effected in 1870 and eight years of meticulous management by Fish.[3]

Another reorganization plan, in effect before Evarts took office in 1877, distributed departmental business among three assistant secretaries, six bureaus, two agencies, a translator, a superintendent of the foreign mail, a telegraph operator, and a private secretary, altogether a surprisingly small staff. The total executive and clerical work force in the department on January 9, 1878, numbered only fifty-one.[4] Evarts made no significant changes in this arrangement, which lasted until 1909.

Fish had also instituted stricter working conditions and far more thorough procedures for handling and recording diplomatic dispatches than his predecessors. For the first time, older records were classified and carefully indexed to obviate the practice of

194

relying upon the memories of experienced personnel for information long buried in the state archives. Under Secretary Fish, the department also moved, in July 1875, from its temporary headquarters (1866–1875) in the Washington Orphan Asylum to the newly completed South Wing of the Executive Office Building.

Fortunately the Hayes administration inherited a strong staff in the State Department, as each of the bureaus was headed by an experienced officer. Sevellon A. Brown, the chief clerk, began his diplomatic career in 1864, John H. Haswell, chief of the Bureau of Archives and Indexes in 1865, and Arthur B. Wood, chief of the Consular Bureau, in 1867. Charles Payson, chief of the Diplomatic Bureau, arrived in 1870. Robert C. Morgan, chief of the Bureau of Accounts, and Ferdinand Jefferson, chief of the Bureau of Rolls and Library, were also holdovers from the Fish period.[5]

For administrative purposes, all diplomatic and consular correspondence was separated into three divisions under the direct supervision of the three assistant secretaries, the key officers who kept the department running smoothly. For the top post, Evarts designated an able former Assistant Secretary, Frederick W. Seward, the son of William H. Seward, Lincoln's Secretary of State. When the younger Seward resigned in the fall of 1879 for reasons of health, Evarts, with the help of a mutual friend, Whitelaw Reid of the New York *Tribune,* persuaded a reluctant John Hay, one of Lincoln's private secretaries and a man with experience in the Paris, Madrid, and Vienna legations, to accept the position. Hay would have preferred the German mission (or after this was denied to him because of his lack of "political standing") some "second-class mission," but he finally agreed to terms and served faithfully for the remaining year and a half of the Hayes presidency. The assignment at least returned him to Washington society and to the company of his literary friends, and it also gave him an intimate knowledge of the routine of office and a familiarity with the methods of diplomacy which would serve him well in his later years as Secretary of State.[6] Seward and Hay often directed the affairs of the department or attended cabinet meetings in Evarts' absence, especially since the Secretary spent part of each summer at his Runnemede estate in Windsor, Vermont.

The post of Second Assistant Secretary again was filled by William Hunter, the most knowledgeable and experienced career man in the department. Coming in 1829 as a translator, and steadily advancing on merit, he compiled an enviable record of fifty-seven years of service, which bridged the lack of experience and the short tenure of so many Secretaries of State. Until the fall of 1877, John A. Campbell, a Grant appointee, temporarily functioned as

Third Assistant Secretary. When the job became vacant and Robert Todd Lincoln declined to serve, it at length was filled by the promotion of Charles Payson, chief of the Diplomatic Bureau.

In turn Evarts reassigned Alvey A. Adee, a "temporary clerk" with seven years prior experience as secretary to Daniel Sickles and Caleb Cushing in the Spanish legation, as the new chief of the Diplomatic Bureau in charge of correspondence with thirty legations. The appointment of Adee proved to be the most remarkable legacy of the Hayes administration to the personnel of the State Department. For the next forty-seven years, scarcely a single diplomatic document escaped his scrutiny. Without the benefit of college training, Adee developed great skill in the drafting of state papers, and he was particularly adept at summarizing a lengthy document in a single paragraph. He also knew French, German, and Spanish. On occasion, under the pressure of heavy business, the bachelor Adee slept on a cot in his office to get the work caught up. Nicknamed "the Anchor of the State Department," Adee, along with Hunter, created a style for the transaction of departmental business that far outlasted the Hayes–Evarts era. Alert to better methods, he introduced the typewriter to the department in the 1880s. For relaxation, Adee traveled through Europe with his bicycle, paddled a canoe in the Potomac, and enjoyed photography.[7]

Outside the executive and clerical ranks of the department, the diplomatic and consular services reflected more of the traditional policy of party patronage even though Evarts tried hard to appoint men of recognized ability. Of the twenty-eight legation heads who held office on March 1, 1877, only eight remained in the diplomatic service four years later. Of the twenty who resigned, only one, George F. Seward at Peking, was dismissed for misconduct.

President Hayes played an active part in the appointment of ministers and of consuls and gave important diplomatic posts to several of his political associates to whom he was indebted. Former Governor Edward F. Noyes, who had headed the Ohio delegation at Cincinnati and had placed Hayes' name in nomination, became minister to France. John A. Kasson and Edward F. Stoughton, erstwhile "visiting statesmen" to Louisiana, received appointments to Austria and Russia. More personal friends were also rewarded. James M. Comly, editor of the *Ohio State Journal*, became minister resident at Honolulu, and Alfred E. Lee, private secretary to Hayes while governor, was named consul-general in Frankfurt, Germany.

Competing factions within the Republican party received equal recognition. James G. Blaine, leader of the Half-Breeds, lobbied successfully in behalf of his former newspaper partner, John L.

Stevens, whom Hayes named minister to Sweden and Norway. Oliver P. Morton, one of the Stalwart bosses, secured the retention of the able John W. Foster at Mexico City.

In line with the President's pacification policy, some southerners received diplomatic posts. Henry W. Hilliard of Georgia represented the Hayes administration in Brazil, and Cassius Goodloe of Kentucky served in Belgium. Two black diplomats were appointed as well: John M. Langston as minister to Haiti and John H. Smyth as minister to Liberia.

Meantime Evarts, and Hayes in particular, used their influence to attract men of distinction from the intellectual community. Although George William Curtis, editor of *Harper's Weekly*, and Whitelaw Reid, editor of the New York *Tribune*, both refused diplomatic assignments, several men of letters—James Russell Lowell, Bayard Taylor, and Bret Harte—accepted appointments to head legations in Madrid and Berlin and a German consulate respectively. Two college presidents—Andrew D. White of Cornell and James B. Angell of Michigan—became United States ministers at Berlin and Peking.[8]

By and large, these diplomats selected by Hayes and Evarts had neither training nor tenure but performed their duties conscientiously. Kasson, a man of vision, even suggested reforming the diplomatic and consular services to ensure a career corps of men carefully trained in the history, the language, and the culture of the countries to which they would be sent.[9] Lowell suffered under the handicap of being known as an impractical "literary fellow," but he gradually learned by doing and enlivened routine diplomatic dispatches with his literary grace and sense of humor. On one occasion when the Spanish government complained that an American firm, in collusion with a Frenchman named Fourcarde, was illegally smuggling refined oil into Spain to avoid duties, Lowell penned a graphic report to Evarts:

> The Frenchman . . . established his storehouses in the suburbs, and then hiring all the leanest and least mammalian women that could be found, he made good all their physical defects with tin cases filled with petroleum, thus giving them what Dr. Johnson would have called the pectorial proportions of Juno. Doubtless he blasphemed the unwise parsimony of Nature in denying to women in general the multitudinous breasts displayed by certain Hindu idols. For some time these milky mothers passed without question into the unsuspecting city and supplied thousands of households with that cheap enlightenment which cynics say is worse than none. Meanwhile M. Fourcarde's pockets swelled in exact proportion to the quaker breastworks of the improvised wetnurses. Could he only have been moderate! Could he only have bethought him in time of the *ne quid nimis*. But one fatal day he sent in a damsel

whose contours aroused in one of the guardians at the gates the
same emotions as those of Maritornes in the bosom of the carrier.
With the playful gallantry of a superior he tapped the object of
his admiration and—it tinkled. He had "struck oil" unawares. Love
shook his wings and fled; Duty entered frowning; and M. Fourcarde's perambulating wells suddenly went dry.[10]

Evarts made his mark best as Secretary of State in improving
the administration and personnel of the counsular service. He
announced he intended to fill all desirable consulships by promotion or on a merit basis. By July 1877, the department had over
seven thousand applications on file and within a year made fifty-
four promotions.[11]

One of Secretary Evarts' primary objectives was to use the State
Department to increase and promote American business abroad.
In emphasizing foreign trade, he acted on the premise that American prosperity depended upon the sale of surplus products abroad.
In a circular letter to all South American consuls, Evarts requested
them to send regular reports outlining some practical measures
to increase United States trade in Latin America. These documents
were then issued monthly in pamphlet form by the State Department for the benefit of American businessmen and manufacturers.
The most important of Evarts' letters of instruction was sent to
all American consuls in Europe and directed them to investigate
five points: rate of wages, cost of living, comparison of wages
for the preceding five years, amount of money in circulation and
condition of trade, and the system of business in the district.
This directive led to the most important effort of the State Department up to that time in employing the consular corps to gather
commercial statistics.[12]

Evarts also facilitated faster communication between consuls and
customs officals, and he required every consul to make a serious
study of the language and history of his host country. New
ministries were established in Colombia and Bolivia (1878) and
Romania (1880).

By the time the Hayes administration left office in March 1881,
American exports had sharply increased, and the President paid
a well-deserved tribute to Evarts' contribution in his annual message of December 1880: "The efforts of the Department of State
to enlarge the trade and commerce of the United States, through
the active agency of consular officers and through the dissemina-
tion of information obtained from them, have been unrelaxed. . . .
The importance and interest attached to the reports of consular
officers are witnessed by the general demand for them by all classes
of merchants and manufacturers engaged in our foreign trade.[13]

President Hayes,
statesman of reunion.
From the
New York Daily Graphic,
April 3, 1877.

Official reception of the first Chinese minister to the United States, September 28, 1878.
From Frank Leslie's Illustrated Newspaper, *October 19, 1878.*

A powwow at the White House.
From Harper's Weekly, January 22, 1881.

During the Hayes administration, there were no great diplomatic issues. Without a large army or a big navy, the United States wisely avoided war and annexed no territory. Expanding commercial ties to sell domestic surpluses and to restore prosperity meant far more to Evarts than territorial gains or newspaper headlines. A great deal of concern had been expressed about the "glut of goods in home markets," and when Hayes in 1880 made the first important plea by a chief executive since 1865 for a larger navy, he was undoubtedly influenced by the fact that in the previous decade, 1870–1880, American export trade had increased more than 200 percent.[14] New markets were opened in Asia, and exports to Europe rose dramatically between 1877 and 1881.

While Secretary of State, Evarts had to resolve certain political questions, such as the murder of American missionaries in Turkey, the drafting of naturalized citizens by Germany, and the expulsion of Jewish-Americans from Russia. The most important diplomatic crises he faced concerned Mexican-American relations, French interests in an interoceanic canal, and the restriction of Chinese immigration.

A variety of elements entered into American diplomatic relations with Mexico between 1877 and 1880: delayed recognition of the Díaz government; Mexico's repeated inability to keep order on the American frontier; intermittent invasions of Mexico by American troops to punish marauding Indians; Mexican fears of American territorial ambitions; and the strong desire of American business promoters to make investments in Mexico. Finally, after three years of trouble, Hayes and Evarts, in a diplomatic about-face, reversed their nonrecognition and "hot pursuit" policies. Good relations returned, and Mexico opened her door to American capital.[15] It would be a mistake, however, to credit Evarts with the new friendship. The improvement in Mexican–American relations came about because of changed circumstances rather than through any negotiated settlement.

In November 1876, Porfirio Díaz overthrew President Sebastian Lerdo de Tejada, drove him from Mexico City, and established himself as a de facto President. Within a few months, Díaz won an easy election victory and, with it, control of virtually the entire country. But in the interim, Indian raiders from Mexico, taking advantage of their country's uncertain leadership, crossed the border and raided towns in northwest Texas and southeast New Mexico. Since the Díaz government could not control these brigands, American forces, in hot pursuit, followed the marauders into Mexican territory.

Unlike most other governments, the United States under Hayes

refused to grant recognition to the Díaz regime until it had proved
its capacity to patrol the border and to maintain order. Another
factor further complicated matters. A free zone (Zona Libre) extending along the whole border aggravated the ordinary nuisance of
smuggling. Since European manufacturers could send goods there
duty free, smuggling became both possible and profitable.

In refusing to recognize a de facto government in Mexico and
in upholding a policy of hot pursuit, Evarts broke with traditional
American policy toward Mexico.[16] The Díaz government was slow
in preventing further border raids because General Escabedo, Lerdo's Minister of War, had launched a counterrevolutionary movement there. Díaz first had to secure the area around the Texas
border.

While the Díaz forces attempted to capture Escabedo, other
outlaws operated freely back and forth across the border. Before
Colonel Vallarta, minister for foreign affairs under Díaz, could
stop these renewed border depradations, Secretary of War George
McCrary issued a fateful order on June 1, 1877, to General Edward
O. Ord, commander of the United States Army in Texas, *authorizing*
him to pursue bandits across the border if and when necessary.
This order, the most aggressive foreign policy action taken by
the Hayes administration, gave credence to Mexico's suspicions
of American annexationist designs upon her territory, while at
home Evarts and Hayes were charged with attempting to divert
attention away from the chief executive's disputed election and
other domestic problems. James G. Blaine, in a Fourth of July
speech at Woodstock, Connecticut, associated the administration's
southern policy with that toward Mexico by proclaiming that the
real purpose of the government was to pacify southerners by annexing the northern states of Mexico.

Contrary to these allegations, Evarts' strong policy actually was
designed to protect Americans along the border. Like President
Hayes, he maintained this protection had to precede recognition.
Hayes replied to Blaine on July 6: "Nothing hostile to Mexico or
detrimental to her interests is intended. As to annexing any part
of the Mexican territory there is no thought of it, and the United
States does not want any more territory in that direction even if
offered as a gift."[17]

John W. Foster, the American minister to Mexico, believed
strongly that the United States should recognize the Díaz regime,
and in the summer of 1877 he requested permission to come to
Washington to present his views. Evarts denied Foster's petition,
and instead instructed him to negotiate a treaty with Mexico settling all outstanding differences between the two nations. As the
price of recognizing Díaz, the American government now insisted

upon an end to border raids and asked that Mexico allow reciprocal crossing of the border in pursuit of ruffians.

The instructions to Foster marked a significant shift in American policy. Initially the United States had asked only that cooperation in the effective suppression of frontier disturbances precede the recognition of Díaz, but now it assumed the more advanced position of requiring Mexico to admit the right of the United States to pursue offenders into Mexico as a condition to a treaty settling all issues between the countries, and, in turn, requiring that such a treaty be a condition for extending recognition to Díaz.[18] Mexico, of course, demanded recognition prior to any settlement of grievances.

The year 1877 ended with negotiations deadlocked between the United States and Mexico. Early in January 1878, Foster arrived in Washington to testify before a House committee. The minister's testimony and private conversations with Evarts persuaded the Secretary to reverse America's Mexican policy, and, in April 1878, the United States finally recognized the Díaz government, nearly a year after it had been recognized by the major powers of Europe.

Contrary to American expectations, settlement of the other outstanding issues between Mexico and the United States did not follow recognition of the Díaz government, largely because Mexico refused to make any agreement on border crossings unless the United States revoked the order of June 1, and Hayes, with the united backing of his cabinet, declined to withdraw the order until border conditions rendered its existence unnecessary.

Díaz nevertheless continued to press for revocation of the order of June 1. By removing troublesome Indians to the Mexican interior during the winter of 1878–1879, he improved border conditions and removed a major source of American complaints. The Texan side of the frontier remained quiet during the summer and autumn of 1879, and General Ord, in his 1879 annual report to Secretary McCrary, indicated he thought the need to cross the border no longer existed. Foster also submitted an encouraging report on the frontier situation. On March 1, 1880, Evarts notified Don Manuel de Zamacona, the Mexican minister to the United States, of the revocation of the controversial order of June 1.[19]

Improved Mexican–American relations thus came about through factors other than diplomacy. For one thing, Díaz decided to suppress raids into Texas. Americans interested in developing trade with Mexico also prompted Evarts to reconsider American policy. They argued persuasively that nonrecognition hurt trade by creating hostility against Americans. The Mexican Congress passed a law decreeing the free importation of flour and grain into the northern states of Mexico and authorized mail steamship service between several Mexican ports and American cities. Díaz employed agents in the United States to court American public opinion in favor of his administration. Meanwhile, John W. Foster and the State Department's diplomatic bureau strongly urged Evarts to recognize Díaz since he had proved his ability to endure, had taken measures to stop border raids, had improved communication with the United States, and had met Mexico's financial obligations. Once the Hayes administration rescinded the order of June 1, trade and investment improved steadily, and, in September 1880, Díaz granted concessions to two American-financed railroad companies in Mexico.

Thus none of the chief issues were really resolved by diplomacy. Improvement in border conditions actually resulted from the growth of federal power in Mexico. In like manner, forced loans on Americans in Mexico disappeared as stability was restored in Mexican affairs. The free zone also became less of a problem as American goods competed favorably with the smuggled European product. The doctrine of hot pursuit, by creating ill-will against the United States, had hampered rather than fostered good relations with Mexico.

In his protracted political struggle with the United States, Díaz won both of his major objectives—diplomatic recognition and revocation of the June 1 order—and surrendered nothing of value. Evarts, while less than a victor, did realize his main goal of protecting American lives and property. By the time he and Hayes left office, border raids were negligible.

While Mexican relations gradually improved, a second diplomatic challenge confronted Hayes and Evarts in Central America. In 1879 a French company, headed by Ferdinand de Lesseps, the builder of the Suez Canal, proposed to construct an interoceanic canal across the Isthmus of Panama.

This new development required President Hayes to reappraise American policy. How would such a project relate to the Monroe Doctrine? How would it affect treaties with Colombia (1846) and Nicaragua (1847), which granted the United States the right of isthmian transit and protection, or another treaty with Great Britain (1850), which promised that neither country would attempt exclusive control over a ship canal? Throughout January and February 1880, Hayes steadily evolved the concept of the "paramount interest" of the United States in hemispheric affairs[20] and in a special message to Congress on March 8, 1880, he vigorously declared that an isthmian canal would be "virtually a part of the coastline of the United States" and that "the policy of this country is a canal under American control."[21]

Until 1879, no country had ever attempted to construct a canal, although the Clayton-Bulwer Treaty of 1850 between England and the United States offered support to the first company which would make the effort. After de Lesseps began to discuss a Central American canal, the United States House of Representatives, in June 1879, requested Hayes to report on American attempts to promote such a canal. Hayes replied promptly through Evarts: "The policy of the United States on the general subject of isthmian transit is understood to have been, and to be, not to undertake the construction of a ship-canal on its own account, even if the practicability of such a work at a reasonable cost were to be shown, but to secure by treaties protection to the capital of such citizens as might be disposed to embark in the enterprise."[22]

Considered by many to be too lenient, the Evarts statement evoked considerable congressional and press criticism in the United States. Meanwhile de Lesseps sought to lessen American opposition to his project by visiting the United States and by offering stock in his construction company to American investors. To further "Americanize" the whole enterprise, he even offered the presidency of the company to General Grant, who declined on Evarts' advice.

Unlike his Secretary of State, who did not sense any real urgency, Hayes believed that the time had come to state strongly American policy with respect to the proposed isthmian canal. He wanted to make it absolutely clear that the United States would not consent to any European power controlling a railroad or a canal across the isthmus.[23] Early in 1880 he sent two naval vessels to the Pacific and Atlantic shores of the isthmus to look for coaling stations, which "will give us a foothold which will be of vast service in controlling the passage from Ocean to Ocean either at Panama or at Nicaragua Lake."[24] On February 10 he took up the matter with his cabinet and enlisted their full support for sending a special message to the Senate, which welcomed the assertion of American power. The President's proclamation extended the Monroe Doctrine and laid the groundwork for all future United States policy in the isthmus: "The policy of this country is a canal under American control. The United States cannot consent to the surrender of this control to any European power, or to any combination of European powers. If existing treaties between the United States and other nations, or if the rights of sovereignty or property of other nations stand in the way of this policy—a contingency which is not apprehended—suitable steps should be taken by just and liberal negotiations to promote and establish the American policy on this subject, consistently with the rights of the nations to be affected by it."[25]

Fortunately for the United States, the French government did not back de Lesseps, and his company, which started digging a canal in 1881, eventually went bankrupt in 1888. For the time being, American fears of a foreign-built canal subsided. Unable to stop the French project at its inception, Hayes and Evarts also refused to back American entrepreneurs, including Admiral Daniel Ammen and James B. Eads, who proposed alternate routes across the isthmus. The principal significance of the Hayes isthmian policy lay in the future. The Monroe Doctrine, originally aimed at European political interference in Latin America, was now enlarged to embrace economic control as well, creating a precedent later followed by Theodore Roosevelt and Henry Cabot Lodge.[26]

A sidelight to the ill-fated de Lesseps Panamanian venture involved Hayes' Secretary of the Navy, Richard W. Thompson. When General Grant refused to associate himself with de Lesseps, that wily promoter enticed Thompson to lend his prestige to the enterprise by accepting a well-paid position as chairman of the American Committee of the Panama Canal Company. Thompson notified Hayes on August 18, 1880, of his interest in accepting the attractive offer but wished to know if such an action "would be, in your view, in any way inconsistent with my relations to the administration and the doctrines of your proclamation."[27] Hayes suggested a personal interview to ascertain the facts more fully, but Thompson's absence from Washington and the President's impending western tour prevented a meeting. Before leaving on his trip, however, Hayes did indicate he presumed Thompson would not accept any other employment while still a member of the cabinet, and he recommended that Thompson see Evarts about the propriety of any association with the de Lesseps American syndicate even after Thompson was no longer an official of the government.[28] In December, when Thompson felt constrained to accept the new job anyway, Hayes promptly cashiered him. To fill the vacancy in the cabinet, the President appointed Nathan Goff, a West Virginia attorney, who filled the post for the remaining two months of the administration.

The third major diplomatic controversy of the Hayes administration concerned the Chinese question, which had its origin in the depression of 1873, and the growing resentment of American laborers toward Chinese workers.[29] News of rioting in eastern cities during the Railway Strike of 1877 touched off a series of violent anti-Chinese demonstrations in San Francisco. The California Workingmen's party had called a meeting on July 22 to express sympathy for their fellow workers in the East. After the meeting, a motley crowd, including hoodlums and workers angered by Chinese labor competition, went to Chinatown, where they smashed windows, burned a laundry, and destroyed fifteen washhouses.[30]

The problem of Chinese immigration had troubled the West for years. Originally welcomed in 1848, when cheap labor was needed for railroad construction, the Chinese grew less acceptable when they turned to other occupations after the railroads were completed. Racial prejudices also appeared, and a minority of American citizens began to agitate for the abrogation of the Burlingame Treaty of 1868, which permitted unrestricted immigration. So strong did the idea of limiting Chinese immigration become that, by 1876, the platforms of both major parties endorsed the principle. Efforts even were made by state and national legislators arbitrarily to abrogate the Burlingame Treaty without executive or State Department action.

Other events further helped to transform the Chinese problem from a local West Coast issue into a question of national importance and interest. A special committee from the California Senate appeared before the House of Representatives in 1877 to present arguments against Chinese immigration. They objected primarily to the failure of the Chinese to assimilate into American society. The committee also listed as complaints the poor position of women in Oriental society, the Chinese acceptance of human slavery, the fact that the Chinese paid little in taxes, unsanitary living conditions, and competition with American labor.[31] Since they ate cheaper food and most of them were "coolies" who did not have to support a family like the American laboring man, the Chinamen were also condemned for contributing to white unemployment.

In contrast to the California committee's petition, the Forty-fifth Congress also received a documentary report from a Joint Comittee of Congress, headed by the late Senator Oliver P. Morton, which had investigated firsthand in California the whole question of Chinese immigration. The Morton Report gave a much more favorable picture of Chinese contributions to California's development, and concluded: "The testimony of many of the witnesses went to show that but for Chinese labor the State would not have half the population, property, and production she has today."[32]

Out of the ensuing congressional debate over the issue came the "Fifteen Passenger Bill," which provided that no more than fifteen Chinese immigrants per ship should be allowed to enter the United States, with violators subject to a fine of one hundred dollars for each passenger and imprisonment for six months. As lawyers, President Hayes and Secretary of State Evarts viewed the bill negatively since they believed the United States could not abrogate a treaty without first approaching China through diplomatic channels. Evarts also opposed congressional interference with the Burlingame Treaty because of his strong desire not to injure American foreign trade.[33] Hayes considered the issue more of a labor problem than an immigration matter since the Chinese did not come to settle in family groups. He opposed the Fifteen Passenger Bill, which amounted to virtual exclusion, as a violation of national faith. Besides, the Burlingame Treaty was of our own making, negotiated by our own minister, urged upon China, and, he concluded, we had profited by it.[34]

These views the President wrote into his veto message of March 1, 1879, utilizing, however, a version written by Evarts similar to his own phraseology. When Congress failed to override the veto, Hayes and Evarts were free to open negotiations with China on revision of the existing treaty. A special three-man commission, headed by James B. Angell, president of the University of Michigan, went to China to seek a new treaty. Angell was accompanied by John T. Swift of California and William H. Trescott, a former State Department official.

Within a few months China agreed to "regulate, limit, or suspend the immigration of Chinese labourers" according to the social and political interests of the United States.[35] At the same time, a new commercial treaty was negotiated. These agreements, signed by China in November 1880, and by the United States in January 1881, capped Hayes' successful four-year Asian policy.

In addition to settling the Chinese issue amicably, Evarts created good relations with Japan by recognizing its claim to tariff autonomy. He also opened Korea further to American trade, successfully defended a reciprocity treaty with Hawaii, and obtained Pago Pago for a naval station, along with commercial privileges in Samoa, before either Great Britain or Germany could seize the initiative.

In Europe, Evarts' diplomacy met with less success. He was unable to secure revocation of French and Austrian bans on American pork products. He did negotiate trademark and consular conventions and opened trade avenues to Serbia and Romania. But he missed a major opportunity to enlarge American trade when he failed to secure a Franco-American commercial treaty.

Evarts also had mixed success in the western hemisphere. While Mexican and isthmian problems subsided, he failed to obtain a commercial union with Canada. He could not stop the Dominican revolt or the War of the Pacific, both of which hurt American trade. He left the fisheries problem unsettled, and he did not achieve his original goal of reciprocity treaties with the Latin American countries.

Nevertheless, all matters considered, the nation's search for prosperity through expanded foreign markets remains the principal legacy of the Hayes administration to American foreign policy.[36]

Notes

1. See Thomas A. Bailey, *A Diplomatic History of the American People,* 4th ed. (New York: Appleton-Century-Crofts, Inc., 1950), 426–442; David M. Pletcher, *The Awkward Years: American Foreign Relations under Garfield and Arthur* (Columbia: University of Missouri Press, 1962), xi–xvi; Milton Plesur, "America Looking Outward: The Years from Hayes to Harrison," *The Historian* 22 (May 1960): 280–295.

2. Two recent dissertations on Evarts should be noted: Sister M. George Bernard Hutton, S.S.N.D., "William M. Evarts, Secretary of State, 1877–1881" (Ph.D. diss., The Catholic University of America, 1966), and Gary Pennanen, "The Foreign Policy of William Maxwell Evarts" (Ph.D. diss., University of Wisconsin, 1969). Graham H. Stuart, *The Department of State* (New York: The Macmillan Company, 1949), 146–151, compares Fish and Evarts as Secretaries of State.

3. Stuart, *Department of State,* 142–146; William Barnes and John Heath Morgan, *The Foreign Service of the United States* (Washington: Historical Office of the Department of State, 1961), 131–139.

4. Pennanen, "Foreign Policy of Evarts," 76. By 1881, when Evarts turned over the conduct of state affairs to his successor, James G. Blaine, the department still employed only thirty-six clerks. Of these, four were women. Salaries ranged from $900 to $1,800 for clerks; $2,100 to $2,500 for bureau chiefs; $3,500 for each of the assistant secretaries; and $8,000 for Secretary Evarts, who nevertheless earned a reputation for "magnificent hospitality." Stuart, *Department of State,* 155. The highest paid American minister received $17,500. Chester L. Barrows, *William M. Evarts* (Chapel Hill: The University of North Carolina Press, 1941), 345.

5. *Congressional Directory,* 1st ed. 45th cong., 1st sess. (Washington: Government Printing Office, 1877), 101; *Register of the Department of State* (Washington: Government Printing Office, 1878), 5–10.

6. Tyler Dennett, *John Hay: From Poetry to Politics* (New York: Dodd, Mead and Company, 1933), 126–129.

7. "Alvey Augustus Adee" in Allen Johnson and Dumas Malone, eds., *Dictionary of American Biography* (New York: Charles Scribner's Sons, 1928–37), I, 105–107.

8. Pennanen, "Foreign Policy of Evarts," 82–84. See also Lyon N. Richardson, "Men of Letters and the Hayes Administration," *New England Quarterly* 15 (March 1942): 110–141.

9. Edward Younger, *John A. Kasson* (Iowa City: State Historical Society of Iowa, 1955), 282–283.

10. James Russell Lowell to William M. Evarts, February 6, 1878, No. 66, National Archives (Fourcarde), cited in Martin Duberman, *James Russell Lowell* (Boston: Beacon Press, 1966), 285–286.

11. Barrows, *Evarts,* 344.

12. Hutton, "Evarts, Secretary of State," 195–197.

13. James D. Richardson, ed., *A Compilation of the Messages and Papers of the Presidents* (New York: Bureau of National Literature, Inc., 1897), X, 4564.

14. Robert Seager II, "Ten Years Before Mahan: The Unofficial Case for the New Navy, 1880–1890," *The Mississippi Valley Historical Review* 40 (December 1953): 494.

15. David M. Pletcher, "Mexico Opens the Door to American Capital, 1877–1880," *The Americas* 16 (July 1959): 1.

16. In part, he and Hayes objected to the method Díaz used in gaining power. "This delay [in recognition] was first due to a prudent hesitation to acknowledge authorities emanating from a revolution which subverted the established constitutional order and endangered the existence of republican government, and to a desire to be assured that his election was approved by the Mexican people and to ascertain whether his administration had stability and a disposition to comply with the rules of international comity and the obligations of treaties." James Morton Callahan, *American Foreign Policy in Mexican Relations* (New York: The Macmillan Company, 1932), 369.

17. New York *Tribune*, July 6, 1877, cited in Pennanen, "Foreign Policy of Evarts," 156.

18. Charles W. Hackett, "The Recognition of the Díaz Government by the United States," *Southwestern Historical Quarterly* 28 (July 1924): 50.

19. See Pennanen, "Foreign Policy of Evarts," 292–312, for the most recent appraisal of the Evarts–Díaz struggle. I have summarized his findings.

20. Hayes, Diary, January 13, February 7, 8, 11, 17, 1880, Hayes Papers, RBHL.

21. Richardson, *Messages and Papers*, X, 4537–4538.

22. U.S., Congress, House, *Message from the President of the United States Transmitting a Report from the Secretary of State Relative to the Steps taken by the Government of the United States to Promote the Construction of an Interoceanic Canal across the Isthmus of Darien, The Darien Interoceanic Canal*, 46th Cong., 1st sess., 1879, Ex. Doc. 10, p. 3, cited in Hutton, "Evarts, Secretary of State," 179.

23. Hayes, Diary, February 11, 1880.

24. Ibid., January 13, 1880.

25. U.S., Congress, Senate, Committee on Foreign Relations, *Message from the President of the United States in Response to Senate Resolution of February 11, 1880, Covering Report of Secretary of State, with Accompanying Documents, in Relation to the Proposed Interoceanic Canal between the Atlantic and Pacific Oceans*, 46th Cong., 2d sess., 1880, cited in Hutton, "Evarts, Secretary of State," 185. Evarts believed the French project would fail anyway without his active opposition. He did not wish to involve the United States in a dispute with England over the Clayton-Bulwer Treaty. Pennanen, "Foreign Policy of Evarts," 328.

26. Pennanen, "Foreign Policy of Evarts," 347–348, 352–353.

27. R. W. Thompson to Hayes, August 18, 1880, Hayes Papers, RBHL.

28. Thompson to Hayes, August 26, 1880, Hayes to Thompson, August 28, 1880, Hayes Papers, RBHL.

29. The most recent article on the controversy over Chinese immigration is Gary Pennanen, "Public Opinion and the Chinese Question, 1876–1879," *Ohio History* 77 (Winter, Spring, Summer 1968): 139–148.

30. Ralph Kauer, "The Workingmen's Party of California," *The Pacific Historical Review* 13, no. 3 (September 1944): 279.

31. U.S., Congress, House, *An Address to the People of the United States upon the Social, Moral, and Political Effect of Chinese Immigration, Prepared*

by a Committee of the Senate of California, Referred to the Committee on Education and Labor, 45th Cong., 1st sess., 1877, Misc. Doc. 9, p. 3, cited in Hutton, "Evarts, Secretary of State," 141.

32. Ibid., 143, citing U.S., Congress, Senate, Views of the late Oliver P. Morton on the Character, Extent, and Effect of Chinese Immigration to the United States, 45th Cong., 2d sess., 1878, Misc. Doc. 20, pp. 5–7.

33. Ibid., 145–146.

34. Hayes, Diary, February 20, 23, 1879. As Hayes understood the problem, very serious questions were at issue: Could one party to a treaty unilaterally repudiate a part of it? And could the Senate by legislation alter the nature of a treaty?

35. William H. Trescott to Evarts, November 8, 1880, Evarts Papers, Library of Congress, cited in Hutton, "Evarts, Secretary of State," 153.

36. My summary of Evarts' record as Secretary of State parallels the résumé given by Pennanen, "Foreign Policy of Evarts," 494–498.

14

The New Union and the
Hayes Tours

In a predominantly newspaper age, long before the advent of radio and television, President Hayes spent much of his four-year term traveling throughout the United States. His purpose was unyielding: to dispel dissension and to restore harmony in American life. Beset by critics in both the political arena and the press, he strove to put his cause and himself directly before the American people. His easy and enthusiastic manner, his cordial and earnest speeches, and his constant appeal to the minds and hearts of individuals took effect as the bitterness of Reconstruction steadily subsided. While many of his trips were avowedly nonpolitical, they definitely helped to project a favorable image of the chief executive, his family, and his advisers. Moreover, the President's many travels strengthened the power and reach of the presidential office and proved to be one of his more effective political maneuvers.

In addition to extended official tours into New England, the South, and the West, Hayes made many shorter trips to attend state and county fairs, dedications, historical anniversaries, and commencement ceremonies. Harvard, Yale, and Johns Hopkins all conferred honorary doctorates on the visiting chief executive.[1] In New York City Hayes participated in the dedication of new buildings for the Museum of Natural History and the Metropolitan Museum of Art, two major landmarks in the nation's cultural progress.[2] Other junkets took him to Mount Vernon and James Madison's estate in Virginia. In the summer of 1879, accompanied by four cabinet officers, he explored the ruins of Westmoreland, Washington's birthplace. After dropping anchor in the Potomac River, he was carried ashore by sailors, and then hiked a mile over marshy ground.[3] What Hayes enjoyed most, however, were soldiers' reunions.

On another trip to see the famous North Dakota wheat fields just before harvest time, he also attended the opening of the Minnesota state fair where an episode typical of the ineptitude of special committees occurred. Ex-Governor Alexander Ramsey and his wife, friends of the Hayes, wished to open their home for a general reception, but the local committee declined their offer in favor of a hotel banquet and reception, adding the suggestion that instead the Ramseys might entertain the President and his party for breakfast. So a club breakfast featuring filet mignon and prairie chicken was prepared by Mrs. Ramsey and her servants. That afternoon when the official party returned from the fair, and Mrs. Ramsey casually inquired of her husband when the committee would arrive to escort President and Mrs. Hayes to the hotel banquet, she was stunned to be told the committee could not manage a banquet for such a large crowd and that only a reception would be held. That meant *she* would be responsible for serving the dinner! With nothing prepared to eat in the house, her servants still at the fair, and no caterer nearby, Mrs. Ramsey frantically searched her wooden icebox and found what remained of the morning meal. Dinner was prepared using the sirloins (from which the filets had been removed) and the legs of the prairie chickens, which she good-naturedly told the President were considered the most delicate part of the bird. In her gracious manner Mrs. Hayes assured her hostess she enjoyed the meal far more than if the official banquet had been held. This was no doubt true. But for Mrs. Ramsey it was not the dinner she would have wished to set before the President and first lady of the land![4]

The President's great concern for education prompted a number of other trips and important speeches. On these occasions he was usually accompanied by Mrs. Hayes. Early in his term they took an interest in Virginia's Hampton Institute.[5] In 1878 and again in 1880 Hayes attended anniversary ceremonies at Hampton, counseling the students "to work—to earn—to save.... If you earn $10—save a little of it. If you earn $100, save more. The difference between spending all and saving something is the difference between misery and happiness."[6] He recognized that peaceful resolution of the problems of a multiracial society was the most pressing challenge still confronting the nation and stressed the importance of fraternal feeling between the sections and equal rights for all citizens: "How to deal with these various classes, these different populations which make up American society.... The main question is how to fuse them into one great, harmonious whole. That question Hampton Institute is solving. It is by dealing with all as children of our great Father.... Sectionalism and race prejudice... are the only two enemies America has any cause to fear."[7]

A return to Gambier, Ohio, was always a favorite pilgrimage of the President. At Kenyon's June 1880 commencement exercises he noted, with pardonable pride, the progress of his alma mater: "Kenyon College plainly now stands on a solid foundation. Situated as it is near the center of the Central State of the Union—easily reached from all parts of the Country—with a site of unsurpassed beauty—perfectly healthy and comfortable for labor and study at all seasons—removed completely from every influence unfriendly to virtue and to scholarly pursuits—with ample grounds and buildings, *and out of debt.*" Drawing upon his own experience, the President praised the virtues of similar institutions:

> The student of the small college who has diligently and thoroughly mastered the studies of his courses will surely find that he is at no disadvantage as compared with the greatest of what are known as the great-Colleges in the training, elementary knowledge, and habits of thought and study which are requisite for success in the professions or in any field of learning or science which he may choose to enter. There are compensations in the little colleges for the well known advantages of the larger institutions. I do not disparage the great colleges. I know by comparison of results. I merely say to you as students of one of the smaller colleges you need not dread more than others the competitions by which in practical life merit is discovered and determined.[8]

Many unusual episodes occurred in the course of Hayes' travels. On a trip to Philadelphia to spend the 1879 Thanksgiving holiday with the family of Methodist Bishop Matthew Simpson, the President departed from the standard official policy of traveling by special railway car. Instead, accompanied by his valet, Isaiah Lancaster, he purchased two coach tickets for the 5:30 P.M. Baltimore and Potomac train. The action was typical, for throughout his public career, Hayes took pleasure in appearing incognito He liked to know what people were thinking without inhibiting their conversation by his high office. Somewhat to his chagrin he discovered the technique did not work so well now that he was President of the United States. An excerpt from Hayes' diary reveals his difficulties:

> I preferred to go without fuss. I had a ticket to Baltimore. But paid forty cents—apparently for Isaiah, but I didn't understand it. A family ticket which I had, included I suppose servants. I was as polite as the conductor, and made no remark. Fare was paid from Baltimore to Phila. for both of us—I think 3:00 [sic] each. On my return I paid $15.00 for fare on B. & O. and for sleeping berth—two sections, leaving Phila. at 11:30 P.M. Soon after lying

down the Conductor told me he had orders to return my fare. I
took it without counting. This morning at 7 P.M. before leaving
the car the conductor told me he had orders to return me the fare
paid on the 26th and gave me 3:00 [*sic*]. This was for fare I suppose
leaving me to pay for *my* own sleeping berth. All of this pleasantly
done, but I suspect I make less trouble if I ask for a special car.

Still he had some measure of success: "On the way up a Mr.
Sutton of the Eastern Shore—clerk in the great wholesale store
of Jacob——& Co., Phila., took a seat by my side. I got much
interesting information about his business and the trade generally."[9]

Of all the Hayes tours, the most dramatic and extended was
a western trip to the Pacific Coast in the fall of 1880, marking
the first time any President had crossed the continent while in
office (although Grant had visited as far west as Utah in 1875).[10]
The trip, personally nonpolitical in nature, with few prepared
speeches, allowed Hayes to do something important during his
final months in office, and left Garfield's men unhampered in their
management of the 1880 Republican presidential campaign. Originally planned for the spring of 1879, the great western tour had
to be postponed for more than a year because an extra session
of Congress required the President's presence in Washington.[11]
Hayes, however, kept in mind the idea of a grand tour as one
way of unifying the nation and promoting pride in America's
material progress and future potential. On June 18, 1880, he publicly announced his intention to make a Pacific trip. General W. T.
Sherman, an old friend, familiar with the terrain to be traversed,
laid out the route and methods of travel, an assignment he dutifully
performed knowing full well he would have to defer to the
President's whims instead of his own preferences on some details.[12] Sherman received help from various army posts and com-
manders scattered throughout the West. Colonel John Jameson of
the Railway Mail Service supervised the day-to-day travel accommodations and kept the accounts.[13] Generally speaking, various
railroads provided a director's car for the President's comfort; the
travelers stopped at military posts en route and used hotels sparingly, receiving their overnight accommodations and hospitality
as a courtesy of army generals or well-known businessmen and
public officials like Irvin McDowell and Leland Stanford. Hayes
kept in constant touch with Washington affairs by telegraph lest
some event require his speedy return to the capital. Fortunately
no emergencies developed, and he kept to his tour schedule.

The size of the official party fluctuated throughout the journey,
but usually averaged about nineteen. A limiting factor, especially
restricting the number of women in the party, was the necessity

of using army field ambulances to cover some five to six hundred miles of rough roads and desert country between railheads.[14] As finally constituted, the official party consisted of President Hayes, army Chief-of-Staff William Tecumseh Sherman, and Secretary of War Alexander Ramsey, together with members of their immediate families, personal friends, and staff assistants. Hayes took his wife Lucy, two sons, Birchard and Rutherford, a favorite niece, Laura (Mrs. John G. Mitchell), and two friends from Cincinnati, Mr. and Mrs. John W. Herron. Isaiah Lancaster attended to the President's personal needs, while Mrs. S. O. Hunt, a young matron from Oakland, California, who had been staying in Washington, came along as a guest of Mrs. Hayes.[15] General Sherman brought his daughter Rachel, Mrs. Joseph Crain Audenreid, the recently widowed wife of his longtime military aide, and General Alexander McDowell McCook, another of his aides. Secretary Ramsey's contingent included his son-in-law, Charles E. Furness of Philadelphia, and his private secretary and personal adviser, Colonel Thomas F. Barr of the War Department, who was accompanied by his wife Julia. Colonel Jameson and Dr. David Lowe Huntington, an army surgeon from the Soldier's Home in Washington, completed the presidential party.

Hayes attended his army reunion in Canton, Ohio, on September 1, 1880, and then departed for Chicago to join the rest of the official party, except for Secretary Ramsey who met them at Omaha. For the next two months, the travelers enjoyed an extraordinary journey of some ten thousand miles, notable for superb weather, grandiose scenery, good health, and freedom from accidents.[16] About eighty cities lay along their route, which they covered by train, stagecoach, army ambulance, steamer, ferryboat, tug, yacht, and ocean vessel. On the way West, stops were made at Cheyenne, Salt Lake City, and Lake Tahoe before the party recuperated for twelve days in the San Francisco area. From here the road lay northward to Oregon and the Washington Territory, with exciting side trips up the Columbia River to Walla Walla and around Puget Sound. Then they embarked at Astoria for the return to San Francisco by ocean steamer. They took a side trip to Yosemite National Park after which the President boarded the Southern Pacific Railway via Los Angeles and headed into the Southwest. Here the army prudently posted pickets and stationed several fresh relays of horses for the hazardous two-day journey by field ambulances across the desert and hostile Apache country. Arriving in Santa Fe on October 28, the President hastened back to Ohio (skipping a planned stop in Denver), in order to reach Fremont just in time to cast his vote for James A. Garfield on November 2. Mrs. Hunt

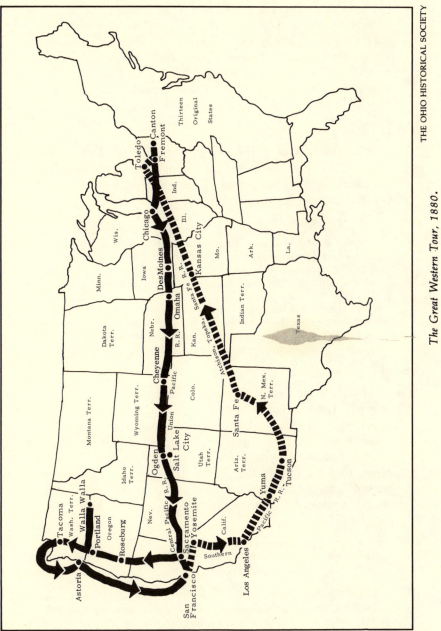

The Great Western Tour, 1880.

THE OHIO HISTORICAL SOCIETY

apparently left the tour upon reaching her home in California, and Birchard returned home ahead of his parents.[17]

A pattern emerged during the first few days of the tour. Local Republican politicians would board the President's train to greet him personally and often to ride along to the next stop. Wherever the train paused briefly, Hayes appeared and spoke a few extempore words. Sherman and Ramsey usually followed with a few felicitous remarks of their own, and then Mrs. Hayes and the other ladies would be presented to the waiting crowd. After cannon, rifle, or whistle salutes, martial music, frequently a band playing "Hail to the Chief" or "Marching Through Georgia," completed the brief festivities.

In his informal way, Hayes used these whistle-stops to personal and political advantage, and he was actually better prepared than his casual manner suggested. A memo written to himself reveals his thoughts on his preparation for the trip:

> As I now see it congratulations on the condition and prospects of our Country will almost always be appropriate. In order to make them of some interest let me gather facts as to restored Union, sound financial condition, increase of exports of Agricultural & Manufacturing products—balance of trade and the like. In order to make the talks practically useful, not merely vain boasting, let me trace the favorable conditions to the adoption of sound principles, and warn the people of some evils existing which threaten our future, such as clipped silver dollars—unredeemed government paper—a redundant currency, popular illiteracy, sectional and race prejudices &c.&c.[18]

If possible the President avoided speechmaking on Sunday. To pass idle time on long stretches between stops, the group played guessing games or sang patriotic and popular songs by the hour.[19]

Lieutenant Charles Rutherford Noyes, son of the President's cousin, Horatio Noyes, stationed in 1880 near Cheyenne, Wyoming, decided to join the official greeting party as his kinsman passed through the territory. A diary kept by Noyes is the only known account by a participant who described the great western tour in detail.

> There were five cars in the train, one carrying the baggage, the second, a C. B. & Q. dining car, the third, a C. B. & Q. director's car occupied by Secretary of War, General Sherman, and the ladies of their party. The fourth, a Pullman sleeper occupied by General McCook and other gentlemen of the party, also by Colonel and Mrs. Barr and Birchard and Rutherford Hayes. The fifth was the Union Pacific Director's car occupied by the President and his party excluding the boys.[20]

Young Noyes accompanied the tour as far as Salt Lake City. Shortly after the train entered Utah, it stopped at the Emory station, and, upon invitation from Rud, Noyes ran forward to join a party of five on the locomotive's cowcatcher for an exciting ride through Echo Canyon. At the same time, the President, Mrs. Hayes, Dr. Huntington, and Mrs. Herron moved up to the engineer's cab. At the end of twenty-five miles, they returned to the passenger cars, much pleased with their unusual experience.[21]

At Salt Lake, the Hayes brothers and Noyes took a brief excursion to Black Rock for a swim in the famous salt water and then rejoined the main party for a tour of Salt Lake City. On September 6, after spending a pleasant weekend in the city, the tourists resumed their journey to California and Noyes returned to his army post. Before parting, he found time to win a rubber of cribbage with Miss Sherman and bid goodbye to each of the passengers. He also wrote a vivid description of the President's accommodations: "Upon arriving at Ogden [the junction for the Far West] the party changed cars to Central Pacific sleeping cars, and the director's car of the Central Pacific was in readiness for the President. This was the finest car which I think I ever saw, its upholstery was of the richest, and all its appointments complete."[22]

On September 8 the presidential party crossed the Sierra Nevada range at beautiful Lake Tahoe and reached San Francisco the following day. After many receptions and some sightseeing in the Bay area, the Hayes caravan headed for Oregon by way of Sacramento where the President delivered one of the few prepared and longer speeches of his tour, sounding his basic theme of nationalism and unity, the principle purpose of his long journey. He observed:

> We have learned something of California. . . . No man can doubt, . . . that here is a soil fit to feed the millions of the earth. . . . Wherever we go we see such provision for education as insures the prosperity of the country. Here people will gather from every known land, and by a process peculiar to the American school-house, be fused into one harmonious whole. . . . What is to be the future of this beautiful land? . . . In my judgment, there is no equal of people anywhere in the United States having such advantages and opportunities to do great service to the nation and mankind as the million or million and a half of people inhabiting what are known as the Pacific States and Territories of the United States. . . . You have your mines of inexhaustible wealth, and your commerce; you have the capacity for a population not less than that of our whole country at the present time; . . . I am glad to meet you in California, and I say to you that we are looking to you as the vanguard of progress. As civilization advances we have generally moved to the westward. You have got to the end of the march. You have reached the margin,

and now it is for you—and I believe you may safely be trusted
with that destiny—to see that in the future, as in the past, American
institutions and the American name shall lose nothing at your
hands.[23]

From the California capital the Oregon division of the Central
Pacific carried the visitors to its terminus at Redding, where the
presidential party divided into three contingents. One went
directly to Portland by sea, while a second section journeyed by
regular stage to Roseburg, Oregon. The third group, comprised
of the President and first lady, the John Herrons, Mrs. Mitchell,
Dr. Huntington, and Colonel Jameson (with General Sherman riding shotgun on the box beside the driver), traveled by a special
stagecoach, drawn by six large and handsome horses, matched
grays, and stopped each night on its way to Roseburg, 275 miles
distant.[24] Sherman had advised this six-day trek by daylight in
order to permit the President to see the magnificent scenery and
to experience the wild and exciting drive along the narrow and
precipitous road from Ashland to Sevens, Oregon, as well as to
observe a government fish hatchery and the local color of several
old mining camps along the way.[25]

On the night of September 27, the presidential stage halted in
Jacksonville, Oregon, a small frontier mining town of one thousand
population. Madam de Robaum's boardinghouse afforded them
overnight accommodations. But next morning the big French-
woman, unlike other proprietors who had entertained the President without charge to gain the added prestige, presented her
guests with an exorbitant bill amounting to one hundred dollars. In
the embarrassing circumstances, John Herron, the President's
former law partner, saved the day. He informed the proprietress
that the party had no intention of buying her hotel, handed her
twenty-five dollars, and bid adieu. Before the flabbergasted woman
could protest further, the stage was gone.[26]

At Roseburg the Portland special of the Oregon and California
Railroad took the travelers by nightfall to the northern border
of the state. Several relaxing days were spent in Portland with
excursions to nearby points. The most interesting of these side
trips was a journey to the Government Indian School at Forest
Grove where Hayes delivered a particularly stirring speech:

> I think it is the wish and prayer of every good citizen that these
> Indian boys and girls should become wise, useful, and good citizens.
> Some people seem to think that God has decreed that Indians should
> die off like wild animals. With this we have nothing to do. If they
> are to become extinct we ought to leave that to Providence, and
> we, as good patriotic, Christian people, should do our best to

improve their physical, mental, and moral condition. We should prepare them to become part of the great American family. If it turns out that their destiny is to be different, we shall have at least done our duty. This country was once theirs. They owned it as much as you own your farms. We have displaced them, and are now completing that work. I am glad that Oregon has taken a step in the right direction.[27]

Going from Portland to Vancouver, the Hayes party spent Sunday with the area military commander, General O. O. Howard. On Monday, October 4 (the President's fifty-eighth birthday), the party ascended the Columbia River, using three steamers and two special trains to penetrate as far as Walla Walla in the Washington Territory. On the afternoon of October 6, 1880, the return journey down the Columbia River began, after the travelers had witnessed at the military post one of the most novel and dramatic episodes of the entire trip, a wild war dance presented by about fifty Umatilla Indians.[28]

Several more pleasant days were passed visiting Kalima, Olympia, Tacoma, and finally Seattle where the President made perhaps his most spectacular entrance to any city on the tour. Laura Mitchell, a gifted letter writer, graphically described this part of the journey for her little cousins back home in Fremont:

> We had a whole week of beauty and delight on Puget Sound following its blue inlets in and out among the many islands and around the rugged fir-hung promotories or gently sloping shores. The Olympic Range seemed attending us in the blue distance, and Mt. Ranier rose in the sky, a snow-crowned shrine for our admiring worship, from time to time. As we drew near Seattle, a fleet of seven vessels—the flag-strung revenue cutter and big and little steamboats, came to meet us, first circled round us, and ranging themselves on either hand escorted us into port.[29]

Returning to Oregon, the presidential party embarked at Astoria aboard the *Columbia* for a calm three-day weekend ocean voyage to San Francisco. "The sea is smooth, almost nobody sick—certainly none of our party," Hayes informed his daughter Fanny. Laura, as usual, was more picturesque:

> Your Mama wishes me to tell you what a superb sailor she has grown. For twenty-four hours we have been on the ocean, and she sings, and talks, and laughs like the jolliest Jack Tar of them all. To be sure, the ocean seems holding its breath, or rising and falling with the gentlest sighs so that we are asailing over it, and proud that we are able bodied people, though a hypochondriac

could hardly imagine himself seasick on this serene sea and in
this smooth-going steamer.... We saw a pair of whales, yesterday,
tossing up their sun-lit spray quite near our steamer.... To be
a whale and *spout* must be the next best happiness to being a
little boy and blowing bubbles.[30]

The party docked at San Francisco early Monday morning,
October 18, and made their way to the Palace Hotel, then probably
the finest hostelry in America. From here they entrained to Madera
where they mounted a six-horse coach of the Yosemite Stage Line
for a delightful excursion through the big tree valley. By Friday
they were back in Madera and ready to travel farther south by
train to Los Angeles, where General Sherman, who had temporarily
left the group, rejoined them. Here they paid quick visits to the
orange groves, the agricultural fair, the new University of Southern
California campus, and Pasadena's vineyards, until they departed
for Mission San Gabriel where they boarded a Southern Pacific
train to Arizona and New Mexico.[31] They made a stop in Tucson
for a military parade and public reception. General O. B. Wilcox
and his staff then joined them for the trip to the end of the railroad
at Shakespeare Ranch, New Mexico, where they arrived on Monday
morning, October 25.[32] Garvey has described this trip as follows:

> From this point wagons carried them to Fort Cummings, a very
> dangerous journey considering threats from Apache raiders and
> wild bands of Cowboys from the notorious San Simon region; but
> Wilcox, avoiding any undue alarm to his charges, ordered a heavy
> military guard and increased picketing along the route, and hurried
> them along to Cow Springs and on to the Memembres River before
> rolling into the fort—covering sixty-four miles in eleven hours.[33]

At dawn they left Fort Cummings by army ambulance and
wagons for Polomas, sixty miles away, and camped there overnight. On Wednesday the caravan covered another twenty-eight
miles up the Rio Grande River near Fort McRea, and then a final
twenty miles to the railhead, where an Atchison, Topeka & Santa
Fe special waited to take them the final two hundred miles to
Santa Fe. On Thursday morning, the presidential train pulled into
Santa Fe, and the rest of that day and evening witnessed a great
celebration culminating in an evening concert and fiesta. The President also purchased some Indian artifacts because of his love of
Americana. From Santa Fe their special train headed northeast,
reaching Kansas early Saturday, October 30. At Dodge City, Hayes
wired Garfield in Mentor, Ohio: "We have had a most delightful
and instructive trip."[34]

In Kansas City the tour party broke up. Secretary Ramsey made
a connection for St. Paul; the Shermans continued on to St. Louis;

and the Hayes contingent boarded a Wabash express for Toledo via Hannibal, Missouri. In the wee hours of the morning, Monday, November 1, 1880, a carriage bearing President and Mrs. Hayes, together with their son Rud, drove up the winding path to their house at Spiegel Grove. The great western tour, the longest journey ever undertaken by a Chief Executive to that time, was over.

Back in the White House by Sunday, November 7, 1880, Hayes penned a modest one-paragraph résumé of his odyssey, the only reference to the event in his entire diary:

> We left W[ashington] on our Pacific tour Thursday evening 26th August and returned Saturday morning after an absence of Seventy one days. Our trip was most fortunate in all of its circumstances. Superb weather, good health and no accidents. A most gratifying reception greeted us everywhere from the people and from noted and interesting individuals.[35]

What pleased the President most, however, was Garfield's victory at the polls, along with Republican gains in the House and the Senate. To Hayes, the presidential election of November 2, 1880, while disappointing in the loss of Nevada and California to the Democrats, was a personal victory since his administration was vindicated by the people's vote of confidence. The Republicans remained in power despite a four-year effort by discontented politicians of both parties to discredit Hayes personally and to brand his administration a fraud and a failure.

Courageous and determined in manner, confident in the ultimate success of his conciliatory policy, Hayes effectively promoted national unity and pride by his travels into many regions of the United States. Moreover, by using presidential tours to manifest the power of the presidency and to develop loyalty for the central government, he revived an important method of maintaining executive authority practiced earlier by Washington and Monroe. Hayes loved to go among the people and to rub elbows with all classes of citizens. He was forever shaking hands, and his friendly, nonpartisan approach to individuals lifted spirits and restored morale. Rutherford Hayes may have entered the White House in the wake of a bitterly contested election, but, four years later, he retired from the presidency as a statesman with the honor and respect of his countrymen.

Notes

1. Hayes received an LL.D. at Harvard, June 27, 1877; an LL.D. at Yale, July 1, 1880; an LL.D. at Johns Hopkins, February 12, 1881.

2. Hayes, Diary, December 26, 1877, April 1, 1880, Hayes Papers, RBHL.

3. Ibid., July 7, 1879.

4. Fargo *Republican*, September 11, 1878, newspaper clipping, Hayes Scrapbook, vol. 112, pp. 139–140, Hayes Papers, RBHL; Marion Ramsey Furness, "Childhood Recollections of Old St. Paul," *Minnesota History* 29 (June 1948): 128–129.

5. "Mrs. Hayes wants to have an interest in your Excellent Institution by contributing enough to support at least one pupil at the Institution. If you will let me know the amount required and when it should be sent &c &c I will remit." Hayes to Gen. Armstrong, August 27, 1877, photostat in RBHL from original letter in the Massachusetts Historical Society.

6. Cited in "Anniversary Day at Hampton," *Southern Workman* 7, no. 6 (June 1878): 46.

7. "Anniversary Day at Hampton," *Southern Workman* 9, no. 6 (June 1880): 68.

8. Original manuscript, pp. 51–52, Benson Scrapbook, Kenyon College Library, Gambier, Ohio.

9. Hayes, Diary, November 28, 1879.

10. See James J. Garvey, "Rutherford B. Hayes: The Great Western Tour of 1880," and Gary Joseph Gonya, "Hayes and Unity (with a Travelogue of the Presidential Tour of 1880)," manuscripts, RBHL.

11. Hayes to Maj. W. D. Bickham, August 19, 1880, Hayes Papers, RBHL.

12. W. T. Sherman to Marian De L. Adams, August 15, 1880, Sherman Papers, RBHL.

13. "His Excellency R. B. Hayes in Account with John Jameson, August 27 to November 6, 1880"; Hayes to F. J. Potter, August 21, 1880, both in Hayes Papers, RBHL.

14. Hayes to W. D. Howells, August 4, 1880, Hayes Papers, RBHL.

15. Hayes Scrapbook, vol. 78, p. 44, Hayes Papers, RBHL. This volume of newspaper clippings and the official Post Route maps for the period, also in the Hayes Library, make it possible to reconstruct the progress of the tour.

16. Hayes, Diary, November 7, 1880.

17. Colonel Jameson's account book with Hayes shows total expenditures of only $575.40 for the nine members of the President's immediate entourage. "Hayes in Account with Jameson."

18. Hayes, Diary, August 19, 1880.

19. Gonya, "Hayes and Unity," 42, 46; Garvey, "Great Western Tour," 40.

20. Extract from "Diary of Charles R. Noyes," 2, typed copy in RBHL.

21. Ibid, 10–11.

22. Ibid., 20.

23. Hayes Scrapbook. Vol. 78, 106, 114–115.

24. Gonya, "Hayes and Unity," 41–42.

25. Sherman to Hayes, August 20, 1880, Hayes Papers, RBHL; Gen. Irvin McDowell to W. T. Sherman, August 13, 1880, with attached notations of Lt. Hoyle, Sherman Papers, copy in RBHL.

26. See Anne Holm Pogue, "Madam De Robaum's Unsettled Claim—1880," in Helen Krebs Smith, ed., *With Her Own Wings* (Portland: Beattie and Company, 1948), 142–144. In fairness, it should be stated that Madam De Robaum was an excellent cook and had gone to consider-

able extra expense to entertain her distinguished guests. A new Brussels carpet was placed in the bedroom occupied by the Hayes, a picture was painted for the dining room, and many food delicacies were imported from distant points.

27. Chicago *Tribune*, October 3, 1880, clipping in Hayes Scrapbook, Vol. 78, p. 127, RBHL.

28. Ibid., p. 124.

29. Laura Platt Mitchell to Fanny and Scott Hayes, October 17, 1880, Hayes Papers, RBHL.

30. Hayes to Fanny Hayes, October 17, 1880; Laura Mitchell to Fanny and Scott Hayes, October 17, 1880, Hayes Papers, RBHL.

31. John E. Baur, "A President Visits Los Angeles: Rutherford B. Hayes' Tour of 1880," *The Historical Society of Southern California Quarterly* 37 (March 1955): 33–47.

32. The return journey is not documented as well as the rest of the trip. Garvey, "The Great Western Tour," 50–55, is the best account.

33. Ibid., 53.

34. Hayes to Garfield, October 30, 1880, Hayes Papers, RBHL.

35. Hayes, Diary, November 7, 1880. Because of the length of the tour there are no entries for the months of September and October.

Part IV

AFTER
THE WHITE HOUSE

15

The Squire of Spiegel Grove

The Garfield inauguration ceremony over, Lucy and Rutherford Hayes watched with pleasure the parade and other festivities in honor of America's twentieth President. Then they quietly moved from the White House to John Sherman's residence to spend one more night in the capital city. How unlike was this stay at the Secretary's home from the one just four years earlier. Then the country was divided and distracted, and every interest depressed; now it was united, harmonious, and prosperous.

Next day, March 5, 1881, accompanied by their children, a party of Ohio friends, and escorted by Cleveland military troops, the former President and first lady eagerly boarded the second section of the Baltimore and Potomac express, and started for their Ohio home. But as they neared Baltimore, their special suddenly smashed head-on into another train of empty passenger cars drawn by two locomotives. John M. Unglaub, engineer of the Hayes train, saw the impending crash and coolly reversed his engine, but not soon enough to avert a collision. Hayes, riding in the fifth coach, was thrown several feet from his seat. Unhurt, he got up and hurried forward to survey the wreckage and to give first aid to the victims. Both engineers were badly injured, and one died from the accident. Unglaub recovered some months later after receiving considerable medical care authorized by his famous passenger. In token of their gratitude for his prompt action in saving their lives, the Hayes family gave the heroic engineer an engraved gold watch and chain, made to order in Philadelphia, as a New Year's present in 1882.[1]

General Sherman expressed the sentiments of many American citizens when he wrote of the presidential family's narrow escape in a wreck that had caused $30,000 damage, killed two persons, and seriously injured twenty others: "I cannot restrain my own feelings in conveying to you my hearty congratulations that not only in this instance but in the long journeys you have made, and risks you have encountered, that your life and health, and those of your cherished family have been almost miraculously spared."[2]

The sad railroad accident delayed the homeward journey, but on Tuesday evening, March 8, the travelers finally reached Clyde, Ohio. Here a reception committee awaited to escort them the last few miles into Fremont where bands, torches, and banners heralded the family's safe return. At Spiegel Grove, another large throng welcomed them home. Some speechmaking and much handshaking followed.

No President left the executive mansion and the arduous duties of the presidential office more gladly and with less regret, or more general content in his own heart with the result of his term than did Hayes.[3] "We have on the whole enjoyed our four years here," he mused, "but the responsibility, the embarrassments, the heartbreaking sufferings which we can't relieve, the ever present danger of scandals and crime among those we are compelled to trust, and a thousand other drawbacks to our satisfaction and enjoyment, by which we are constantly surrounded, leave us no place for regret upon retiring from this conspicuous scene to the freedom, independence, and safety of our obscure and happy home in the pleasant grove at Fremont."[4] He welcomed retirement from politics: "I am soon to become a private citizen . . . to have the right to manage my own private affairs without intrusion."[5]

Only fifty-eight years of age, with an estate large enough to insure financial independence, Hayes might easily have withdrawn to a comfortable and private seclusion for the remainder of his life, free to enjoy his family, his library, and his beautiful home and wooded estate. Instead, Rutherford Hayes became one of the most active and distinguished retired Presidents in the cause of his fellowman that America has ever known.

He explained to the people who welcomed him back to Fremont his idea of what a former President should do as a private citizen: "Let him, like every good American citizen, be willing and prompt to bear his part in every useful work that will promote the welfare and the happiness of his family, his town, his state, and his country. With this disposition he will have work enough to do, and that sort of work that yields more individual contentment and gratification than belong to the more conspicuous employments of life from which he was retired."[6]

For the last twelve years of his life, Hayes conscientiously practiced his theory. He traveled widely, making more trips and delivering more speeches on behalf of educational, humanitarian, and reform causes than any previous ex-President down to his time. He interspersed these activities with innumerable army reunions and heavy involvement in the affairs of Fremont. The management of his investments and the further development of Spiegel Grove took much of his time. The one pursuit he completely avoided was any active participation in politics, although he remained an interested private observer.

To maintain such a busy life required a discipline in habits and daily routine. Hayes described his method as follows:

> I rise with the sun both winter and summer, and seldom use the gas to dress by. This makes me get up very early in the long days of the year, but in winter I sometimes lie abed as late as 7 o'clock, though I usually try to get out by six. I dress and come down to my library and work from that time until breakfast. I do my disagreeable work before breakfast, and I solve my most knotty problems at that time. I think one's brain is clearer in the morning and I find this to be my best working period. My correspondence is quite large and it covers all sorts of subjects. I do all my work myself and pen answers to all my letters with my own hand. At 8 o'clock I have my breakfast, and shortly after this I go to work again and write away until about 11, when I drop my writing for the day.... I walk at least six miles every day and often more.... I have my lunch at 1 o'clock and after it is over I read and walk about the grounds here.... Later in the afternoon I take a drive.[7]

He spent his evenings with his family and guests.

Spiegel Grove contributed much to Hayes' happiness. Part of a quarter section purchased by Uncle Sardis in 1845, it was a beautiful site of deep primeval woods, reflecting pools of water, and abundant wildlife situated on the western edge of Fremont. A large variety of native American trees, in particular, oaks, hickories, elms, and pines, adorned the grounds. Hayes planted others —willows from the seeds of trees on Washington's grave at Mount Vernon, two oaks grown from acorns of the Charter Oak at Hartford, Connecticut, and tulip trees from Montpelier, the home of James Madison.

The original two-and-one-half-story house, erected by Sardis Birchard in 1863, underwent several structural changes over the next quarter-of-a-century until it became a large rambling three-story brick mansion. Hayes inherited the property in 1873 and remodeled and enlarged it three times to suit his family needs. First he built a wooden appendage, containing a kitchen, woodhouse, and privy, to the rear of the original brick section. At the same time he extended the front porch and rearranged the existing rooms to provide for a library and larger drawing room. In 1880, just prior to his retirement from the presidency, he made the most important changes, virtually doubling the size and redecorating the interior. Webb supervised the entire project, which added a matching gabled brick wing to the north side. This made possible a new reception room and a larger library. Meanwhile a square-balconied fourth-story cupola, used by Mrs. Hayes as a conservatory for house plants, and a bigger veranda, a favorite place Hayes used for exercise and relaxation, were completed. In 1889 another large brick addition to the rear provided a new kitchen and a larger dining room, plus an extra eleven bedrooms on the upper floors. One of Fremont's first telephones was installed there in November 1881, and four years later, hydrant water replaced the spring previously used on the property.

From the time of his inheritance of the estate, Hayes steadily improved and beautified the grounds, preserving and accentuating its natural advantages by clearing out indifferent trees, extending the lawns immediately about the house to let in sunlight, opening vistas to throw into relief some superb old oak or elm, and planting a hemlock avenue of spruces and pines. He rearranged the driveways so as not to have people sitting on the porch disturbed by persons driving about the place.[8]

Hayes began his adjustment to private life by immersing himself in local affairs. He rejoined the Odd Fellows and affiliated with the Fremont post of the GAR. He helped to found a community board of trade and became director of a new savings bank. While he never officially joined a church, he participated actively in Lucy's Methodist congregation. He contributed generously for a new brick church and renewed the pledge when fire tragically destroyed the edifice. He even used his influence to reinstate the pastor, D. D. Mather, after the unfortunate minister was temporarily removed on a controversial charge of showing improper interest in women parishioners.

One of the most unusual aspects of Hayes' retirement was his mounting interest and concern in liberal social movements. The older he became and the longer he reflected upon American society, the more he became a dedicated opponent of privilege and the exploitation of any group. He greatly feared the effect of the concentration of wealth in a few hands. He read works of social criticism by Mark Twain and William Dean Howells, and especially Henry George's *Progress and Poverty*. While not ready to accept the single tax solution George proposed, Hayes sympathized strongly with the author's analysis.[9]

Hayes firmly believed that universal education was the best approach to the elimination of social injustice and the promotion of harmony in American life. To this end he devoted many long hours of his retirement years. Since he felt the South was too poor to finance an adequate educational system, he favored the Blair Bill, which called for federal aid to education. Meantime, he served on the board of trustees of the Peabody Education Fund established for the purpose of promoting education in the South. In 1882, another large fund, created by Connecticut manufacturer John F. Slater specifically to assist Negro education in the South, drew Hayes' attention and he became its first president.

In a small but meaningful way, these activities gave Hayes a direct opportunity to further his concept of solving the racial question by better education for both whites and blacks.[10] Of the individuals he aided through Slater scholarship funds, the most distinguished in later life was W. E. B. Du Bois.

Contemporary with these activities, Hayes became a pioneer advocate and a great crusader for industrial or manual arts training, the belief that from the age of fourteen to the end of formal schooling, children should give two or three hours each day to careful instruction in skilled labor. Such a policy, he maintained, would inculcate respect for labor and develop character and self-reliance. He thought all liberally educated persons should know how to use their hands and their minds. In support of his argument he cited the examples of St. Paul, a tentmaker, and Jesus, a carpenter.

The elder statesman also accepted appointment to the board of trustees of several colleges and universities—Western Reserve University, Ohio State University, Ohio Wesleyan University, and Kenyon College.[11] More educational institutions sought his services as a commencement or special occasion speaker than he could possibly honor although he tried to be generous with his time. A typical episode involved Heidelberg College, located in Tiffin about eighteen miles south of Fremont.

Several times during the 1880s, Heidelberg's president, George Williard, had formally requested President Hayes to speak at the college. The latter, unusually busy with many humanitarian and philanthropic activities, always declined. In the spring of 1887 Dr. Williard again invited Hayes to Tiffin. With commitments already on his June calendar to speak at Green Springs Academy, Western Reserve University, Ohio State University, and Ohio Wesleyan University, Hayes sent his usual note of regret to Heidelberg. So it might have been had not the men of the senior class refused to be denied. Organizing a committee, they walked to Fremont and personally presented their petition to the squire of Spiegel Grove. This show of determination so touched their venerable host that he consented to deliver the commencement address and to present diplomas to the graduating class on June 16, 1887. Hayes spoke without a manuscript but used a brief outline still preserved among his papers at the presidential library in Fremont. His theme, as anticipated, was typical of his thinking at the time: the importance of training the hands and the mind for a complete education. In his diary Hayes recorded a pleasant trip and visit with "the folks at Tiffin."

Still other causes occupied the ex-President's attention. In 1883 he accepted the leadership of the National Prison Association, a post he held for nearly a decade. In his mind, crime prevention was related to manual training. A way to reduce crime, or to reform men convicted of a crime, was to teach all persons to respect labor. Hayes also worked to expedite court procedures and to eliminate political interference with judicial proceedings. Another movement he backed in the closing years of his life was the annual Lake Mohonk Conference on the problems of Indians and Negroes.

Without a doubt, however, of all the many kinds of meetings Hayes attended in his busy life, none pleased him more than a reunion with old army comrades. He never missed a meeting of his regiment. The annual state and national GAR encampments invariably found him present and on the program. His military career meant a great deal to him. Frequently he was called upon to unveil monuments or to participate in Memorial Day services in the North and the South. Always he tried to make these occasions joint federal and confederate ceremonies and to heal sectional hatred. Union veterans considered him a godfather, and he received hundreds of letters asking for assistance. Often he wrote a letter of recommendation or advocated legislation favoring hospitalization and pensions for those who had suffered permanent damage to their health in war.

The death of President Garfield from the effects of an assassin's bullet in September 1881 was the first of several bereavements during the next ten years, which claimed major figures of the Hayes presidential era. At Garfield's funeral, Hayes rode with ex-President Grant; four years later he sat beside President Arthur at Grant's obsequies; in 1886 he joined President Cleveland in services marking Arthur's demise. That same year Samuel J. Tilden died, followed closely by Thomas J. Hendricks (1885) and Hayes' running mate, William A. Wheeler (1886). Stanley Matthews, Associate Justice of the Supreme Court and a close friend of Hayes from college days at Kenyon, was buried in 1889. Famed Union Generals Philip H. Sheridan and William Tecumseh Sherman passed away in 1888 and 1891. These deaths saddened Hayes and made him aware that his own life was almost over.

The hardest blow came on June 25, 1889, with the loss of his beloved Lucy after forty years of near perfect wedlock. He never really recovered from the shock of her passing. In his diary, he poured out his feelings, and his longing for death that he might be reunited with her.

On January 9, 1893, he went to Columbus on university business; a few days later he arrived in Cleveland to interview a candidate for the post of director of manual training at Ohio State University, a task he finished. On Saturday afternoon, January 14, while standing in the Cleveland railway station, about to board the train for Fremont after a long trudge through deep snow in near-zero temperature, Hayes was suddenly stricken by a severe pain in his chest. Sensing the nearness of the end, he doggedly got on the train and began his final journey, accompanied by his son Webb. "I would rather die at Spiegel Grove than to live anywhere else," he said.[12] His wish was fulfilled at eleven o'clock on the night of January 17, 1893.

Friday morning, January 20, 1893, the day of the funeral, dawned bright and clear in snow-covered Fremont, after temperatures the night before had dropped to five below. The oaks about the mansion at Spiegel Grove shown in the sunshine. Everything was a tracery of frost looking like a delicate wax work on the broad veranda the deceased President loved so much. The entire Grove was beautiful beyond description. It seemed as if even harsh winter had donned a charming role to honor him who that afternoon was laid to rest in Oakwood Cemetery beside Lucy.[13]

Notes

1. Hayes, Diary, March 9, 1881; Hayes to Thomas C. Donaldson, December 22, 1881; Washington *Evening Star*, January 5, 1882; Scrapbook of R. B. Hayes, 1876–1881, kept by Sarah Jane Grant; all in Hayes Papers, RBHL.

2. W. T. Sherman to Hayes, March 6, 1881, Hayes Papers, RBHL.

3. Hayes to Guy M. Bryan, January 1, 1881, Hayes Papers, RBHL.

4. Hayes, Diary, January 16, 1881.

5. Ibid., January 2, 1881.

6. Cited in Charles Richard Williams, *The Life of Rutherford Birchard Hayes* (Boston: Houghton Mifflin Company, 1914), II, 335–336.

7. Cited in Asa E. Martin, *After the White House* (State College, Pa.: Penns Valley Publishers, Inc., 1951), 294–295.

8. Samuel C. Townsend, *Spiegel Grove* (Fremont: Lesher Printers, 1965), passim; Hayes, Diary, March 10, 1881.

9. Hayes Diary, March 18, 19, 1886, December 4, 1887, March 11, 1888.

10. See Louis D. Rubin, Jr., *Teach the Freeman: The Correspondence of Rutherford B. Hayes and the Slater Fund for Negro Education, 1881–1893* (Baton Rouge: Louisiana State University Press, 1959), I, xiii–lv.

11. For examples of Hayes' concern for education see Walter S. Hayes, Jr., "Rutherford B. Hayes and The Ohio State University," *Ohio History* 77 (Winter, Spring, Summer 1968): 168–183, and Henry L. Swint, "Rutherford B. Hayes, Educator," *The Mississippi Valley Historical Review* 39 (June 1952): 45–60.

12. Williams, *Life of Hayes*, II, 397.

13. In 1915, the remains of President and Mrs. Hayes were reinterred in Spiegel Grove.

The Hayes mansion and The Rutherford B. Hayes Library,
Spiegel Grove, Fremont, Ohio.

Epilogue

The presidency of Rutherford Hayes is best described as a time of turmoil and transition, of tragedy and triumph. For many years, the controversy surrounding the contested election of 1876 and the poor reputation of the Gilded Age generally have made it very difficult to evaluate dispassionately either Hayes the man or the significance of his administration in American history. On the occasion of the sesquicentennial of his birth in 1822, it is time to recognize an undeservedly forgotten President's accomplishments.

Hayes entered the White House under extremely great handicaps: a disputed title; a hostile Congress with a Democratic majority in both houses for most of the next four years; little respect for presidential authority; a cumbersome bureaucracy and an entrenched patronage system to resist civil service reform; a business depression; powerful opposition to a "sound" dollar; intense sectional hatred; and racial unrest involving black, Indian, and Chinese minorities.

To cope with these problems, Hayes brought with him to Washington a thorough classical and legal education, solid experience in local, state, and national politics, and, above all, great strength of character and moral purpose. Hayes epitomized the best middle-class, moderate Victorian standards in contemporary American life. He was not brilliant or colorful, but he was kind, high-principled, public-spirited, unaffected, loyal, and singularly decent and honest, a man without pretense, without egotism. No scandal stained his personal or public life. A strong sense of duty guided his actions. By temperament, he was essentially a harmonizer who strove to bring out the better instincts of his fellow men. All these qualities made him an excellent presiding officer in any group, and a particularly good choice to lead the nation in a period of transition away from bitter wartime memories and Reconstruction policies into a new age of national unity and growth.

He did not resolve all of the issues confronting the country. Saddest of all, he failed to advance or to protect the rights of Negro citizens. Hayes believed he had secured valid pledges guaranteeing fair treatment of southern blacks, but he greatly underestimated the time required to overcome a deeply rooted social evil. When he realized his error, he rejected force and turned to universal education as the only way to ameliorate social injustice. The tragedy of the abandonment of the Negro after Reconstruction is that this unhappy circumstance utterly contradicted everything else President Hayes had stood and worked for in his career. His wholehearted support of the Fourteenth and Fifteenth amendments is undeniable. His concept of democracy is equally well-defined: "Our Government has been called the white man's government. Not so. It is not the Government of any class, or nationality, or race. It is a Government founded on the consent of the governed.... It is not the Government of the native born, or of the foreign born, of the rich man, or of the poor man, of the white man, or of the colored man—it is the government of the *freeman*...."[1]

While President, he did not fully comprehend the importance of the great technological and social forces at work, which were rapidly transforming American life and creating a new order. His handling of the Railway Strike of 1877 and the money question suggest a narrow viewpoint. After Hayes retired, however, he gradually modified his older ideas and developed a deep sympathy for workingmen and farmers caught in the web of monopoly and concentration of wealth.

In other respects, he definitely pointed the government in new directions and made several significant departures from the policies of his predecessors. He absolutely refused to be put down by attacks upon his person and high office based upon charges of accepting a fraudulent election. Instead he remained remarkably cool and demonstrated he was more than equal to the occasion, until the Democrats were finally compelled to withdraw the accusation. The failure of the opposition party to renominate Tilden or Hendricks in 1880, the election of Garfield (who was intimately associated with Hayes as a member of the Electoral Commission and later as Republican minority floor leader in the House), and the appearance of President-elect Grover Cleveland at Hayes' funeral demonstrated public acceptance of the decision of the Electoral Commission.

Not only did Hayes stoutly defend his legal right to the presidency, he recovered and strengthened the power and the prestige of the executive branch after it had reached a low ebb under Grant. By naming his own cabinet, by resisting legislative riders to appropriation bills, by winning the New York Custom House struggle, and by elevating the tone of official life, President Hayes restored confidence in presidential leadership and redressed the balance of power among the three branches of government. Unable to function as a legislative leader without a working majority, he resorted to administrative action to win respect for his office.

He struck the first effective presidential blows for civil-service reform. In this work he was most effectively aided by Carl Schurz, the one cabinet official who took seriously the President's order to make appointments on a merit basis. Schurz also launched a new era in Indian affairs by treating the native Americans with human dignity. Meanwhile, John Sherman, the financial wizard of the Republican party, ably promoted the President's economic policy. Resumption of specie payment came off smoothly and on schedule. Because or in spite of it, business revived, and the economy recovered rapidly.

Of all the causes Hayes believed in, the one closest to his heart was national unity. It fell to his lot, however, that he, who was not a vindictive man, should run for office in campaigns noted for their exceptional bitterness. Almost all of the elections in which he was prominent were marked by close divisions and more than usual rancor. He began his political career by winning the office of city solicitor of Cincinnati by a majority of one; he closed it by winning the presidency by a single electoral vote.

Narrow victory margins necessitated conciliatory policies. Hayes knew what was required of him and did his job well. There is no doubt that his administration served a useful purpose in the transition from sectional antagonism to national harmony, and from the old methods of dealing with the public service as party spoils to the new method of placing merit and fitness above party service or requirements.

He served his party best because he served his country best. Of the five Republican Presidents from 1869 to 1893, Rutherford Hayes most deserved to be reelected, but he did not wish to be known as just another successful party politician. Characteristically, in his letter of acceptance of July 8, 1876, he deliberately inserted a self-denying proclamation of his "inflexible purpose" to serve for only a single term. Thus, at the beginning of his administration, he effectively removed himself from any further partisan political activity and freed his hands to accomplish the greater good of healing a strife-torn nation. He became the President whose administration symbolized the birth of a new union. This was his greatest triumph.

Notes

1. "Union and Liberty," Hayes Campaign Address, Lebanon, Ohio, August 5, 1867, Hayes Papers, RBHL.

A Note on Sources

The chapter notes reveal some of my sources and suggest further reading on specific topics. The following highly selective bibliography represents only a very small portion of the primary sources and secondary works I have used. A comprehensive Hayes bibliography appears in Harry Barnard, *Rutherford B. Hayes and His America* (Indianapolis: The Bobbs-Merrill Company, Inc., 1954), 571–588. Rather than simply citing these same references again, I have considered it more important to describe briefly the major collections in the Hayes Library. In addition I have appended several checklists covering dissertations and theses, books, and articles, which for the most part have appeared since Barnard completed his work.

Manuscript Collections

My study of the Hayes presidency is based primarily upon the rich resources of the Rutherford B. Hayes Library in Fremont, Ohio, which contains the President's addresses and speeches, correspondence, diaries, personal library of over ten thousand volumes, pictures and photographs, scrapbooks, and hundreds of objects associated with his life. The library, originally erected by the State of Ohio, and since greatly remodeled and expanded by the Hayes Foundation and the Ohio Historical Society, has been open to the public since 1916. It is recognized as the prototype of the presidential library concept adopted by the federal government beginning with the construction of the Franklin D. Roosevelt Library at Hyde Park, New York, in 1939. The principal Hayes sources I have examined include the following primary materials

RUTHERFORD BIRCHARD HAYES PAPERS, 1835–1893 (160 FEET)

Correspondence, letter books, speeches, account books and financial records, real estate records, law cases, campaign and other political notebooks, White House desk pad notes, lists of guests and visitors, calling cards, material on social events, autograph books, school notebooks (1838–1841), college essays, genealogical records of the Hayes family, estate papers, notes and records about the Twenty-third Regiment of Ohio Infantry, notes on local history, Civil War papers, catalogs of Hayes' private library, scrapbooks and clippings on baseball and other topics, maps, and pictures. Concerns his family and personal affairs; his military service in the Civil War; his business and law practice; his political career as city solicitor in Cincinnati, U.S. Congressman, Governor of Ohio, and President; and his activities as presiding officer or trustee of John F. Slater Fund, Military Order of the Loyal Legion of the United States, Mohonk Conference on the Negro, Mount Union College, National Prison Association, Ohio Historical Society, Ohio State University, Ohio Wesleyan University, Peabody Education Fund, the Twenty-third Volunteer Infantry Association, and Western Reserve University.

LUCY WEBB HAYES PAPERS, 1841–1890 (8 FEET)

Civic leader and wife of President Hayes. Correspondence, account books, school essays, tributes, clippings, and pictures. Many letters concern Mrs. Hayes' interest in the women's missionary societies of the Methodist Episcopal Church, the Woman's Christian Temperance Union, the Ohio Soldiers' and Sailors' Orphans Home, Xenia, Ohio, and other benevolent activities.

BIRCHARD AUSTIN HAYES PAPERS, 1862–1926 (3 FEET)

Lawyer, and son of Rutherford B. Hayes. Correspondence (family and business), diaries, account books, notebooks, scrapbooks, abstracts, clippings, and photos.

WEBB COOK HAYES PAPERS, 1868–1934 (28 FEET AND 15 BOXES)

Secretary to his father, President Hayes, army officer, industrialist, world traveler, and philanthropist. Correspondence, a letter book (1893–1899), diaries, notebooks, account books and other financial papers, military service records, a narrative of operations in the Philippine Insurrection, recommendations, school papers, scrapbooks, address books, greeting cards, and hundreds of pictures illustrating several phases of Hayes' life. Includes material on his interests in National Carbon Co., Pemiscot Land & Cooperage Co., and Whipple Manufacturing Co., and his other investments; his political activity while serving as secretary to his father as governor of Ohio and President; his military service in the Spanish-American War, the Boxer Rebellion, the Mexican border troubles in 1911, and World War I; his chairmanship of the Cuba-China Battlefield Commission; the gift of Spiegel Grove to the State of Ohio; the Rutherford B. Hayes Library; his trusteeship of Ohio Historical Society and Western Reserve Historical Society; and his travels, military honors, and philanthropies, as well as correspondence with family and friends.

RUTHERFORD PLATT HAYES PAPERS, 1864–1911 (3 FEET)

Librarian, scientific farmer, and son of Rutherford B. Hayes. Correspondence (family and business), notes, school papers, and photos.

Frances Hayes Papers, 1878–1950 (2 feet)

Correspondence (chiefly family), diaries, account books, logbooks, school records and notebooks, a scrapbook, exercise books, autograph books, clippings, and photos of Rutherford B. Hayes' daughter.

Scott Russell Hayes Papers, 1873–1929 (1 foot)

Business executive and son of Rutherford B. Hayes. Correspondence (family and business), essays, autograph album, clippings, and photos.

William King Rogers Papers, 1830–1922 (22 boxes)

Lawyer and land developer. Correspondence (family, general, and while private secretary to President Hayes), diary (1873); business papers relating to railroads, mining, and the Chiriqui Investment Company; documents, legal papers, clippings, maps, and photos.

I have also used Hayes manuscripts owned by the Library of Congress, the Ohio Historical Society, the Western Reserve Historical Society, and The National Archives. These institutions have custody of the papers of many of Hayes' opponents, as well as close political associates and friends of President Hayes: cabinet officers; judges; legislators; statesmen; soldiers; literary figures; and newspapermen. Much of this material is available in the Hayes Library on microfilm, in photocopy, or transcription. "The Memoirs of Thomas C. Donaldson," from the Indiana State Historical Society holdings, is a prime example.

Government documents are another primary source of information. Hayes' legislative record in the House of Representatives is outlined in the pages of the *Congressional Globe* covering the Thirty-ninth and Fortieth congresses. Papers relating to Hayes' work as city solicitor of Cincinnati and his executive records as governor of Ohio are in the Hayes Library. The story of Congress during his presidency is detailed in the twenty-four volumes of the *Congressional Record* for the Forty-fifth and Forty-sixth congresses (1877–1881). James D. Richardson, ed., *A Compilation of the Messages and Papers of the Presidents, 1789–1897* (New York: Bureau of National Literature, Inc., 1897), 10 vols., contains some of Hayes' executive orders and proclamations, besides his inaugural address, annual messages, and vetoes.

The Hayes Library possesses a fine collection of nineteenth-century newspapers and periodicals. Among those I have found particularly helpful are: Chicago *Daily Tribune*, Cincinnati *Commercial*, Cincinnati *Gazette*, Dayton *Journal*, *Frank Leslie's Illustrated Weekly*, Fremont *Journal*, *Harper's Weekly*, Louisville *Courier-Journal*, *The Nation*, New York *Daily Graphic*, New York *Sun*, *New York Times*, New York *Tribune*, New York *World*, *Ohio State Journal*, *Puck*, *Scribner's Monthly*, Springfield *Republican*, Toledo *Blade*, Washington *National Republican*.

Dissertations and Theses

Abshire, David M. "David M. Key: A Study of Statesmanship in Post

Reconstruction Politics." Ph.D. dissertation, Georgetown University, 1959.

Adler, Selig. "The Senatorial Career of George Franklin Edmunds, 1866 –1891." Ph.D. dissertation, The University of Illinois, 1934.

Andrews, Richard Allen. "Years of Frustration: William T. Sherman, The Army, and Reform, 1869–1883." Ph.D. dissertation, Northwestern University, 1968.

Bartha, William. "The Early Political Career of Rutherford B. Hayes with Especial Reference to His Congressional Years." Master's thesis, The Ohio State University, 1963.

Bartlett, Catherine S. "The Prison Reform Activities of Rutherford B. Hayes, 1868–1893." Master's thesis, The Ohio State University, 1958.

Bickham, Sylvia Carroll. "Rutherford Birchard Hayes and the Southern Problem, 1860–1893." Master's thesis, Miami University, 1950.

Binkley, Wilfred E. "The Operation of the Check and Balance System of the Federal Government of the United States, 1875–1897." Master's thesis, The Ohio State University, 1926.

Bogarad, Allen Boyd. "A Historical and Rhetorical Analysis of Rutherford Birchard Hayes." Master's thesis, The Ohio State University, 1957.

Campion, Martin Clare. "The Gilded Age in American Historiography." Ph.D. dissertation, University of Minnesota, 1970.

Corwin, John Chaney. "Rutherford B. Hayes and Civil Service Reform." Master's thesis, The Ohio State University, 1941.

Flack, James Kirkpatrick, Jr. "The Formation of the Washington Intellectual Community, 1870–1898." Ph.D. dissertation, Wayne State University, 1968.

Flynn, James J. "The Disputed Election of 1876." Ph.D. dissertation, Fordham University, 1953.

Frazier, Frank G. "The Dissension among Ohio Republicans over the Policies of President Rutherford B. Hayes." Master's thesis, The Ohio State University, 1961.

Garvey, James J. "The Great Western Tour of 1880." Senior seminar paper submitted to Dr. Robert McCluggage, Loyola University of Chicago, 1966.

Geer, Emily Apt. "Lucy Webb Hayes: An Unexceptionable Woman." Ph.D. dissertation, Western Reserve University, 1962.

Gilcreast, Everett Arthur. "Richard Henry Pratt and American Indian Policy, 1877–1906: A Study of the Assimilation Movement." Ph.D. dissertation, Yale University, 1967.

Gonya, Gary Joseph. "Hayes and Unity (With a Travelogue of the Presidential Tour of 1880)." Master's thesis, St. Meinrad Seminary, 1965.

Gray, Edgar Laughlin. "The Career of William Henry Smith, Politician –Journalist." Ph.D. dissertation, The Ohio State University, 1951.

Grillot, Mary L. "A Literary Profile of Rutherford Birchard Hayes." Master's thesis, Bowling Green State University, 1968.

Hardy, Bill Benson. "Rutherford Hayes: Political Paradox." Master's thesis, Southern Methodist University, 1947.

Harrington, Margaret. "Lucy Webb Hayes as First Lady of the United States." Master's thesis, Bowling Green State University, 1956.

Hayes, Walter Sherman. "Rutherford B. Hayes and His Connection with The Ohio State University." Master's thesis, The Ohio State University, 1962.

Hess, James William. "George F. Hoar, 1826–1884." Ph.D. dissertation, Harvard University, 1964.

Houdek, John Thomas. "James A. Garfield and Rutherford B. Hayes: A Study in State and National Politics." Ph.D. dissertation, Michigan State University, 1970.

Huth, Edward Andrew. "President Rutherford B. Hayes: Civil Service Reformer." Ph.D. dissertation, Western Reserve University, 1943.

Hutton, Sister M. George Bernard, S.S.N.D. "William M. Evarts, Secretary of State, 1877–1881." Ph.D. dissertation, The Catholic University of America, 1966.

Krebs, Frank John. "Hayes and the South." Ph.D. dissertation, The Ohio State University, 1950.

Kunkler, Joel W. "The Literary and Economic Influences on Rutherford B. Hayes' Social Attitude." Master's thesis, Bowling Green State University, 1970.

Kuntz, Norbert A. "The Electoral Commission of 1877." Ph.D. dissertation, Michigan State University, 1969.

Leland, Earl. J. "The Post Office and Politics, 1876–1884: The Star Route Frauds." Ph.D. dissertation, The University of Chicago, 1964.

MacDonald, Curtis C. "Ansequago, A Biography of Sardis Birchard." Ph.D. dissertation, Western Reserve University, 1958.

McHargue, Daniel S. "Appointments to the Supreme Court of the United States: The Factors That Have Affected Appointments, 1789–1932." Ph.D. dissertation, University of California at Los Angeles, 1949.

Palmer, Upton S. "An Historical and Critical Study of the Speeches of Rutherford B. Hayes, with an Appended Edition of His Addresses." Ph.D. dissertation, University of Michigan, 1950.

Pennanen, Gary. "The Foreign Policy of William Maxwell Evarts." Ph.D. dissertation, University of Wisconsin, 1969.

Polakoff, Keith Ian. "The Disorganized Democracy: An Institutional Study of the Democratic Party, 1872–1880." Ph.D. dissertation, Northwestern University, 1968.

Porter, Dallas E. "The Educational Activities and Ideas of Rutherford Birchard Hayes." Master's thesis, The Ohio State University, 1938.

Price, Ruth P. "The Reform Activities of Rutherford B. Hayes." Master's thesis, The University of Toledo, 1948.

Ranson, Frederick D. "Rutherford B. Hayes in the Civil War." Master's thesis, West Virginia University, 1966.

Rick, Sister Mary Clarisena. "Guy M. Bryan and President Hayes' Southern Policy." Master's thesis, Xavier University, 1958.

Riddle, Judith Anne. "The Ragged Shirt versus the Bloody Shirt: The Campaign and Election of 1876 in Ohio." Master's thesis, University of Cincinnati, 1965.

Sholars, Fannie Baker. "Life and Services of Guy M. Bryan." Master's thesis, University of Texas, 1930.

Sopko, Sister Mary Carnath, R.S.M. "Religious Issues in Ohio Politics, 1875." Master's thesis, Xavier University, 1953.

Stukes, Joseph Taylor. "The American Nation in 1876." Ph.D. dissertation, University of South Carolina, 1962.

Swift, Donald Charles. "The Ohio Republicans, 1866–1880." Ph.D. dissertation, University of Delaware, 1967.

Tucker, David Milton. "The Mugwumps and the Money Question, 1865–1900." Ph.D. dissertation, State University of Iowa, 1965.

Waltmann, Henry George. "The Interior Department, War Department and Indian Policy, 1865–1887." Ph.D. dissertation, University of Nebraska, 1962.

Weinstein, Allen. "Origins of the Silver Question: Myths, Policies and Politics of a Monetary Issue, 1867–1878." Ph.D. dissertation, Yale University, 1967.

Books and Monographs

The Gilded Age, long a much maligned era, has in recent years enjoyed more sympathetic treatment by historians. The older, less favorable, interpretation is represented by such works as Vernon L. Parrington, *Main Currents in American Thought* (New York: Harcourt, Brace and Co., 1927–1930); Charles A. Beard and Mary Beard, *The Rise of American Civilization* (New York: Macmillan, 1927); and Matthew Josephson, *The Politicos, 1865–1896* (New York: Harcourt, Brace and Co., 1938). Revisionist approaches to the period include John A. Garraty, *The New Commonwealth, 1877–1890* (New York: Harper & Row, 1968); H. Wayne Morgan, *From Hayes to McKinley* (Syracuse: Syracuse University Press, 1969); and Robert H. Wiebe, *The Search for Order, 1877–1920* (New York: Hill and Wang, 1967).

Standard works for the study of Hayes' life and career are:

Barnard, Harry. *Rutherford B. Hayes and His America*. Indianapolis: The Bobbs-Merrill Company, Inc., 1954.

Bishop, Arthur, ed. *Rutherford B. Hayes, 1822–1893: Chronology–Documents–Bibliographical Aids*. Dobbs Ferry, N.Y.: Oceana Publications, Inc., 1969.

Burgess, John W. *The Administration of President Hayes*. New York: Charles Scribner's Sons, 1916.

Eckenrode, Hamilton J. *Rutherford B. Hayes: Statesman of Reunion*. New York: Dodd, Mead & Company, 1930.

Howard, J. Q. *The Life, Public Services and Select Speeches of Rutherford B. Hayes*. Cincinnati: Robert Clarke & Company, 1876.

Howells, William Dean. *Sketch of the Life and Character of Rutherford B. Hayes*. New York: Hurd and Houghton, 1876.

Myers, Elisabeth P. *Rutherford B. Hayes*. Chicago: Reilly & Lee, 1969.

Robinson, Lloyd. *The Stolen Election: Hayes versus Tilden—1876*. Garden City, N.Y.: Doubleday & Company, Inc., 1968.

Stillwell, Lewis Dayton. *The Hayes Administration, 1877–1881*. Hanover, N.H.: 1954.

Williams, Charles Richard. *The Life of Rutherford Birchard Hayes*. 2 vols. Boston: Houghton Mifflin Company, 1914.

———, ed. *Diary and Letters of Rutherford Birchard Hayes*. 5 vols. Columbus: F. J. Heer Printing Company, 1922–1926.

Williams, T. Harry. *Hayes of the Twenty-Third: The Civil War Volunteer Officer*. New York: Alfred A. Knopf, 1965.

———, ed. *Hayes: The Diary of a President, 1875–1881*. New York: David McKay Company, Inc., 1964.

The following titles are examples of newer works, which reinterpret various aspects of the Hayes period:

Abshire, David M. *The South Rejects a Prophet: The Life of Senator D. M. Key, 1824–1900*. New York: Frederick A. Praeger, 1967.

Ambrose, Stephen E. *Duty, Honor, Country: A History of West Point.* Baltimore: The Johns Hopkins Press, 1966.

Bain, Richard C. *Convention Decisions and Voting Records.* Washington: The Brookings Institution, 1960.

Brown, Dee. *Bury My Heart at Wounded Knee.* New York: Holt, Rinehart & Winston, 1970.

————. *The Year of the Century: 1876.* New York: Charles Scribner's Sons, 1966.

Brown, Harry J., and Williams, Frederick D. *The Diary of James A. Garfield, 1848–1874.* 2 vols. East Lansing: Michigan State University Press, 1967.

Bruce, Robert V. *1877: Year of Violence.* New York: The Bobbs-Merrill Co., 1959.

Burbank, David T. *Reign of the Rabble: The St. Louis General Strike of 1877.* New York: Augustus M. Kelley, 1966.

Burnham, W. Dean. *Presidential Ballots, 1836–1892.* Baltimore: The Johns Hopkins Press, 1955.

Clancy, Herbert J. *The Presidential Election of 1880.* Chicago: Loyola University Press, 1958.

Cooper, William J. *The Conservative Regime: South Carolina, 1877–1890.* Baltimore: The Johns Hopkins Press, 1968.

Dearing, Mary R. *Veterans in Politics: The Story of the G. A. R.* Baton Rouge: Louisiana University Press, 1952.

De Santis, Vincent P. *Republicans Face the Southern Question: The New Departure Years, 1877–1897.* Baltimore: The Johns Hopkins Press, 1959.

Dunham, Allison, and Kurland, Philip B., eds. *Mr. Justice.* Rev. Ed. Chicago: The University of Chicago Press, 1964.

Durbin, Louise. *Inaugural Cavalcade.* New York: Dodd, Mead and Company, 1971.

Eaton, Herbert. *Presidential Timber, A History of Nominating Conventions, 1868–1960.* New York: Free Press of Glencoe, 1964.

Eggert, Gerald T. *Railroad Labor Disputes: The Beginnings of Federal Strike Policy.* Ann Arbor: The University of Michigan Press, 1967.

Evans, Frank B. *Pennsylvania Politics, 1872–1877: A Study in Political Leadership.* Harrisburg: The Pennsylvania Historical and Museum Commission, 1966.

Fleming, Thomas J. *West Point: The Men and Times of the United States Military Academy.* New York: William Morrow & Company, Inc., 1969.

Franklin, John Hope. *Reconstruction: After the Civil War.* Chicago: The University of Chicago Press, 1961.

Friedman, Leon, and Israel, Fred L., eds. *The Justices of the United States Supreme Court, 1789–1969: Their Lives and Major Opinions.* 4 vols. New York: Chelsea House Publishers, 1969.

Fritz, Henry E. *The Movement for Indian Assimilation, 1860–1890.* Philadelphia: University of Pennsylvania, 1963.

Galloway, George Barnes. *History of the House of Representatives.* New York: Thomas Y. Crowell Company, 1961.

George, Sister Mary Karl. *Zachariah Chandler: A Political Biography.* East Lansing: Michigan State University Press, 1969.

Ginger, Ray. *Age of Excess: The United States from 1877 to 1914.* New York: The Macmillan Company, 1965.

Green, Constance McLaughlin. *Washington, 1800–1950.* 2 vols. Princeton: Princeton University Press, 1962–63.

Haynes, George Henry. *The Senate of the United States: Its History and Practice.* 2 vols. New York: Russell & Russell, 1960.

Hirshson, Stanley P. *Farewell to the Bloody Shirt.* Bloomington: Indiana University Press, 1962.

Holley, Edward G. *Raking the Historic Coals: The A. L. A. Scrapbook of 1876.* Chicago: Lakeside Press, 1967.

Hoogenboom, Ari. *Outlawing the Spoils: A History of the Civil Service Reform Movement, 1865–1883.* Urbana: University of Illinois Press, 1961.

Jackson, Carlton. *Presidential Vetoes, 1792–1945.* Athens: University of Georgia Press, 1967.

Jones, Howard Mumford. *The Age of Energy: Varieties of American Experience, 1865–1915.* New York: The Viking Press, 1971.

Jordan, David M. *Roscoe Conkling of New York: Voice in the Senate.* Ithaca: Cornell University Press, 1971.

Kane, Joseph N. *Facts about the Presidents, A Compilation of Biographical and Historical Data.* New York: The H. W. Wilson Company, 1959.

Kirkland, Edward Chase. *Industry Comes of Age: Business, Labor and Public Policy, 1860–1897.* Chicago: Quadrangle Books, 1967.

LaFeber, Walter. *The New Empire: An Interpretation of American Expansion, 1860–1898.* Ithaca: Cornell University Press, 1963.

Logan, Rayford W. *The Betrayal of the Negro.* New York: Collier Books, 1965.

Lorant, Stephen. *The Glorious Burden.* New York: Harper & Row, 1968.

Magrath, C. Peter. *Morrison R. Waite, The Triumph of Character.* New York: The Macmillan Company, 1963.

Mardock, Robert W. *The Reformers and the American Indian.* Columbia: University of Missouri Press, 1971.

Martin, Asa E. *After the White House.* State College, Pa.: Penns Valley Publishers, Inc., 1951.

Marx, Rudolph. *The Health of the Presidents.* New York: Putnam, 1961.

Merrill, James M. *William Tecumseh Sherman.* Chicago: Rand McNally and Company, 1971.

Morgan, H. Wayne. *The Gilded Age: A Reappraisal.* Syracuse: Syracuse University, 1963.

———. *The Gilded Age.* Rev. ed. Syracuse: Syracuse University Press, 1970.

———. *Unity and Culture: The United States, 1877–1900.* Baltimore: Penguin Books, Inc., 1971.

Nugent, Walter T. K. *Money and American Society, 1865–1880.* New York: The Free Press, 1968.

Ohio Historical Society. *The Governors of Ohio.* Columbus: The Stoneman Press, 1954.

Plesur, Milton. *America's Outward Thrust: Approaches to Foreign Affairs, 1865–1890.* De Kalb, Illinois: Northern Illinois University Press, 1971.

Pletcher, David M. *The Awkward Years: American Foreign Relations under Garfield and Arthur.* Columbia: University of Missouri Press, 1962.

Pollard, James E. *The Presidents and the Press.* New York: The Macmillan Company, 1947.

Randel, William Peirce. *Centennial: American Life in 1876.* Philadelphia: Chilton Book Company, 1969.

Rawley, James A. *Edwin D. Morgan, 1811–1883: Merchant in Politics.* New York: Columbia University Press, 1955.

Roseboom, Eugene H. *A History of Presidential Elections*. New York: The Macmillan Company, 1957.

Rothman, David J. *Politics and Power: The United States Senate, 1869–1901*. Cambridge: Harvard University Press, 1966.

Rubin, Louis D. *Teach the Freeman: The Correspondence of Rutherford B. Hayes and the Slater Fund for Negro Education, 1881–1893*. 2 vols. Baton Rouge: Louisiana University Press, 1959.

Sage, Leland L. *William Boyd Allison*. Iowa City: State Historical Society of Iowa, 1956.

Schlesinger, Arthur M., Jr. and Israel, Fred L., eds. *History of American Presidential Elections, 1789–1968*. New York: Chelsea House Publishers, 1971.

Shadgett, Olive Hall. *The Republican Party in Georgia from Reconstruction through 1900*. Athens: University of Georgia Press, 1964.

Shannon, Fred A. *The Centennial Years*. Garden City, N.Y.: Doubleday & Company, Inc., 1967.

Sievers, Harry J., S.J. *Benjamin Harrison, Hoosier Statesman: From the Civil War to the White House, 1865–1888*. New York: University Publishers Incorporated, 1959.

Smith, G. Wayne. *Nathan Goff, Jr., A Biography*. Charleston, West Virginia: Education Foundation, Inc., 1959.

Sproat, John G. *"The Best Men": Liberal Reformers in the Gilded Age*. New York: Oxford University Press, 1968.

Sutherland, Arthur E. *The Law at Harvard: A History of Ideas and Men, 1817–1967*. Cambridge, Mass.: The Belknap Press of Harvard University, 1967.

Sutton, Walter. *The Western Book Trade: Cincinnati as a Nineteenth-Century Publishing and Book-Trade Center, containing a Directory of Cincinnati Publishers, Booksellers, and Members of Allied Trades, 1796–1880*. Columbus: Ohio State University Press, 1961.

Taylor, John M. *Garfield of Ohio: The Available Man*. New York: W. W. Norton & Company, 1970.

Unger, Irwin. *The Greenback Era, A Social and Political History of American Finance, 1865–1879*. Princeton: Princeton University Press, 1964.

Walker, Robert H. *Everyday Life in the Age of Enterprise, 1865–1900*. New York: G. P. Putnam's Sons, 1967.

Webb, Ross A. *Benjamin Helm Bristow: Border State Politician*. Lexington: The University Press of Kentucky, 1969.

Weinstein, Allen. *Prelude to Populism: Origins of the Silver Issue, 1867–1878*. New Haven: Yale University Press, 1970.

Welch, Richard E., Jr. *George Frisbie Hoar and the Half-Breed Republicans*. Cambridge: Harvard University Press, 1971.

White, Leonard D. *The Republican Era: 1869–1901, A Study in Administrative History*. New York: The Macmillan Company, 1958.

Woodward, C. Vann. *Origins of the New South, 1877–1913*. Baton Rouge: Louisiana University Press, 1951.

———. *Reunion and Reaction: The Compromise of 1877 and the End of Reconstruction*. 2d ed., rev. Garden City, N.Y.: Doubleday & Company, Inc., 1956.

Articles

Baur, John E. "A President Visits Los Angeles: Rutherford B. Hayes' Tour of 1880." *The Historical Society of Southern California Quarterly* 37 (March 1955): 33–47.

Bestor, Arthur E., Jr. "The Transformation of American Scholarship, 1875 –1917." *The Library Quarterly* 23 (July 1953): 164–179.

Bigelow, Martha M. "The Political Services of William Alanson Howard." *Michigan History* 42 (March 1958): 1–25.

Bone, Fanny Z. Lovell. "Louisiana in the Disputed Election of 1876." *Louisiana Historical Quarterly* 14 (July and October 1931): 408–440, 549–566; 15 (January and April 1932): 93–116, 234–267.

Clendenen, Clarence C. "President Hayes' 'Withdrawal' of the Troops —An Enduring Myth," *South Carolina Historical Magazine* (October 1969): 240–250.

Cotner, Robert C., and Marchman, Watt P., eds. "Correspondence of Guy M. Bryan and Rutherford B. Hayes: Additional Letters." *Ohio State Archaeological and Historical Quarterly* 63 (October 1954): 349–377.

Davison, Kenneth E., and Thurston, Helen M., eds. "Rutherford B. Hayes Special Edition." *Ohio History* 77 (Winter, Spring, Summer 1968): 1–208.

D'Elia, Donald J. "The Argument Over Civilian or Military Indian Control, 1865–1880." *The Historian* 24 (February 1962): 207–225.

De Santis, Vincent. "American Politics in the Gilded Age." *Review of Politics* 25 (October 1963): 551–561.

————. "Catholicism and Presidential Elections, 1865–1900." *Mid-America* 42 (April 1960): 67–79.

————."President Hayes's Southern Policy." *The Journal of Southern History* 21 (November 1955): 476–494.

————. "Republican Efforts to 'Crack' the Democratic South." *Review of Politics* 14 (1952): 244–264.

————. "The Republican Party and the Southern Negro, 1877–1897." *The Journal of Negro History* 45 (April 1960): 71–87.

Dippre, Harold C. "Corruption and the Disputed Election Vote of Oregon in the 1876 Election." *Oregon Historical Quarterly* 67 (September 1966): 257–272.

Eidson, William G. "Who Were the Stalwarts?" *Mid-America* 52 (October 1970): 235–261.

Ekland, Roy E. "The 'Indian Problem': Pacific Northwest, 1879." *Oregon Historical Quarterly* 70 (June 1969): 100–137.

Ellis, Richard N. "General John Pope and the Southern Plains Indians, 1875–1883." *Southwestern Historical Quarterly* 72 (October 1968):152 –169.

Evans, Frank B. "Wharton Barker and the Republican National Convention of 1880." *Pennsylvania History* 27 (January 1960): 28–43.

Farrelly, David G. "John M. Harlan's One-Day Diary, August 21, 1877." *The Filson Club Quarterly* 24 (April 1950): 158–168.

Ferrell, Robert H., ed. "Young Charley Dawes Goes to the Garfield Inauguration: A Diary." *The Ohio Historical Quarterly* 70 (October 1961): 332–342.

Frank, John P. "The Appointment of Supreme Court Justices: Prestige, Principles and Politics." *Wisconsin Law Review* (March 1941): 172–347.

Gignilliat, John L. "Pigs, Politics, and Protection: The European Boycott of American Pork, 1879–1891." *Agricultural History* 35 (January 1961): 3–12.

Goff, John S. "Justice John Marshall Harlan of Kentucky." *Register of the Kentucky Historical Society* 55 (April 1957): 109–133.

Grob, Gerald N. "The Railroad Strikes of 1877." *Midwest Journal* (Winter 1954–1955): 16–34.

Gruener, Claude Michael. "Rutherford B. Hayes's Horseback Ride Through Texas." *The Southwestern Historical Quarterly* 68 (January 1965): 353–360.

Hacker, Barton C. "The United States Army as a National Police Force: The Federal Policing of Labor Disputes, 1877–1898." *Military Affairs* 33 (April 1969): 255–264.

Harris, William C. "A Mississippi Whig and the Ascension of Rutherford B. Hayes to the Presidency." *Journal of Mississippi History* 30 (August 1968): 202–205.

Hartman, William. "The New York Custom House: Seat of Spoils Politics." *New York History* 34 (April 1953): 149–163.

Hendricks, Gordon. "The Eakins Portrait of Rutherford B. Hayes." *The American Art Journal* 1 (Spring 1969): 104–114.

Hickerson, Frank R. "The Educational Contribution of Rutherford B. Hayes." *Northwest Ohio Quarterly* 33 (Winter 1960–1961): 46–53.

House, Albert V. "Republicans and Democrats Search for New Identities, 1870–1890." *Review of Politics* 31 (October 1969): 466–476.

Kindahl, James K. "Economic Factors in Specie Resumption: The United States, 1865–79." *The Journal of Political Economy* 69 (February 1961): 30–48.

Kleber, Louis C. "The Presidential Election of 1876." *History Today* 20 (November 1970): 806–813.

Koenig, Louis W. "The Election That Got Away." *American Heritage* 11 (October 1960): 4–7, 99–104.

Kuntz, Norbert. "Edmund's Contrivance: Senator George Edmunds of Vermont and the Electoral Compromise of 1877." *Vermont History* 38 (Autumn 1970): 305–315.

Lancaster, Clay. "The Philadelphia Centennial Towers." *Journal of the Society of Architectural Historians* 19 (March 1960): 11–15.

————. "Taste at the Philadelphia Centennial," *Magazine of Art* 43 (December 1950): 293–297, 308.

Lewis, Ellwood W., III. "The Appointment of Mr. Justice Harlan." *Indiana Law Journal* 29 (Fall 1953): 46–74.

McPherson, James. M. "Coercion or Conciliation? Abolitionists Debate President Hayes's Southern Policy." *The New England Quarterly* 39 (December 1966): 474–497.

Marchman, Watt P. "Lucy Webb Hayes in Cincinnati: The First Five Years, 1848–1852." *Bulletin of the Historical and Philosophical Society of Ohio* 13 (January 1955): 38–60.

————, ed. "The Washington Visits of Jenny Halstead, 1879–1881." *Bulletin of the Historical and Philosophical Society of Ohio* 12 (July 1954): 179–193.

Marszalek, John F., Jr. "A Black Cadet at West Point." *American Heritage* 22 (August 1971): 30–37, 104–106.

Meier, August. "The Beginning of Industrial Education in Negro Schools." *Midwest Journal* 7 (Spring 1955): 21–44.

————. The Vogue of Industrial Education." *Midwest Journal* 7 (Fall 1955): 241–266.

Moore, Dorothy. "William A. Howard and the Nomination of Rutherford B. Hayes for the Presidency." *Vermont History* 38 (August 1970): 316–319.

Nichols, Jeannette P. "Rutherford B. Hayes and John Sherman." *Ohio History* 77 (Winter, Spring, Summer 1968): 125–138.

Parker, Wyman W. "The College Reading of a President." *The Library Quarterly* 21 (April 1951): 107–112.

———. "Rutherford B. Hayes as a Student of Speech at Kenyon College." *The Quarterly Journal of Speech* 39 (October 1953): 291–295.

Pennanen, Gary. "Public Opinion and the Chinese Question, 1876–1879." *Ohio History* 77 (Winter, Spring, Summer 1968): 139–148.

———. "Sitting Bull: Indian Without a Country." *Canadian Historical Review* 51 (June 1970): 123–140.

Peskin, Allan. "Garfield and Hayes: Political Leaders of the Gilded Age." *Ohio History* 77 (Winter, Spring, Summer 1968): 111–124.

Plesur, Milton. "America Looking Outward: The Years From Hayes to Harrison." *The Historian* 22 (May 1960): 280–295.

Pletcher, David M. "Mexico Opens the Door to American Capital, 1877–1880." *The Americas* 16 (July 1959): 1–14.

Porter, Daniel R. "Governor Rutherford B. Hayes." *Ohio History* 77 (Winter, Spring, Summer 1968): 58–75.

Reeves, Thomas C. "Chester A. Arthur and Campaign Assessments in the Election of 1880." *The Historian* 31 (August 1969): 573–582.

———. "Chester A. Arthur and the Campaign of 1880." *Political Science Quarterly* 84 (December 1969): 628–637.

Roberts, Derrell. "Joseph E. Brown and the Florida Election of 1876." *The Florida Historical Quarterly* 40 (January 1962): 217–225.

Rogers, Ben F. "William Gates Le Duc, Commissioner of Agriculture." *Minnesota History Bulletin* 34 (Autumn 1955): 287–295.

Rogers, Joseph M. "How Hayes Became President." *McClure's Magazine* 23 (May 1904): 76–88.

Shofner, Jerrell H. "Florida Courts and the Disputed Election of 1876." *The Florida Historical Quarterly* 48 (July 1969): 26–46.

———. "Florida in the Balance: The Electoral Court of 1876." *The Florida Historical Quarterly* 47 (October 1968): 122–150.

———. "Fraud and Intimidation in the Florida Election of 1876." *The Florida Historical Quarterly* 42 (April 1964): 321–330.

Singletary, Otis A. "The Election of 1878 in Louisiana." *The Louisiana Historical Quarterly* 40 (January 1957): 46–53.

Sinkler, George. "Race: Principles and Policy of Rutherford B. Hayes." *Ohio History* 77 (Winter, Spring, Summer 1968): 149–167.

Slaner, Philip A. "The Railroad Strikes of 1877." *Marxist Quarterly* 1 (April–June 1937): 214–236.

Sternstein, Jerome L., ed. "The Sickles Memorandum: Another Look at the Hayes–Tilden Election-Night Conspiracy." *Journal of Southern History* 32 (August 1966): 342–357.

Swift, Don C. "Ohio Republicans and the Hayes Administration Reforms." *Northwest Ohio Quarterly* 42 (Fall 1970): 99–106; 43 (Winter 1971): 11–22.

Swint, Henry L. "Rutherford B. Hayes, Educator. *Mississippi Valley Historical Review* 39 (June 1952): 45–60.

Thelen, David P. "Rutherford B. Hayes and the Reform Tradition in the Gilded Age." *American Quarterly* 22, no. 2, pt. 1 (Summer 1970): 150–165.

Timberlake, Richard H. "Ideological Factors in Specie Resumption and Treasury Policy." *Journal of Economic History* 24 (March 1964): 29–52.

Tindall, George B. "Southern Strategy: A Historical Perspective." *North Carolina Historical Review* 48 (Spring 1971): 127–141.

Tunnell, T. B., Jr. "The Negro, the Republican Party, and the Election of 1876 in Louisiana." *Louisiana History* 7 (Spring 1966): 101–116.

Unger, Irwin. "Business and Currency in the Ohio Gubernatorial Campaign of 1875." *Mid-America* 41 (January 1959): 27–39.

———. "Business Men and Specie Resumption." *Political Science Quarterly* 74 (March 1959): 46–70.

———. "The Business Community and the Origins of the 1875 Resumption Act." *Business History Review* 35 (Summer 1961): 247–262.

Vaughn, William P. "West Point and the First Negro Cadet." *Military Affairs* 35 (October 1971): 100–102.

Wall, Joseph F. "Henry Watterson and the 'Ten Thousand Kentuckians.'" *The Filson Club History Quarterly* 24 (October 1950): 335–345.

Westin, Alan F. "John Marshall Harlan and the Constitutional Rights of Negroes: The Transformation of a Southerner." *The Yale Law Journal* 66 (April 1957): 636–710.

Wittke, Carl F. "Carl Schurz and Rutherford B. Hayes." *The Ohio Historical Quarterly* 65 (October 1956): 337–355.

Wright, Peter M. "The Pursuit of Dull Knife from Fort Reno in 1878–1879." *The Chronicles of Oklahoma* 46 (Summer 1968): 141–154.

Yearley, Clifton K., Jr. "The Baltimore and Ohio Railroad Strike of 1877." *Maryland Historical Magazine* 50 (September 1956): 188–211.

Index